Georgia Real Estate Postlicensing for Salespersons

1st Edition

PERFORMANCE
PROGRAMS
COMPANY

Stephen Mettling
Ryan Mettling
David Cusic

Material in this book is not intended to represent legal advice and should not be so construed. Readers should consult legal counsel for advice regarding points of law.

Georgia Real Estate Postlicensing for Salespersons

Table of Contents

Georgia Real Estate Postlicensing for Salespersons

Course Overview

The Georgia Postlicensing for Real Estate Salespersons Course (the "GAP" Program) has been developed to satisfy Georgia's official 25-hour postlicensing requirement. The course also fulfills the Real Estate Commission's objective of giving Georgia real estate licensees a carefully developed reinforcement of key real estate brokerage principles, concepts, and practices necessary to initiate a productive, professional career in real estate.

Beyond an initial review of key principles, the GAP Program takes on a further examination of essential skills and practices that will be necessary to meet client and customer transactional requirements within Georgia's legal framework. Such skills examined include handling trust funds, listing and selling, financial qualification, pricing property, managing closing-related activities, risk management, insurance, safety precautions and other primary activities.

Finally, Georgia Postlicensing for Real Estate Salespersons stresses the importance of adopting professional practices. These include compliance with law and regulations, full and proper disclosure to all parties, and maintaining ethical standards as promulgated by the National Association of Realtors® and the Real Estate Commission. By combining a critical concept review with key skills and professional practices, we hope Georgia Postlicensing for Real Estate Salespersons will make a valuable contribution to your early success and fulfillment in the world of Georgia real estate. Good luck!

ABOUT THE AUTHORS

For nearly fifty years, Stephen Mettling has been actively engaged in real estate education. Beginning with Dearborn in 1972, then called Real Estate Education Company, Mr. Mettling managed the company's textbook division and author acquisitions. Subsequently he built up the company's real estate school division which eventually became the country's largest real estate, insurance and securities school network in the country. In 1978, Mr. Mettling founded Performance Programs Company, a custom training program publishing and development company specializing in commercial, industrial, and corporate real estate. Over time, Performance Programs Company narrowed its focus to real estate textbook and exam prep publishing. Currently the Company's texts and prelicense resources are used in hundreds of schools in over 48 states. As of 2021, Mr. Mettling has authored over 100 textbooks, real estate programs and exam prep manuals.

Ryan Mettling, partner and publisher of Performance Programs, is an accomplished online curriculum designer, author, and course developer. He is responsible for the company's strategic planning, general management, printing and production, e-pub and retail platforms, and multi-channel marketing. Mr. Mettling is a member of the Real Estate Educators Association (REEA), and graduated Valedictorian from the University of Central Florida's College of Business Administration.

David Cusic, Ph.D., has been a training consultant, author, and Performance Programs Company partner for over forty years. As an educator with international real estate training experience, Dr. Cusic has been engaged in vocation-oriented education since 1966. Specializing in real estate training since 1983, he has developed numerous real estate training programs for corporate and institutional clients nationwide. Dr.

Cusic is co-author of the Company's flagship title, Principles of Real Estate Practice by Mettling and Cusic, now complemented by over 19 state supplements and 22 exam prep texts.

KEY CONTRIBUTOR

Jane Somers. Jane Somers has been a writer and educator for more than 30 years. She has directed the academic programs for a multi-campus college and has in recent years become an accomplished developer of online and classroom real estate curricula for a national real estate licensing organization, specializing in state licensing laws. Ms. Somers is also active in condominium association management and has served as president of a condominium owners association for ten years.

SECTION I: THE REGULATORY ENVIRONMENT

Unit 1: The Georgia Real Estate Commission

Unit 2: Fair Housing, ADA, and Antitrust Laws

Unit 3: The Georgia Residential Mortgage Fraud Act

UNIT 1:

THE GEORGIA REAL ESTATE COMMISSION

Unit One Learning Objectives: When the student has completed this unit, he or she will be able to:

- Characterize the role of the Georgia Real Estate Commission as a licensing and regulatory entity.
- Summarize the powers and duties of the Georgia Real Estate Commission.
- Identify acts that violate Georgia's real estate laws and describe the disciplinary process for such violations.

GA REAL ESTATE COMMISSION POWERS AND DUTIES

Purpose

The Georgia Real Estate Commission is the regulatory entity empowered to enforce Georgia license laws. Its primary purpose is to protect the interests of the public. Its duty is not to protect consumers, nor is its duty to protect real estate professionals. It is to ensure that due process is served. It does not advocate for real estate professions or for consumers.

Composition of GREC

The Commission is composed of six members, all of whom are appointed by the Governor and confirmed by the Senate. Five members must have been actively licensed and residents of Georgia for a minimum of five years. The sixth member must have no connection with the real estate industry and must have a recognized interest in consumer concerns. Commission members serve five-year terms and receive compensation for time spent performing official duties, for time spent traveling to meetings, and for actual expenses.

Duties and powers

The Commission's authority is based on statutory law which allows it to adopt rules and regulations designed to clarify, enforce, and administer the law. The rules can never be in conflict with License Law or other laws.

The Commission has the authority to provide licensing requirements, promulgate rules and regulations to enforce professionalism of licensees, and administer license law by enforcing the rules and regulations. The Commission also has the authority to establish licensing fees, renewal fees and late fees, and to issue, revoke, censure or suspend licenses.

The Commission protects the interests of the public by denying a license, or terminating a license, of any individual the Commission feels is not qualified or morally fit to be a part of the real estate industry. The Commission also safeguards the ethical standards of the industry by denying or terminating licenses, or disciplining licensees. The Commission ensures that both consumers and licensees receive due process rights under the law.

Fees established by the Commission must be reasonable and are determined by the cost of Commission operations. All fees are deposited into the state treasury to cover administration costs of the Commission and enforcement of license law.

The Commission maintains records in order to certify the license history of licensees and may also prepare and distribute educational material to licensees and the public.

The Commission will supply declaratory rulings regarding the applicability of the statutes or rules when requested but will not provide a ruling not on matters related to investigative hearings that are pending. A Commission member must recuse himself or herself from voting if a conflict of interest is present.

GEORGIA LICENSE LAW VIOLATIONS

It is imperative for a licensee to have a thorough understanding of what constitutes a violation of License Law or the Rules and Regulations. Being found guilty of unfair trade practices and other prohibited activities can result in disciplinary action, in some cases even loss of license.

Unfair trade practices

Discrimination. The first unfair practice covered in license law is discrimination -- fair housing violations based on family status, race, sex, color, disability, religion, or national origin (the seven federally protected classes). Violations include:

- refusing to rent, lease or sell, or to negotiate the rental, lease or sale, or in any way make unavailable, or deny real estate to any person; or, discriminating based on terms, conditions, or privileges related to the sale, rental, services or facilities.
- publishing or printing any ad that indicates any limitation, preference, or discrimination; or in any way representing that real estate is not available for viewing, rental or sale when it is available. Licensees should advertise the property, not who should live there.
- indicating that change can occur in an area in order to induce or discourage listing, purchasing, selling, or renting, or indicating that change may occur in an area based on any protected class and that change will result in lowering property values, increase in criminal or antisocial behavior, or decline in quality of school (referred to as "blockbusting").

Other unfair trade practices

- Performing any real estate activity without a real estate license or with a lapsed license
- Advertising using misleading or inaccurate terms, policies, values or services
- Failing to account for or remit any money and other items of value in the licensee's possession belonging to others
- Failing to make certain written disclosures
- Representing a broker or accepting compensation from anyone other than the broker with whom the licensee is affiliated, without the knowledge and consent of the broker
- Acting as agent and undisclosed principal in a transaction
- Guaranteeing future profits which may result from the resale of real property
- Offering real estate for sale or lease without the knowledge and consent of the owner
- Inducing a party to break an existing contract; obtaining a contract when another broker has an existing exclusive brokerage agreement; altering another licensee's commission
- Negotiating directly with a party who has an exclusive brokerage agreement with another broker
- Performing any licensing activity relative to property located in another state without being properly licensed or otherwise complying with that state's brokerage laws
- Paying commission or compensation to an unlicensed person for performing a licensing activity

- Failing to include an expiration date or including an automatic extension clause in any written listing agreement
- Failing to deliver, within the designated time, a completed copy of the purchase agreement, offer, or complete closing statement to the appropriate parties
- Making any substantial misrepresentations; demonstrating incompetency or dishonesty; making any false statement of material fact on an application; falsifying any real estate document
- Indicating a price opinion is an appraisal
- Acting as an undisclosed dual agent
- Failing to comply with trust fund laws including earnest money deposits and record retention
- Creating a lien that casts a cloud on a title
- A community association manager performing an act that may be performed only by a licensee
- Failing to comply with referral requirements
- Failing to include financing terms in offers if a financing contingency exists; failing to include the correct amount of earnest money, security deposit, or terms in any sales contract or lease
- Conducting real estate business under a name that is not registered with the Commission.
- Failing to comply with reporting requirements (address change; new trust accounts; personal real estate activities; final disposition of any administrative, civil, or criminal action)

Other violations

Additional violations may include a licensee failing to affiliate with a new company or become inactive when leaving a firm, failing to respond to a Commission request, submitting a check to the Commission with insufficient funds, a non-broker licensee performing broker acts or duties, accepting an unapproved bonus, paying a commission to a licensee representing another party to the transaction without the consent of all parties, or other activities that could harm the public of other licensees.

Whenever a licensee is convicted of any of the following offenses, the licensee must notify the commission within 10 days of the conviction: felony; forgery; embezzlement; obtaining money under false pretenses; theft, extortion or conspiracy to defraud; sexual offense; probation violation; or crime involving moral turpitude.

Disciplinary process

Actions. The Commission may initiate actions; investigate the actions of any applicant, licensee, real estate course, or instructor; and investigate applicants' licensure, fraudulent conduct, mishandling of trust funds, or violations which have been litigated.

The Commission may issue subpoenas to obtain documents or other material and may apply to the superior court of the county in which a person disobeying a subpoena resides for an order requiring him or her to comply. The investigative report determines whether or not a possible violation occurred. If the Commission determines that no violation occurred, the file is closed.

If the investigation determines that a violation did occur, disciplinary actions may be taken. The Commission can never censure, revoke or suspend a license without first providing an opportunity for a hearing. Hearings are held in the county of domicile of the Commission. Failure to comply with a final order may result in the Commission imposing a sanction on the license. The Commission may

- censure the licensee
- administer a reprimand
- require a licensee to complete a course in real estate brokerage
- refuse to grant or renew a license
- revoke or suspend the license

9

- downgrade a broker license to a salesperson's license
- impose monetary assessments and fines
- obtain a court injunction to prohibit a licensee from performing any activity in violation of License Law
- obtain a cease-and-desist order to prohibit the individual from illegally practicing real estate
- issue a confidential letter of findings if the alleged violation did not harm any third parties

If the Commission denies an application for the applicant's failure to meet requirements, it notifies the applicant of the denial and offers him or her the opportunity to request a hearing before the Office of State Administrative Hearings. The party may request a review of the initial decision within 30 days.

The licensee must immediately forward his or her wall certificate of licensure and pocket card to the Commission when receiving a notice of suspension or revocation. If the licensee is a broker, he or she must also forward all affiliated licensees' wall certificates and pocket cards. A licensee who surrendered his or her license or had the license revoked must apply for licensure as an original applicant if requesting reinstatement. When a broker's or associate broker's license is revoked or surrendered, the individual must wait at least ten years before reapplying for licensure.

An aggrieved party may request judicial review in the superior court of the Commission's county.

Education, Research and Recovery Fund

The purpose of the Recovery Fund to compensate consumers who suffer losses due to licensees' violations of License Law, Rules or Regulations. Twenty dollars of each license application is paid into the Recovery Fund. The Fund must have a minimum balance of $1 million. If the balance drops below $1 million, the Commission may assess $30 per year for all license renewals to rebuild the Fund. Income from the invested Fund is used for real estate education and research.

The aggrieved party must first obtain a judgment against the licensee. If the court feels the aggrieved party is unable to collect from the licensee, the court directs the Commission to pay from the Fund. The fund may reimburse actual or compensatory damages, or both. The maximum amount per transaction, regardless of number of persons aggrieved, is $25,000, so no party can ever establish a claim for more than $25,000 from the Fund. The maximum liability of the Fund for the acts of any one licensee is $75,000. The statute of limitations on claims made against a licensee is two years from the time of the cause of action.

When the Fund pays an aggrieved party as a result of a licensee's violation, his or her license is automatically revoked. If the judgment is against the firm, the qualifying broker's license is automatically revoked and may not be relicensed until the payment is repaid in full, plus interest.

==

SNAPSHOT REVIEW: UNIT ONE

THE GEORGIA REAL ESTATE COMMISSION

GA REAL ESTATE COMMISSION POWERS AND DUTIES

Purpose

- regulate Georgia licensing activity and licensees and protect the interests of the public

Composition of GREC

- six members, appointed by Governor: five brokers and one unlicensed to represent the pubic; serve five-year terms and receive compensation

Duties and powers

- establishes fees, adopts and promulgates rules and regulations, regulates licensure and licensing activities; can revoke, suspend or deny a license, and discipline licensees
- supplies declaratory rulings regarding the applicability of the statutes or rules

GEORGIA LICENSE LAW VIOLATIONS

- activities that can result in disciplinary actions, including revocation of license

Unfair trade practices

- discrimination; deceptive advertising; accounting negligence; failure to disclose; representing another broker; undisclosed interest; guaranteeing profits; unauthorized representation; agency interference; out-of-jurisdiction practice; compensating non-licensees; listing non-compliance; document delivery; material misrepresentations; representing value opinion as an appraisal; undisclosed dual agency; earnest money depositing; creating liens; dishonesty; records retention; community association-related violations; altering commissions; referrals in violation; financing disclosure; business name; undisclosed real estate activities; trust fund violations; brokerage activity with lapsed license; not notifying Commission of legal proceedings; misrepresented applications

Other violations

- specific activities that are violations and could harm the public or other licensees; additional violations covered in license law that can also result in disciplinary action

Disciplinary process

- Commission may investigate licensees, firms, schools, instructors, courses within three years of occurrence
- no disciplinary action without a hearing; if guilty, result can be revocation, suspension, censure, reprimand, fine, downgrade broker license to salesperson, required completion of course in brokerage; citation and letter of finding option if no one harmed by violation

Education Research and Recovery Fund

- to compensate someone injured by licensee's violation, after party has successful lawsuit but unable to collect

==

Check Your Understanding Quiz:

Unit One: The Georgia Real Estate Commission

Carefully read each question and provide your best answer based on what you learned in this unit. Then check your answers against the Answer Key which immediately follows the quiz questions.

1. From where does the Georgia Real Estate Commission obtain its authority?

    a. The rules and regulations
    b. Common law
    c. Statutory law
    b. The governor

2. How do individuals become members of the Commission?

    a. State level general election
    b. Appointment by the Governor
    c. Application to the existing Commission
    d. Selected by the State Senate

3. Which of the following is NOT the Commission's duty?

    a. Provide licensing requirements
    b. Administer license law
    c. Issue declaratory rulings
    d. Advocate for real estate professionals

4. When a licensee is convicted of embezzlement, he or she must notify the Commission within _____ of the conviction.

    a. 10 days
    b. 30 days
    c. 45 days
    d. The licensee is not required to notify the Commission since embezzlement is not a license law violation.

5. Discrimination as an unfair trade practice can be based on a person's

    a. level of education.
    b. age.
    c. living arrangements.
    d. disability.

6. Which of the following is a violation of fair-trade practices?

    a. Disclosing a dual agency
    b. Including an expiration date in a listing agreement
    c. Explaining that a price opinion is the same as an appraisal
    d. Including financing terms in an offer

7. After an investigation determines a license law violation did occur, what is the next step before the Commission can revoke or suspend a license?

    a. The Commission must provide an opportunity for a hearing.
    b. The Commission must find the violator guilty as a result of a hearing.
    c. The violator must request a judicial review.
    d. The aggrieved party must request payment from the Education, Research, and Recovery Fund.

8. To receive payment from the Recovery Fund, the aggrieved party must first

    a. present witnesses to the Commission.
    b. obtain a judgment against the licensee.
    c. provide an itemized list of expenses and costs to the Commission.
    d. justify a payment over $25,000.

===

Answer Key:

Unit One: The Georgia Real Estate Commission

1. **c. Statutory law**
2. **b. Appointment by the Governor**
3. **d. Advocate for real estate professionals**
4. **a. 10 days**
5. **d. disability.**
6. **c. Explaining that a price opinion is the same as an appraisal**
7. **a. The Commission must provide an opportunity for a hearing.**
8. **b. obtain a judgment against the licensee.**

==

UNIT 2:

FAIR HOUSING, AMERICANS WITH DISABILITIES ACT, ANTITRUST LAWS

Unit Two Learning Objectives: When the student has completed this unit, he or she will be able to:

- Describe the various practices that constitute discrimination in housing based on race, color, religion, national origin, sex, handicap, and families with children and the consequential penalties.
- Explain the purpose and five components of the Americans with Disabilities Act.
- Discuss the ADA requirements landlords must meet as well as the legal concerns and requirements of the ADA employers and building managers face for both employees and members of the public.
- Identify antitrust laws and the practices those laws prohibit.

FAIR HOUSING

Federal and state governments have enacted laws prohibiting discrimination in the national housing market. The aim of these **fair housing laws,** or **equal opportunity housing laws,** is to give all people in the country an equal opportunity to live wherever they wish, provided they can afford to do so, without impediments of discrimination in the purchase, sale, rental, or financing of property. It is incumbent upon real estate students to learn Georgia fair housing laws and note where these laws differ from national fair housing laws.

State Fair Housing Laws. While states have enacted fair housing laws that generally reflect the provisions of national law, each state may have slight modifications of national law. For that reason, it is incumbent upon real estate students to learn their Georgia laws and, in particular, note where these laws differ from national fair housing laws.

Fair Housing and Local Zoning. The Fair Housing Act prohibits practices that discriminate against individuals on the basis of race, color, religion, sex, national origin, familial status, and disability. The Act does not pre-empt local zoning laws but prohibits municipalities and other local governments from making zoning or land use decisions or implementing land use policies that exclude or otherwise discriminate against protected persons, including individuals with disabilities.

Fair Housing Laws

Civil Rights Act of 1866. The original fair housing statute, the Civil Rights Act of 1866, prohibits discrimination in housing *based on race*. In 1962, the President issued **Executive Order 11063** to *prevent discrimination in residential properties financed by FHA and VA loans*. The order facilitated enforcement of fair housing where federal funding was involved.

Civil Rights Act of 1968. Title VIII of the Civil Rights Act of 1866, known today as the **Fair Housing Act**, prohibits discrimination in housing *based on race, color, religion, or national origin*. The Office of Fair

Housing and Equal Opportunity (FHEO) administers and enforces Title VIII under the supervision of the Department of Housing and Urban Development (HUD).

Fair Housing Amendments Act of 1988. Amendments to federal fair housing laws prohibit discrimination based on sex and discrimination against handicapped persons and families with children.

Illegal Discrimination

Discrimination by the agent. The Fair Housing Act specifically prohibits such activities in residential brokerage and financing as the following:

- **Discriminatory misrepresentation.** An agent may not conceal available properties, represent that they are not for sale or rent, or change the sale terms for the purpose of discriminating.
- **Discriminatory advertising.** An agent may not advertise residential properties in such a way as to restrict their availability to any prospective buyer or tenant.
- **Providing unequal services.** An agent may not alter the nature or quality of brokerage services to any party based on race, color, sex, national origin, or religion.
- **Steering.** Steering is the practice of directly or indirectly channeling customers toward or away from homes and neighborhoods. An agent may not describe an area in a subjective way for the purpose of encouraging or discouraging a buyer about the suitability of the area.
- **Blockbusting.** An agent may not induce owners in an area to sell or rent to avoid an impending change in the ethnic or social makeup of the neighborhood that will cause values to go down.
- **Restricting MLS participation.** It is discriminatory to restrict participation in any multiple listing service based on one's race, religion, national origin, color, or sex.
- **Redlining.** Redlining is the residential financing practice of refusing to make loans on properties in a certain neighborhood regardless of a mortgagor's qualifications.

Discrimination by the client. Fair housing laws apply to home sellers as well as to agents. If an agent goes along with a client's discriminatory act, the agent is equally liable for violation of fair housing laws. Examples include refusing a full-price offer from a party, removing the property from the market to sidestep a potential purchase by a party, and accepting an offer from one party that is lower than one from another party. It is thus imperative to avoid complicity with client discrimination. Further, an agent should withdraw from any relationship where client discrimination occurs.

Listing agreements. Before entering into a listing agreement, a licensee should explain that it is necessary to comply with fair housing laws and obtain the potential client's acknowledgment and agreement. The agent should make it clear that the agent will

- reject the use of terms indicating race, religion, creed, color, national origin, sex, handicap, age or familial status to describe prospective buyers.
- terminate the listing if the seller uses race, religion, creed, color, national origin, sex, handicap, age, or familial status in the consideration of an offer.
- inform the broker if the seller makes any attempt to discriminate illegally.

Offers. A seller cannot refuse to sell a property to an individual based on the individual's belonging to a protected class, and if this is attempted, the real estate professional must not be involved. If the seller asks about the color, religion, creed, national origin, ethnicity, age, or familial status of a buyer, the agent must explain that it is illegal to give out such information. The best risk reduction procedure is to treat all buyers and sellers equally, showing no preference for one over another.

Exemptions

The Fair Housing Act allows for exemptions under a few specific circumstances:

- A privately owned single-family home where no broker is used and no discriminatory advertising is used, with certain additional conditions
- Rental of an apartment in a 1-4 unit building where the owner is also an occupant, provided the advertising is not discriminatory
- Facilities owned by private clubs and leased non-commercially to members
- Facilities owned by religious organizations and leased non-commercially to members, provided membership requirements are not discriminatory

Further, federal fair housing laws do not prohibit age and family status discrimination under the following circumstances:

- in government-designated retirement housing
- in a retirement community if all residents are 62 years of age or older
- in a retirement community if 80 % of the dwellings have one person who is 55 years of age or older, provided there are amenities for elderly residents
- in residential dwellings of four units or less, and single-family houses if sold or rented by owners who have no more than three houses

In 1968, the Supreme Court ruled in *Jones v. Mayer* that all discrimination in selling or renting residential property based on race is prohibited under the provisions of the Civil Rights Act of 1866, with no exemptions. Anyone who feels victimized by discrimination *based on race* may seek legal recourse under the 1866 law.

In 1972, HUD instituted a requirement that brokers display a standard HUD poster. The poster affirms the broker's compliance with fair housing laws in selling, renting, advertising, and financing residential properties. Failure to display the poster may be construed as discrimination.

Enforcement

Persons who feel they have been discriminated against under federal fair housing laws may file a complaint with the Office of Fair Housing and Equal Opportunity (FHEO) within HUD, or they may file suit in a federal or state court.

An FHEO complaint. Complaints alleging fair housing violations must be filed with the FHEO within one year of the violation. HUD then initiates an investigation in conjunction with federal or local enforcement authorities. If HUD decides that the complaint merits further action, it will attempt to resolve the matter out of court. If HUD efforts to resolve the problem fail, the aggrieved party may file suit in state or federal court. In addition to or instead of filing a complaint with HUD, a party may file suit in state or federal court within two years of the alleged violation.

Penalties. If discrimination is confirmed in court, the respondent may be enjoined to cease practicing his or her business. The plaintiff may be compensated for damages including humiliation, suffering, and pain. The injured party may seek equitable relief, including forcing the guilty party to complete a denied action such as selling or renting the property. Also, the courts may impose civil penalties for first-time or repeat offenders.

AMERICANS WITH DISABILITIES ACT (ADA)

Purpose

The ADA, which became law in 1990, is a civil rights law that prohibits discrimination against individuals with disabilities in all areas of public life, including employment, education, transportation, and facilities that are open to the general public. The purpose of the law is to make sure that people with disabilities have the same rights and opportunities as everyone else.

The Americans with Disabilities Act Amendments Act (ADAAA) became effective on January 1, 2009. Among other things, the ADAAA clarified that a disability is "a physical or mental impairment that substantially limits one or more major life activities." This definition applies to all titles of the ADA and covers private employers with 15 or more employees, state and local governments, employment agencies, labor unions, agents of the employer, joint management labor committees, and private entities considered places of public accommodation.

Components

The law consists of five parts.

- Title I (Employment) concerns equal employment opportunity. It is enforced by the U.S. Equal Employment Opportunity Commission.
- Title II (State and Local government) concerns nondiscrimination in state and local government services. It is enforced by the U.S. Department of Justice.
- Title III (Public Accommodations) concerns nondiscrimination in public accommodations and commercial facilities. It is enforced by the U.S. Department of Justice.
- Title IV (Telecommunications) concerns accommodations in telecommunications and public service messaging. It is enforced by the Federal Communications Commission.
- Title V (Miscellaneous) concerns a variety of general situations including how the ADA affects other laws, insurance providers, and lawyers.

Real estate practitioners are most likely to encounter Titles I and III and should acquire familiarity with these.

Requirements

The act requires landlords in certain circumstances to modify housing and facilities so that disabled persons can access them without hindrance.

The ADA also requires that disabled employees and members of the public be provided access that is equivalent to that provided to those who are not disabled.

- Reasonable accommodations must be made to enable disabled employees to perform essential functions of their jobs.
- Modifications to the physical components of a building may be necessary to provide the required access to tenants and their customers, such as widening doorways, changing door hardware, changing how doors open, installing ramps, lowering wall-mounted telephones and keypads, supplying Braille signage, and providing auditory signals.
- Existing barriers must be removed when the removal is "readily achievable," that is, when cost is not prohibitive. New construction and remodeling must meet a higher standard.
- If a building or facility does not meet requirements, the landlord must determine whether restructuring or retrofitting or some other kind of accommodation is most practical.

Legal concerns

The Americans with Disabilities Act requires managers to ensure that disabled employees and members of the public have the same level of access to facilities as is provided for those who are not disabled. Employers with at least fifteen employees must follow nondiscriminatory employment and hiring practices. Reasonable accommodations must be made to enable disabled employees to perform essential functions of their jobs. Modifications to the physical components of the building may be necessary to provide the required access to tenants and their customers, such as widening doorways, changing door hardware, changing how doors open, installing ramps, lowering wall-mounted telephones and keypads, supplying Braille signage, and providing auditory signals. Existing barriers must be removed when the removal is "readily achievable," that is, when cost is not prohibitive. New construction and remodeling must meet a higher standard. Managers must be aware of the laws and determine whether their buildings meet requirements. If not, the manager must determine whether restructuring or retrofitting or some other kind of accommodation is most practical.

Penalties

Violations of ADA requirements can result in citations, business license restrictions, fines, and injunctions requiring remediation of the offending conditions. Business owners may also be held liable for personal injury damages to an injured plaintiff.

ANTITRUST LAWS

Antitrust laws

Brokerage companies, like other businesses, are subject to antitrust laws designed to prevent monopolies and unfair trade practices.

Sherman Antitrust Act. Enacted in 1890, the Sherman Antitrust Act prohibits restraint of interstate and foreign trade by conspiracy, monopolistic practice, and certain forms of business combinations, or mergers. The Sherman Act empowers the federal government to proceed against antitrust violators.

Clayton Antitrust Act. The Clayton Antitrust Act of 1914 reinforces and broadens the provisions of the Sherman Act. Among its prohibitions are certain exclusive contracts, predatory price cutting to eliminate competitors, and inter-related boards of directors and stock holdings between same-industry corporations. The Clayton Act also legalizes certain labor strikes, picketing, and boycotts.

Fair Business Practices Act. The Georgia Fair Business Practices Act (§ 10-1-390) prohibits unfair and deceptive acts that involve the sale, lease or rental of goods, services or property for personal, family or household purposes. There are many prohibited activities. Some of these have a direct application to real estate licensees.

The Act prohibits making misleading statements about another business or its products or services. Another prohibited activity in the Act is advertising goods or services with the intent not to sell them as advertised.

Deceptive Trade Practices Act. Georgia's Uniform Deceptive Trade Practices Act (§ 10-1-372) prohibits deceptive acts or omissions and permits an injured party to take legal action. It also prohibits disparaging the goods, services, or business of another by false or misleading representation. This would also be in violation of the REALTOR® Code of Ethics.

Prohibited practices

Anti-competitive behavior. The effect of antitrust legislation is to prohibit trade practice and trade restraints that unfairly disadvantage open competition. Business practices and behaviors which violate antitrust laws include collusion, price fixing, market allocation, bid rigging, restricting market entry, exclusive dealing, and predatory pricing.

Collusion. Collusion is the illegal practice of two or more businesses joining forces or making joint decisions which have the effect of putting another business at a competitive disadvantage. Businesses may not collude to fix prices, allocate markets, create monopolies, or otherwise interfere with free market operations.

Price fixing. Price fixing is the practice of two or more brokers agreeing to charge certain commission rates or fees for their services, regardless of market conditions or competitors. In essence, such pricing avoids and disturbs the dynamics of a free, open market.

For instance, the two largest brokerages in a market jointly decide to cut commission rates by 50% in order to draw clients away from competitors. The cut-rate pricing could destroy smaller agencies that lack the staying power of the large companies.

Market allocation. Market allocation is the practice of colluding to restrict competitive activity in portions of a market in exchange for a reciprocal restriction from a competitor: "we won't compete against you here if you won't compete against us there."

For example, Broker A agrees to trade only in single family re-sales, provided that Broker B agrees to focus exclusively on apartment rentals and condominium sales. The net effect is an illegally restricted market where collusion and monopoly supplant market forces.

Tie-in agreements. In a tie-in agreement, the sale of one product or performance of a service is tied to the sale of another, less desirable product or service. For instance, "I will sell you this car, but you have to hire my brother-in-law to drive it." Or, more likely, "I will list and sell your old home if you hire me to find you a new home to purchase." Tie-ins restrict competition and limit the freedom of the consumer.

Advertising compliance

Brokers have the responsibility of reviewing all advertising for compliance with license law, fair housing laws, antitrust laws and any other applicable statutes.

Violations

Violations of fair trade and antitrust laws may be treated as felonies, and penalties can be substantial. Loss of one's license is also at stake. Brokers are well-advised to understand and recognize these laws.

SNAPSHOT REVIEW: UNIT TWO

FAIR HOUSING, ADA, ANTITRUST LAWS

FAIR HOUSING LAWS

- enacted to create equal opportunity and access to housing and housing finance
- state laws generally reflect federal fair housing laws; federal laws do not pre-empt local zoning laws but prohibit them from discriminating

Civil Rights Act of 1866

- no discrimination in selling or leasing housing *based on race*
- Executive Order 11063: no race discrimination involving FHA- or VA-backed loans

Civil Rights Act of 1968

- Title VIII (Fair Housing Act): no housing discrimination based on race, color, religion, national origin
- certain exceptions permitted

Fair Housing Amendments Act of 1988

- no discrimination based on sex or against the handicapped or families with children

Jones v. Mayer

- no race discrimination, without exception

Equal Opportunity in Housing Poster

- must be displayed by brokers

Discrimination by the agent

- misrepresentation, advertising, unequal services, steering, blockbusting, MLS restrictions, redlining

Discrimination by the client

- agent liable for complying with client's discriminatory acts

Exemptions

- **Title VIII** - privately-owned single-family with no broker and no discriminatory advertising; 1-4 unit apartment building where owner is resident and no discriminatory advertising; private club facilities leased to members; religious organization-owned facilities for members and no discrimination
- **Federal fair housing laws** – no age and family status discrimination in government-designated retirement housing, a retirement community if all residents are 62 years of age or older, a retirement community if 80 % of the dwellings have one person who is 55 years of age or older, residential dwellings of four units or less, and single-family houses if sold or rented by owners who have no more than three houses

Enforcement

- file HUD complaint, sue in court, or both; may obtain injunction, damages; violators subject to prosecution

ADA

- no discrimination against those with disabilities; applies to employment, education, transportation, public facilities; equivalent access
- Titles I (employment) and III (public accommodation) most common for real estate agents

ANTITRUST LAWS

- Sherman Act and Clayton Act pioneered antitrust laws to prohibit unfair trade practices, trade restraints, and monopolies
- Fair Business Practices Act prohibits unfair practices in sale, lease, rental of goods, services, and property; no misleading statements about a competitor; no false advertising
- Deceptive Trade Practices Act prohibits deceptive acts or omissions, disparaging of competitors, false advertising
- illegal to collude, disadvantage competitors; fix prices; allocate markets; force tie-ins

===

Check Your Understanding Quiz:

Unit Two: Fair Housing, ADA, Antitrust Laws

Carefully read each question and provide your best answer based on what you learned in this unit. Then check your answers against the Answer Key which immediately follows the quiz questions.

1. Executive Order 11063 prohibited discrimination in housing

    a. based on national origin.
    b. financed with a mortgage loan.
    c. financed by FHA and VA loans.
    d. in Georgia.

2. Which fair housing law added families with children as a protected class?

    a. Civil Rights Act of 1866
    b. Civil Rights Act of 1968
    c. Fair Housing Amendments Act of 1988
    d. Executive Order 11063

3. When an agent channels customers away from certain neighborhoods, the agent is guilty of

    a. blockbusting.
    b. steering.
    c. redlining.
    d. none of the above.

4. If an agent changes a property's sale terms for the purpose of discriminating, the agent is guilty of

    a. discriminatory advertising.
    b. providing unequal services.
    c. discriminatory misrepresentation.
    d. redlining.

5. Which of the following statements is false?

    a. Fair housing laws apply to home sellers.
    b. There is no need for an agent to withdraw from a client relationship if the client discriminates.
    c. Refusing a full-price offer from a party may be discrimination on the part of the seller.
    d. Agents should avoid complicity with client discrimination.

6. Which of the following is exempt from fair housing laws?

   a. Rental of an apartment where the owner advertises for adults with no children.
   b. Facilities owned by private clubs that limit rentals to Asian American members.
   c. Sale of a privately owned single-family home where no broker is used and with advertising that specifies maintaining a Jewish-only community.
   d. A religious organization renting only to members.

7. *Jones v. Mayer* resulted in no allowable exemptions for discrimination in housing based on

   a. race.
   b. age.
   c. sex.
   d. familial status.

8. Which of the five components of the Americans with Disabilities Act are real estate professionals most likely to encounter?

   a. Titles I Employment and II State and Local government
   b. Titles III Public Accommodations and V Miscellaneous
   c. Titles I Employment and III Public Accommodations
   d. Titles II State and Local government and III Public Accommodations

9. The ADA requires that employers with at least _____ employees must follow nondiscriminatory employment and hiring practices.

   a. 10
   b. 15
   c. 25
   d. 45

10. Certain labor strikes, picketing, and boycotts were legalized by which antitrust law?

   a. Sherman Antitrust Act
   b. Clayton Antitrust Act
   c. Georgia Fair Business Practices Act
   d. Georgia's Uniform Deceptive Trade Practices Act

11. In addition to prohibiting deceptive acts or omissions, Georgia's Uniform Deceptive Trade Practices Act prohibits

   a. price fixing.
   b. colluding to restrict competition in the market in exchange for a reciprocal restriction from a competitor.
   c. predatory pricing.
   d. disparaging the goods, services, or business of another by false or misleading representation.

12. _____ is the illegal practice of two or more businesses joining forces or making joint decisions which have the effect of putting another business at a competitive disadvantage.

    a. Market allocation
    b. Collusion
    c. Price fixing
    d. Tie-in agreement

==

Answer Key:

Unit Two: Fair Housing, ADA, Antitrust Laws

1. c. financed by FHA and VA loans.
2. c. Fair Housing Amendments Act of 1988
3. b. steering.
4. c. discriminatory misrepresentation.
5. b. There is no need for an agent to withdraw from a client relationship if the client discriminates.
6. d. A religious organization renting only to members.
7. a. race.
8. c. Titles I Employment and III Public Accommodations
9. b. 15
10. b. Clayton Antitrust Act
11. d. disparaging the goods, services, or business of another by false or misleading representation.
12. b. Collusion

===

UNIT 3:

GEORGIA RESIDENTIAL MORTGAGE FRAUD

Unit Three Learning Objective: When the student has completed this unit, he or she will be able to:

- Explain how the Georgia Residential Mortgage Fraud Act applies to residential mortgage loans for properties located in Georgia and the penalties for violating the Act.

RESIDENTIAL MORTGAGE FRAUD

Mortgage

It is common to use borrowed money to purchase real estate. A borrower may give a note promising to repay the borrowed money and execute a mortgage on the real estate for which the money is being borrowed as security.

A mortgage is a legal document stating the pledge of the borrower (the **mortgagor**) to the lender (the **mortgagee**). The mortgage document pledges the borrower's ownership interest in the real estate in question as collateral against performance of the debt obligation.

The loan application

The process of initiating a mortgage loan begins when a borrower completes a loan application and submits it to a lender for evaluation by the lender's underwriters. Most lenders use some version of the "Uniform Residential Loan Application" promulgated by Fannie Mae. This form requests the borrower to provide information about the property and the borrower. In addition, the application must include supporting documentation, such as a credit report, income and employment verification, a purchase contract, and an appraisal report.

Completion. The application must be complete for the lender to consider it. The form must be signed and dated by the applicant(s) and delivered to the lending institution. The **initiation** of the application process occurs when the lender receives the completed application package from the applicant. Federal law requires the lender to accept all applications and to give applicants notice concerning the disposition of the application.

The Georgia Residential Mortgage Fraud Act

The Georgia Residential Mortgage Fraud Act (§ 16-8-100 through -106) applies only to residential property located in Georgia; it does not apply to loans made for commercial properties, properties larger than one to four units, nor does it apply to loans made in Georgia for properties located out of state. However, other laws may apply to loans made for those properties.

The Georgia Act makes any misrepresentation or omission in the mortgage lending process illegal. Anyone who uses, files, or causes someone to use a misstatement, omission, or misrepresentation, or receives any proceeds as a result of misrepresentation, is in violation of the Act. This includes appraisals, loan applications, closing statements, personal qualifying documents of the borrower for the loan application, and other loan documents.

If the lender denies the loan application because of fraudulent information on the application form, the borrower has no claim to a refund of the application fee.

Penalties

District attorneys and the Attorney General have the authority to prosecute residential mortgage fraud cases. Penalties can include imprisonment for not less than one year or more than ten years, a fine of up to $5,000.00, or both. An individual who is proved to be involved in a pattern of residential mortgage fraud may face imprisonment of three to twenty years, a fine of up to $100,000.00, or both.

GA RESIDENTIAL MORTGAGE FRAUD

MORTGAGE FRAUD

Mortgage loan application

- borrower provides personal and property data; supporting documentation: appraisal report, credit report, purchase contract, income and/or employment verification

Georgia Residential Mortgage Fraud Act

- applies only to GA residential properties of four units or fewer; outlaws misrepresentation and omission in lending process

==

Check Your Understanding Quiz:

Unit Three: GA Residential Mortgage Fraud

Carefully read each question and provide your best answer based on what you learned in this unit. Then check your answers against the Answer Key which immediately follows the quiz questions.

1. A mortgage document associated with a mortgage loan serves as

   a. security on the loan.
   b. incentive to borrow money to purchase real estate.
   c. proof of the property's value.
   d. proof of the borrower's ability to repay the loan.

2. Submission of the _____ is considered the initiation of the mortgage loan process.

   a. offer to purchase
   b. credit report
   c. loan application
   d. purchase contract

3. The GA Residential Mortgage Fraud Act applies to which of the following?

   a. Apartment properties larger than 4 units
   b. Single-family homes
   c. A single-family home located outside of Georgia
   d. Property with 10 college dorm rooms

4. Which of the following is illegal under the GA Residential Mortgage Fraud Act when related to a mortgage loan application?

   a. Misrepresenting the actual location of the auto repair shop for which the loan is being sought
   b. An accidental error on the appraisal of a commercial building
   c. Any omission on a closing statement for a single-family home
   d. All of the above

5. Which of the following is false?

   a. Anyone who causes someone to omit a relevant fact on a GA mortgage loan application is in violation of the GA Residential Mortgage Fraud Act.
   b. The GA Residential Mortgage Fraud Act only applies to residential property located in GA.
   c. The GA Residential Mortgage Fraud Act sometimes apples to properties located outside of GA.
   d. Anyone who receives compensation for covering up a lie on a GA mortgage loan application is in violation of the GA Residential Mortgage Fraud Act.

6. Anyone who is involved in a pattern of residential mortgage fraud may be imprisoned for

    a. 1 to 3 years.
    b. 3 to 20 years.
    c. 10 to 35 years.
    d. up to 15 years.

7. Who has the authority to prosecute residential mortgage fraud cases?

    a. Any attorney handling a related law suit
    b. Any prosecuting attorney
    c. A district attorney
    d. The U.S. Attorney General

8. What is the highest fine an individual can face for residential mortgage fraud in GA?

    a. $5,000
    b. $10,000
    c. $25,000
    d. $100,000

9. If a lender denies a mortgage loan application for fraudulent information, the borrower

    a. may file a lawsuit against the lender.
    b. will lose the loan application fee.
    c. will automatically be fined up to $5,000.
    d. will never again be allowed to apply for a mortgage loan.

10. The GA Residential Mortgage Fraud Act does not apply to

    a. appraisals.
    b. loan applications.
    c. purchase contracts.
    d. closing statements.

==

Answer Key:

Unit Three: GA Residential Mortgage Fraud

1. a. security on the loan.
2. c. loan application
3. b. Single-family homes
4. c. Any omission on a closing statement for a single-family home
5. c. The GA Residential Mortgage Fraud Act sometimes apples to properties located outside of GA.
6. b. 3 to 20 years.
7. c. A district attorney
8. d. $100,000
9. b. will lose the loan application fee.
10. c. purchase contracts.

===

SECTION II: BROKERAGE FIRM OPERATION AND REGULATION

Unit 4: Management Responsibilities of the Brokerage Firm

Unit 5: Broker-Salesperson Relationship, Unlicensed Assistants

Unit 6: Advertising Regulations

Unit 7: General Office Rules and Policies

Unit 8: Trust Accounts and Handling Trust Funds

UNIT 4:

MANAGEMENT RESPONSIBILITIES
OF THE BROKERAGE FIRM

Unit Four Learning Objectives: When the student has completed this unit, he or she will be able to:

- Identify the broker or qualifying broker requirements for each type of brokerage.
- Describe the brokerage operations requirements including but not limited to agreements, training, and supervisory requirements.
- Explain the process of transferring licensees in and out of the firm

MANAGEMENT RESPONSIBILITIES

Brokerage operations requirements

Requirement by type of firm. Each type of brokerage must have a broker or qualifying broker who is responsible for communications with the Commission and who is held accountable for actions of the brokerage firm.

In a *sole proprietorship*, the licensed broker/owner is accountable to the Commission for the acts of all affiliated licensees and non-licensed personnel. A sole proprietorship must be owned entirely by the broker.

In a *partnership*, one of the partners must serve as the qualifying broker and be accountable to the Commission for acts of the firm. If all the partners are corporations, the qualifying broker must be one of the partner corporation's officers whose actions are binding to both the corporation and partnership.

The qualifying broker for a *limited partnership* must be the general partner. If the general partner is a corporation, the qualifying broker must be one of that corporation's officers whose actions are binding on both the corporation and the general partner.

A *limited liability company* must have a qualifying broker who is a member, or if the articles of organization confer management of the company to a manager, the manager may serve as qualifying broker.

The qualifying broker for a *corporation* must be an officer of the corporation.

The broker must have signatory powers on all brokerage trust accounts.

Death, resignation or termination of the qualifying broker. Upon the death, resignation or termination of the qualifying broker, the brokerage company must obtain a new qualifying broker within 60 days or cease all real estate brokerage activity until a new qualifying broker is secured. While seeking a new qualifying broker, the brokerage firm must designate an individual to sign documents and applications required to be filed with the Commission, and to disburse trust funds as required by license law. In a partnership, one of the partners must be designated. A limited liability company must designate a member, and a corporation must designate one of the corporation's officers to disburse funds and sign documents.

In a partnership, one of the partners must be designated. A limited liability company must designate a member, and a corporation must designate one of the corporation's officers to disburse funds and sign documents.

Licensee's employee v. independent contractor status. Georgia license law does not stipulate whether an affiliated licensee of the broker is an employee or an independent contractor. The decision as to the working relationship between the broker and licensees is determined by the broker and included in the contract between the broker and the affiliated licensee based on the amount of control over the brokerage activities that the broker wishes to maintain, the type of government-required paperwork for each type, and whether the brokerage wishes to pay benefits such as insurance or paid vacations.

Multiple offices. Licensees who operate from more than one place of business must comply with all applicable local business ordinances affecting their business operations.

Change of address. The broker must notify the Commission in writing within 30 days of a change of the broker's place of business.

Broker and qualifying broker requirements

Name of firm. The broker may not conduct business under any name other than the name in which the broker's license is issued.

Brokerage activities supervised by broker or qualifying broker. All real estate brokerage activities must be under the direct management and supervision of a broker or qualifying broker, who is held responsible by the Commission for all company activities, including the real estate actions of all affiliated licensees and unlicensed personnel. He or she has responsibility for any violations of License Law and the Rules and Regulations unless he or she can demonstrate that reasonable procedures were in place for supervising the affiliates' actions, and that he or she did not participate in nor affirm the violation.

Violation notifications. The broker must notify the Georgia Real Estate Commission of any violations of License Law or the Rules and Regulations. This affects better protection of the public as well as a more professional industry.

Each firm applying for a license must authorize its qualifying broker to bind the firm to any settlement of a contested case before the Commission if the firm is named as a respondent.

Training responsibility. Not only is training of licensees required by the Rules, it is to the broker's advantage to fulfill his or her responsibility as prescribed in the rules to instruct and review (ongoing training) affiliated licensees regarding applicable laws and rules. As a matter of risk management, the broker should also have ongoing training covering fair housing laws, contract law, environmental issues, changes in financial laws and trends, etc.

Advertising compliance. The broker also has the responsibility of reviewing all advertising for compliance with license law, fair housing laws, antitrust laws and any other applicable statutes.

Contract review. The broker must review, within 30 days of the date of an offer or contract, all listing and sales contracts, management agreements, and offers to buy, sell, lease, or exchange property that are obtained or secured by the affiliated licensees. The firm's trust accounting practices must be reviewed by the broker, including ensuring that property disbursements are made from the accounts.

Records maintenance. The broker is responsible for safekeeping of all records related to the transaction, including sales contracts, listing agreements, buyer agency agreements, property management agreements, community association management agreements, closing statements, leases and any other documents related to a transaction that may be required by law to be maintained.

Affiliate compensation agreements. The firm and all licensed affiliates must enter into a written agreement specifying compensation term for licensees during the time of their affiliation. That agreement must also specify how the licensees are to be compensated for work begun but not completed prior to the termination of the affiliation. The Commission does not regulate the content of the agreements nor enforce provisions of the agreements. The broker is responsible for ensuring compliance with this requirement.

Transaction compliance. The broker or qualifying broker must also ensure that an individual with appropriate management authority is reasonably available to assist licensees and the public in real estate transactions handled by the firm. Although the broker or qualifying broker may delegate any of the management duties, he or she is responsible for the acts of the person to whom the duties are delegated.

The broker or qualifying broker must ensure that any licensing activity is performed only by licensees. The firm may not pay commissions to inactive licensees or any unlicensed person, including support personnel. The broker or qualifying broker is also held responsible for establishing, implementing, and continuing procedures for all these areas, and providing all licensed personnel with written policies and procedures under which they are expected to operate.

Transferring licensees in and out of the firm. When an affiliated licensee leaves a broker, that broker must immediately cause the license of that licensee to be forwarded either to the Commission or to the new broker for whom the licensee will act. If the wall certificate of licensure is forwarded to the new broker, the broker releasing the licensee must notify the Commission in writing and furnish other information regarding the termination of the licensee as the Commission may require including a release signed by the broker and the licensee.

If the licensee assumes responsibility for delivery of the license to the new broker, he or she must deliver it as soon as possible after receipt.

When the broker returns the wall certificate to the Commission, he or she must include a release signed by the broker and the licensee.

When a broker is releasing the licensee for any reason other than licensee's request and is unable to obtain licensee's signature, the broker must send the Commission a copy of the letter mailed to the licensee's last known address indicating that the broker is returning the license to the Commission, and that the licensee has one month from the Commission's receipt of the licensee's wall certificate to transfer to another broker or place the license on inactive status.

Disputes over agreement terms between the broker and licensee cannot be grounds for the broker's refusal to sign release and forward wall certificate to the Commission, nor for the parties to file a complaint with the Commission.

Any licensee whose license is released by a broker cannot engage in real estate activities until the licensee personally delivers to the Commission an approved application to transfer the license to a new broker or has the United States Postal Service postmark a letter containing an application; or receives a wall certificate of licensure from the Commission authorizing the licensee to serve as the broker or the qualifying broker of a firm.

A licensee transferring to a new broker may continue to act as a licensee for the former broker with regard to transactions begun prior to the transfer, if both brokers agree in writing as to the licensee's actions and list in the agreement the specific transactions in which the licensee will be acting on behalf of the former broker. The written agreement must also state how the licensee will be compensated by the former broker. The former broker must agree in writing to be responsible for the licensee's activities related to the listed transactions.

The transferring licensee is prohibited from using any written brokerage engagement obtained through the firm, unless authorized by the broker. The names of prospective customers or clients given in writing to the transferring licensee during his or her affiliation must be accounted for to that broker. All property plats, keys, transaction records, and other property belonging to the broker must be returned in person by the transferring licensee. Brokerage engagements belong to the broker and must remain with the broker.

The licensee's failure to meet these requirements is not grounds for the broker's refusal to sign the release and forward the wall certificate, but can be grounds for filing a formal written complaint with the Commission.

The broker wanting the licensee to affiliate with his or her firm must enter into a written agreement expressing terms for transferring from the previous broker.

The licensee must transfer his or her license to another broker or apply for inactive status within one month of the Commission's receipt of the wall certificate.

Wall certificate of licensure. Newly licensed salespersons or community association managers may not begin brokerage activities until the broker receives the licensee's wall certificate. The licensee may not begin brokerage activities until the wall certificate is received.

Qualifying brokers affiliated with multiple firms. An individual licensed as broker or qualifying broker may serve as broker or qualifying broker with more than one licensed firm. An associate broker affiliated with a licensed firm may serve as broker or qualifying broker for more than one licensed firm provided that he or she notified the broker with whom the associate broker is affiliated of intending to provide services with another firm. This notice must be in writing.

MANAGEMENT RESPONSIBILITIES OF THE BROKERAGE FIRM

MANAGEMENT RESPONSIBILITIES OF REAL ESTATE FIRMS

Brokerage operations requirements

- each type of firm required to have broker or qualifying broker
- must assign new qualifying broker within 60 days of death or termination of qualifying broker
- employee v. independent contractor determined by broker

Broker and qualifying broker requirements

- conduct business in firm's name, train licensees, review contracts and trust account records, ads, brokerage agreements; contract with affiliated licensees and support personnel; transferring licensees; notify Commission of violations

==

Check Your Understanding Quiz:

Unit Four: Management Responsibilities of the Brokerage Firm

Carefully read each question and provide your best answer based on what you learned in this unit. Then check your answers against the Answer Key which immediately follows the quiz questions.

1. If a qualifying broker resigns, the brokerage company must obtain a new qualifying broker

    a. within 60 days.
    b. within 30 days.
    c. as soon as possible.
    d. when the appropriately qualified individual becomes available.

2. Which of the following is not a determining factor in deciding if a licensee will be an employee or an independent contractor?

    a. The amount of control the broker wishes to have over the brokerage activities
    b. The licensee's preference
    c. The type of paperwork required by the government
    d. Whether or not benefits are to be paid

3. Under what name must the broker conduct real estate business?

    a. The broker's legal name
    b. The name of the brokerage company
    c. The name on the broker's license
    d. Any name the broker so chooses

4. The broker is responsible when any affiliated licensee violates license law

    a. unless the broker can show existing procedures for supervising the licensee and that the broker did not participate in the violation.
    b. in every case since the broker is responsible for supervising the licensee's activities.
    c. unless the broker can show that training in complying with license law has been provided.
    d. The broker is never responsible for a licensee violating license law; only the licensee is to be held responsible.

5. The broker is responsible for reviewing offers or contracts within _____ of the document's date.

    a. 5 business days
    b. 10 days
    c. 20 business days
    d. 30 days

6. Which of the following statements is false?

   a. The broker is responsible for entering into a written agreement with all licensed affiliates regarding compensation.
   b. The employment agreement must specify how the licensee is to be compensated for work not completed upon the licensee's termination.
   c. The Commission regulates the content of the employment agreement.
   d. The Commission does not enforce the provisions of employment agreements.

7. Which of the following is true?

   a. The broker is responsible for orally explaining policies and procedures which the licensee must follow.
   b. The broker may pay commissions to support personnel.
   c. The firm may pay commissions to inactive licensees but not any unlicensed person.
   d. The broker or qualifying broker must ensure that any licensing activity is performed only by licensees.

8. A licensee transferring from the affiliated broker has _____ from the Commission's receipt of the licensee's wall certificate to transfer to another broker.

   a. 5 days
   b. 14 days
   c. 1 month
   d. 6 months

9. When a licensee is transferring out of a firm and the broker returns the wall certificate to the Commission, what else must the broker include with the certificate?

   a. A letter explaining the circumstances leading to the licensee's transfer
   b. A copy of the broker's own wall certificate
   c. A release signed by both the broker and the licensee
   d. A copy of the agreement between the broker and licensee signed at the beginning of the licensee's affiliation with the broker

10. If a licensee fails to meet the requirements to transfer to another firm, the broker

    a. may file a written complaint with the Commission.
    b. may refuse to sign the release.
    c. may refuse to forward the licensee's wall certificate to the Commission or the new broker.
    d. has no recourse.

Answer Key:

Unit Four: Management Responsibilities of the Brokerage Firm

1. a.   within 60 days.
2. b.   The licensee's preference
3. c.   The name on the broker's license
4. a.   unless the broker can show existing procedures for supervising the licensee and that the broker did not participate in the violation.
5. d.   30 days
6. c.   The Commission regulates the content of the employment agreement.
7. d.   The broker or qualifying broker must ensure that any licensing activity is performed only by licensees.
8. c.   1 month
9. c.   A release signed by both the broker and the licensee
10. a.   may file a written complaint with the Commission.

UNIT 5:

BROKER-SALESPERSON RELATIONSHIP, UNLICENSED ASSISTANTS

Unit Five Learning Objectives: When the student has completed this unit, he or she will be able to:

- Explain the specifics of a broker relationship with independent contractors as it differs from the relationship with employees.
- Identify the obligations of both the broker and the sales agent in an employment relationship and explain how compensation is determined.
- Define ministerial activities and list those permitted by unlicensed assistants, licensees, and unlicensed property management assistants.
- Identify the required agreements related to employing unlicensed support personnel.

BROKER-SALESPERSON RELATIONSHIP

Only a broker with an active broker's license can hire and employ a licensed salesperson. A licensed salesperson may work only for the employing broker and may not work for or receive direct compensation from any other broker.

Salesperson's employment status

A sales agent may be an independent contractor (IC) or an employee. In either case, the broker is responsible and liable for the sales agent's actions. Brokers are subject to guidelines of the U.S. Equal Employment Opportunity Commission (EEOC), a federal agency that enforces laws against workplace discrimination.

Independent contractor / broker relationship. Generally, a broker has limited control over the actions of a contractor. Specifically:

- a broker can require performance results, but is limited in demanding *how* a contractor performs the work. For example, a broker may not prescribe selling methods, meeting attendance, or office hours.
- an IC is responsible for income and social security taxes; the broker does not withhold taxes
- a broker cannot provide an IC with employee benefits such as health insurance or pension plans

Employee / broker relationship. A broker has greater control over the actions of an employee. Specifically:

- a broker can impose a sales methodology. In addition, a broker can enforce all office policies, including hours, meeting attendance, and telephone coverage.
- a broker must withhold income taxes and pay unemployment compensation tax on behalf of an employee
- an employee may receive the benefits enjoyed by the broker's non-selling employees

A written agreement between broker and employee or independent contractor should clearly state each party's duties and responsibilities to the other. In addition, the agreement should clarify the agent's compensation program as well as who is to pay for incidental business expenses.

Obligations and responsibilities

Sales agent's duties and responsibilities. In accepting employment from a broker, a salesperson generally makes a commitment to:

- work diligently to sell the broker's listings
- work diligently to procure new listings
- promote the business reputation of the broker
- abide by the broker's established policies
- fulfill the fiduciary duties owed clients as their subagent
- maintain insurance policies as required by the broker
- have transportation for conducting business, as required by the broker
- conform to ethical standards imposed by broker and trade organization
- uphold all covenants and provisions of the employment agreement

Broker's obligations to the sales agent. In employing a salesperson, a broker generally makes a commitment to:

- make the brokerage's listings available
- make the brokerage's market and property data available
- provide whatever training was promised at the time of hiring
- provide whatever office support was promised at the time of hiring
- uphold the commission structure and expense reimbursement policy
- conform to ethical standards imposed by the broker's trade organization
- uphold all covenants and provisions of the employment agreement

Agent compensation

An agent employee of a broker may receive wages, salary, additional commissions, expense reimbursements, and benefit plans. An independent contractor's compensation is a normally a combination of commissions and free office support. Most sales agents work as independent contractors who earn a commission.

Commission splits. A sales agent earns compensation for procuring listings and for procuring buyers or tenants, whenever a transaction results. In the jargon of brokerage, these are the two "sides" to a commission: the listing side and the selling side. An agent who procures a listing receives a share of the broker's listing side commission, according to the agent's commission schedule. An agent who sells a listing, i.e., finds the customer, receives a share of the broker's selling side of the commission, according to the commission schedule. An agent who procures both listing and customer receives a share of the broker's listing side commission and selling side commission.

Commission schedules. An agent's commission schedule is a comprehensive summary of commission splits under various circumstances, including:

- listing and selling side
- salesperson's level of sales performance
- broker's level of expense reimbursement to agent
- the particular policies or organization of the agency

- prevailing commission splits in the market

In view of these circumstances, an agent's commission schedule can vary widely. For example, an agent who is the highest sales producer in the market may be able to secure a 70% or 80% commission split with the broker, regardless of side. If the broker is paying an inordinate amount of selling expenses, an agent's commission split may only be 40%. Some brokerages have a policy of not paying any expenses except the rent. In such cases, agents may receive an 80% or 90% commission split. In almost all cases, broker and agent negotiate the schedule of commissions in the environment of competitive market conditions.

Calculating commissions. The following exhibit illustrates how commissions might be split in a hypothetical transaction.

Calculating Commissions

Sale price: $500,000   Co-brokerage splits: 50%
Commission: 6%, or $30,000   Agent splits: 50% on both sides

Situation A: a cooperating broker is involved

	Commission $	Commission %
Listing broker	7,500	1.5%
Listing agent	7,500	1.5%
Selling broker	7,500	1.5%
Selling agent	7,500	1.5%

Situation B: no cooperating broker; listing agent finds buyer

Listing broker	15,000	3.0%
Listing agent	15,000	3.0%

Situation C: no cooperating broker; another agent *in the same agency* finds buyer

Listing broker	15,000	3.0%
Listing agent	7,500	1.5%
Selling agent	7,500	1.5%

UNLICENSED ASSISTANTS

Real estate assistant or personal assistant

Brokers and salespersons may hire licensed or unlicensed employees to assist them with a variety of tasks. Unlicensed assistants may perform clerical or ministerial acts, but nothing requiring a license. Licensed assistants may perform tasks requiring a license. Unlicensed assistants usually may be compensated directly by the salesperson they work for, but licensed assistants must be compensated by the employing broker and are subject to that broker's supervision.

Support personnel activity. [Rule 520-1-.07 (6)]. When a licensee affiliated with a firm engages support personnel to help in conducting real estate business, both the firm and the affiliated licensee are responsible for the acts of the support personnel and for assuring that the support personnel comply with the requirements of License Law and the Rules and Regulations.

Written agreement(s) required. A firm that employs or contracts with support personnel to assist in conducting real estate activities must have a written agreement with the support personnel specifying the duties that the support personnel may perform on behalf of the firm or on behalf of an affiliated licensee of the firm, and the tasks that support personnel are prohibited from performing.

If an affiliated licensee employs or contracts with the support personnel, the broker must enter into a written agreement with the affiliated licensee authorizing the use of the support personnel and specifying the duties that the support personnel may perform for the affiliated licensee and tasks that the support personnel are prohibited from performing. The agreement must also include the broker's approval of any compensation arrangement the affiliated licensee has with the support personnel. Additionally, the affiliated licensee and the support personnel must have a separate written agreement specifying duties permitted and prohibited by the support personnel.

To recap, there are three separate written agreements regarding support personnel:

- an agreement between the broker and the support personnel
- an agreement between the broker and the affiliated licensee, if the affiliated licensee is using the services of the support personnel
- an agreement between the affiliated licensee and support personnel.

An individual actively licensed with one firm may work as support personnel for a different firm or for a licensee of a different firm only after obtaining written consent of the broker of both firms. An inactive licensee may also work as support personnel for a firm or an affiliated licensee.

Ministerial acts

Ministerial activities permitted by unlicensed support personnel. Ministerial acts are those acts that are informative but do not rise to the level of representation. Ministerial acts as listed here are those acts related to real estate activities that support personnel may perform and that do not require discretion or the exercise of the support personnel's own judgment.

The Commission has identified certain tasks that support personnel are permitted to perform, as guidelines for brokerage firms, affiliated licensees, and support personnel. Although the list of permissible items does not include every permitted activity, it should be remembered that unlicensed support personnel may not perform any real estate licensing activity on behalf of the broker or affiliated licensee.

Support personnel may

- schedule appointments with the owner or owner's agent to show listed property;
- schedule inspections, mortgage applications, pre-closing (final walk-through) inspections, closings and open houses
- answer and forward phone calls and emails
- submit listing and listing change data to a multiple listing service
- assemble documents for closings
- compute commission checks
- verify the status of a loan commitment
- have keys made for the company's listings
- install or remove lock boxes
- place and remove signs
- type contract forms as directed by the broker or affiliated licensee
- write ads and promotional materials for approval by the firm
- place ads in media as directed and approved by the broker
- record and deposit earnest money, rents and security deposits
- obtain documents from the courthouse or other public resources

- act as a courier in obtaining or delivering keys and documents
- monitor personnel files and license reports from the Commission
- order routine repair items and perform physical maintenance tasks

Support personnel sometimes accompany a licensee to an open house or showing for security purposes only. The support personnel may not answer any questions regarding the property, contracts, the neighborhood, etc. Questions must be answered only by the licensee.

Prohibited activities for unlicensed support personnel. The Commission has identified certain following tasks that cannot be performed by unlicensed support personnel. Again, items covered here are not all-inclusive, but are provided as guidelines. For instance, support personnel may not make cold calls or do any type of prospecting. Keep in mind that prospecting for clients is an activity requiring a real estate license. Support personnel are also prohibited from holding or hosting open houses, or hosting kiosks, home show booths or fairs.

Support personnel may prepare promotional material or ads only with the review and approval of a licensee. They may not write or place ads on their own, without the direction of a licensee.

They cannot show real estate, respond to questions regarding financing, closings or title, nor can they answer questions regarding listings except price and amenities as authorized in writing by a licensee. This can be difficult to adhere to, because consumers inherently have additional questions. If the support personnel answered some questions regarding the property, it is difficult for the consumer to understand why that person is unable to answer additional questions. Support personnel may not discuss amenities or features of real estate under any circumstances, with a prospective purchaser or tenant; neither can they discuss the terms or conditions of real estate offered for sale or lease with the owner. Support personnel are also prohibited from providing owners or prospective purchasers or tenants with any advice or recommendations regarding the sale, purchase, exchange, or leasing of real estate.

Support personnel are prohibited from discussing or explaining any contracts, offers, brokerage agreement, or other real estate documents with anyone outside the brokerage firm. They may not negotiate or agree to any commission, commission split, referral fee, or management fee, on behalf of the broker, nor can they collect or hold deposits, rent, or anything of value received from owner, purchasers, renters, or any consumer.

Unlicensed support personnel and inactive licensees may not indicate in any way, orally or in writing, as being actively licensed or affiliated with a particular brokerage company or broker as a licensee.

Ministerial activities permitted by licensees. These are acts related to the real estate transaction that a licensee or the licensee's employee may perform which do not require discretion or the exercise of the licensee's own judgment. Ministerial acts do not include providing advice or counsel; they are not agency duties.

A broker who represents a seller, buyer, tenant or landlord may provide assistance to the other party in the transaction by performing ministerial acts without violating the terms of the brokerage engagement.

Ministerial acts include identifying property for sale, lease, or exchange for the customer. Ministerial acts also include providing customers with real estate statistics and property information. The licensee can provide to the customer specific information on the property or on real estate in general.

Licensees may provide consumers with preprinted real estate form contracts, leases, and other related forms, and can complete contract forms as directed by a customer (act as a scribe). Some examples of a licensee providing these ministerial acts are providing or completing contracts as directed by the customer:

- for the seller on behalf of a buyer client who is interested in buying the seller's unlisted property;
- for the buyer who attends the open house of a property listed by the licensee,
- for a landlord when representing the tenant, or
- for the tenant when representing the landlord.

Ministerial acts include assisting the customer by locating professionals, such as inspectors, lenders, engineers, surveyors, insurance agents, attorneys, or home warranty companies. Licensees are often asked for names of professionals whose services are needed in a real estate transaction. Licensees should consult their broker or office policy regarding the company's policy. Some brokerages require affiliated licensees to provide at least three names for any type of professional services, and companies often have a list of several. Also, some brokerages use a specific form providing names of professionals, indicating that the company is providing names but is not endorsing the service providers.

Licensees are also permitted to perform the ministerial acts of identifying schools, places of worship, shopping areas, local activity centers and other similar facilities for the parties of a real estate transaction.

To recap, ministerial acts are acts performed for a customer and are not agency duties.

Ministerial activities permitted by unlicensed property management assistants. Unlicensed individuals employed by a broker to assist in property management services may perform ministerial activities if the activities are authorized in the agreement between the broker and employee and are limited to:

- delivering, receiving and executing lease applications, leases, or amendments, executing rental agreements, and receiving rent payments, security deposits, or related payments to be delivered to and made payable to the broker or owner, and providing information authorized by the broker about the rental units, the applications, or leases
- showing rental units, when directly instructed to do so by the broker
- providing the owner with information regarding financial accounts and payments from owner's tenants
- providing a tenant information about the status of his or her security deposit or rent payments
- performing ministerial acts as authorized by the broker in the written agreement between the broker and the employee

A broker utilizing the services of an unlicensed employee is held responsible for activities of that employee.

BROKER-SALESPERSON RELATIONSHIP, UNLICENSED ASSISTANTS, TEAMS

BROKER-SALESPERSON RELATIONSHIP

Legal relationships

- salesperson is agent, fiduciary of broker; acts in broker's name; subagent of client
- **may not:** have two employers; be paid by other parties; bind clients contractually

Salesperson's employment status

- may be employee or contractor; relationship defined by agreement; assistant may be licensed or unlicensed; if licensed, supervised and paid by employing broker

Obligations and responsibilities

- agent to broker: obtain & sell listings; follow policies and employment provisions; promote ethics and broker's reputation
- broker to agent: provide data, office support, compensation, training; uphold ethics, policies, and employment agreement

Agent compensation

- commissions per schedule after splits with cooperating brokers

UNLICENSED ASSISTANTS

Support personnel and ministerial activities

- may conduct ministerial acts, no licensing activity; must have agreements with firm and licensee
- ministerial acts performed fora customer; do not require the licensee's judgment or discretion
- permitted by property management assistant if authorized in agreement between broker and employee; limited activities+

===

Check Your Understanding Quiz:

Unit Five: Broker-Salesperson Relationship, Unlicensed Assistants

Carefully read each question and provide your best answer based on what you learned in this unit. Then check your answers against the Answer Key which immediately follows the quiz questions.

1. From whom may a licensed salesperson receive direct compensation?

    a. The client
    b. The affiliated broker
    c. An unaffiliated broker
    d. Anyone to whom the salesperson provides services

2. Which of the following applies to an independent contractor?

    a. Taxes are withheld from compensation.
    b. Benefits such as health insurance are provided by the broker.
    c. Performance results may be required.
    d. Working hours and overtime may be required.

3. Which of the following does not apply to a broker's employee?

    a. The broker has limited control of the employee's methodologies.
    b. The broker can require meeting attendance.
    c. Income tax is withheld from compensation.
    d. A sales methodology may be imposed.

4. How does a broker normally compensate an independent contractor?

    a. Salary
    b. Commission split
    c. Wages
    d. Benefit plan

5. Which of the following is not typically figured into an agent's commission schedule?

    a. The agent's level of sales performance
    b. The organization of the agency
    c. The market's prevailing commission splits
    d. The office support provided

6. In a situation where the listing agent finds the buyer with no cooperating broker, where the sale commission is 6%, and where the agent split is 50% on both sides, how much commission will the agent receive on a $300,000 sale price?

   a. $18,000
   b. $15,000
   c. $9,000
   d. $7,500

7. In a situation where the listing agent works with a cooperating broker whose salesperson found the buyer, where the sale commission is 6%, and where the agent split is 50% on both sides, how much commission will the listing agent receive on a $300,000 sale price?

   a. $18,000
   b. $9,000
   c. $4,500
   d. $3,750

8. If the sale price is $300,000, the commission rate is 6% and there is a cooperating broker, how much commission will the cooperating broker receive on the sale?

   a. $18,000
   b. $9,000
   c. $4,500
   d. $3,750

9. If a licensee employs support personnel to assist in conducting the licensee's activities, what agreement(s) must be in place?

   a. An agreement between the licensee's affiliated broker and the support personnel
   b. An agreement between the broker and the support personnel and an agreement between the licensee and the support personnel
   c. An agreement between the broker and the licensee, an agreement between the licensee and the support personnel, and an agreement between the broker and the support personnel
   d. No agreements are necessary since the support personnel is an employee and not an independent contractor.

10. When a licensee hires support personnel to assist in conducting specific tasks, who is responsible for the support personnel's activities and compliance with license law?

    a. Both the licensee and the affiliated broker
    b. Just the licensee
    c. Just the affiliated broker
    d. The support personnel

11. What are ministerial acts?

   a. Acts performed by religious leaders
   b. Acts all licensees are required to perform for clients
   c. Acts that do not require discretion, judgment, or licensure
   d. Acts that are informative and rise to the level of representation

12. Which of the following statements is true?

   a. Unlicensed support personnel may verify the status of a loan commitment.
   b. Unlicensed support personnel may perform any real estate licensing activity on behalf of the broker.
   c. Support personnel are not permitted to submit listings to a multiple listing service.
   d. Support personnel may hold open houses on behalf of the broker.

13. Support personnel are prohibited from

   a. performing ministerial activities.
   b. depositing earnest money.
   c. scheduling inspections.
   d. explaining contracts to clients.

14. Which of the following is a ministerial act that a licensee is permitted to perform for the non-represented party in a transaction?

   a. Providing the other party with advice about the client's property
   b. Recommending offer terms to the other party regarding the client's property
   c. Identifying properties for sale for the customer
   d. A licensee is not permitted to perform ministerial acts for anyone other than a signed client.

15. Which of the following is an unlicensed property management assistant prohibited from doing?

   a. Showing rental units without direct instructions from the broker
   b. Providing a tenant with the status of his security deposit
   c. Providing the owner with information about tenant rent payments
   d. Executing lease applications

==

Answer Key:

Unit Five: Broker-Salesperson Relationship, Unlicensed Assistants, Teams

1. b. The affiliated broker
2. c. Performance results may be required.
3. a. The broker has limited control of the employee's actions.
4. b. Commission split
5. d. The office support provided
6. c. $9,000
7. c. $4,500
8. c. $4,500
9. c. An agreement between the broker and the licensee, an agreement between the licensee and the support personnel, and an agreement between the broker and the support personnel
10. a. Both the licensee and the affiliated broker
11. c. Acts that do not require discretion, judgment, or licensure
12. a. Unlicensed support personnel may verify the status of a loan commitment.
13. d. explaining contracts to clients.
14. c. Identifying properties for sale for the customer
15. a. Showing rental units without direct instructions from the broker

UNIT 6:

ADVERTISING REGULATIONS

Unit Six Learning Objectives: When the student has completed this unit, he or she will be able to:

- Explain Georgia real estate advertising rules specifically addressing misleading advertising, internet advertising, and the use of firm and trade names in advertising.
- Identify requirements licensees must meet when advertising real estate in Georgia.

ADVERTISING REGULATIONS

Advertisement regulations

Advertising is an important tool in marketing properties and procuring buyers. It is, however, subject to regulation and restrictions.

Advertising (Rule 520-1-.09)

The Rules provide guidelines with regard to advertising. Advertising includes any means in which a licensee uses any media to inform the general public of real estate for sale, lease, rent or exchange.

Media includes television, radio, Internet (including websites, blogs, vlogs, etc.), newspapers, photographs, magazines, business cards, posters, billboards, flyers, office signs, for sale signs, for lease signs, sold signs, directional signs, signs on vehicles, newsletters, voicemail, email, email farming, fax transmissions, bulletin boards, social networking, text messages, banner ads. In short, anything that is created or used to market property in any way that the public can see or hear is advertising.

The license laws of most states list illegal advertising actions subject to discipline such as:

- making any substantial and intentional misrepresentation
- making any promise that might cause a person to enter into a contract or agreement when the promise is one the licensee cannot or will not abide by
- making continued and blatant misrepresentations or false promises through affiliate brokers, other persons, or any advertising medium
- making misleading or untruthful statements in any advertising, including using the term "Realtor" when not authorized to do so and using any other trade name, insignia or membership in a real estate organization when the licensee is not a member.

Committing such acts may result in license suspension or revocation.

Misleading advertising. Advertising must not be misleading or inaccurate regarding material facts, nor can it in any way misrepresent real estate or its features. When a licensee becomes aware that a principal is advertising to sell, buy, rent, lease, or exchange real estate in any way that does not comply, the licensee must immediately take steps to stop the advertising until it is in compliance.

Licensees are prohibited from intentionally using advertising that is misleading, inaccurate or in any way misrepresents property, terms, values, policies, or services. The broker has the responsibility of overseeing all advertising to ensure compliance.

Advertising requirements

All advertising by associate brokers, salespersons, and community association managers must be under the direct supervision of their broker and in the name of their firm. Ads that do not contain the name of the firm are referred to as "blind ads" because the consumer might assume the advertiser is a seller or landlord advertising property for sale, rather than a real estate licensee.

Licensees are prohibited from advertising real estate unless the licensee first obtains written permission of the owner or the owner's authorized agent. Licensees are prohibited from placing a sign on property without the written consent of the owner. Signs must be removed within ten days after the listing expires. Leaving the sign longer than ten days beyond expiration constitutes illegally advertising property no longer listed by the licensee.

Discriminatory advertising is strictly prohibited. A licensee must not advertise to sell, buy, exchange, rent, or lease real estate when the ad is directed at persons of a certain race, color, national origin, religion, gender, handicap, or familial status. Ads must be confined to information regarding the real estate. Violations include making any type of ad that indicates any preference, limitation, or discrimination. Keep in mind that discriminatory advertising is a violation of License Law, federal fair housing laws, and the REALTOR® Code of Ethics.

When permission is granted by the listing firm, a licensee advertising real estate listed with another firm must conspicuously disclose that fact and the name of the listing firm, unless the listing firm agreed in writing to waive that disclosure.

Internet advertising

Licensees advertising real estate on the Internet must disclose the name and phone number of the licensee's firm on every viewable webpage of the site. When advertising in electronic messages that are limited in size, a license may instead use a direct link to a display that has the firm's name and phone number. When advertising on an internet website not owned or controlled by the licensee or the licensee's firm, and that website's terms of use limit the licensee's ability to comply, the advertising must provide a direct link on every viewable webpage of the website.

Updating the site. Outdated information on a website maintained by a licensee must be revised or removed from the website within thirty days of the information becoming outdated. If a licensee's website is maintained by an authorized third party, the licensee must provide the party a timely written notice of outdated information or information to be removed from the website. A licensee who provides timely notice will not be in violation if the third party fails to affect an information change as requested by the licensee.

These advertising requirements apply to information on a website that is within the licensee's ownership or direct control. Licensees are not responsible for any information taken from the licensee's website, or other advertising, if placed on a website or in other advertising outside the licensee's direct control and without the licensee's consent.

Trade names and franchise names

The term "trade name" includes trademark and service mark and also includes advertising done by others on behalf of the licensee. Firms using a trade name, or any franchisee, must clearly and unmistakably include the firm's name as registered with the Commission in a manner that attracts the attention of the public. The firm's name must appear adjacent to any specific real estate the firm advertises so that the public can identify the firm that has the real estate listed.

In advertising real estate, the name of the firm must be in equal or greater size, prominence, and frequency than the names of any affiliated licensees. Any firm using a trade name or any franchisee must clearly include the firm's name as registered with the Commission on any contracts or other documents related to real estate transactions, and clearly include the firm's name on office signs.

Firm names and telephone numbers in advertising. When advertising real estate firms must include the name of the firm as registered with the Commission and a telephone number for the firm. The name and telephone number of the firm advertising the real estate for sale, rent, or exchange must appear in equal or greater size, prominence, and frequency than the name of any affiliated licensees.

The phone number must reach a broker or a manager of the firm without going through an affiliated licensee listed in the ad. A block advertisement in any print media that advertises the firm's listings and includes the name of the listing agent next to each listing will be in compliance if the name of the firm appears only once at the top of the ad in equal or greater prominence and print size than any of the listing licensee's names. The firm's name may be located in other positions in block advertisements if the firm name appears larger and more prominently displayed than the name of any other licensee in the ad.

Licensees advertising as principals

A licensee may not advertise real estate in any way indicating that the offer is being made by a private, unlicensed party. Every associate broker, salesperson, and community association manager is prohibited from advertising under the licensee's individual name to buy or offer for sale, rent, or lease real estate. All advertising must be under the direct supervision of the broker and in the name of the firm. However, when a licensee wishes to advertise real estate owned by the licensee, the licensee may do so if the broker holding the licensee's license has been notified in writing of the specific real estate to be advertised, gives written consent, and approves the ad.

Regardless of whether the licensee's license is actively licensed or on inactive status, any advertisement must include one of the following:

- "(seller, buyer, landlord, tenant) _____ holds a real estate license"
- "Georgia Real Estate License # _____."

A licensee must make every reasonable attempt in advertising to assure that consumers know that they are being contacted by a licensee.

Licensees advertising approved schools

A licensee may not advertise that the licensee offers, sponsors, or conducts Commission approved courses or does so in conjunction with an approved school or other approved organization unless the licensee is approved by the Commission to offer the courses.

Telephone Consumer Protection Act

The TCPA (Telephone Consumer Protection Act) addresses the regulation of unsolicited telemarketing phone calls. Rules include the following:

- telephone solicitors must identify themselves, on whose behalf they are calling, and how they can be contacted
- telemarketers must comply with any do-not-call request made during the solicitation call
- consumers can place their home and wireless phone numbers on a national Do-Not-Call list which prohibits future solicitations from telemarketers.

CAN-SPAM Act

The CAN-SPAM Act (Controlling the Assault of Non-Solicited Pornography and Marketing Act of 2003) supplements the Telephone Consumer Protection Act (TCPA). It

- bans sending unwanted email 'commercial messages' to wireless devices
- requires express prior authorization
- requires giving an 'opt out' choice to terminate the sender's messages

SNAPSHOT REVIEW: UNIT SIX

ADVERTISING REGULATIONS

ADVERTISING

- in name of firm; broker supervision; authorized by property owner; nondiscriminatory, not misleading
- special requirements for Internet
- use of trade names, franchise names, and firm name; firm telephone numbers
- license to obtain broker approval when advertising licensee's own property
- no advertising schools unless approved by Commission
- requirements for telemarketing calls
- requirements for email advertising

Check Your Understanding Quiz:

Unit Six: Advertising Regulations

Carefully read each question and provide your best answer based on what you learned in this unit. Then check your answers against the Answer Key which immediately follows the quiz questions.

1. If a licensee becomes aware that a principal is advertising property for sale in a way that is out of compliance with advertising rules, the licensee must

    a. immediately notify the Commission.
    b. notify the affiliated broker.
    c. take steps to stop the advertising.
    d. do nothing since it is the principal and not the licensee who is advertising the property.

2. Blind ads are those that

    a. do not include photos of the property.
    b. do not include the property's address.
    c. do not include the asking price of the property.
    d. do not include the firm's name.

3. Signs placed on a property for sale must be removed within _____ of the listing expiration date.

    a. 5 days
    b. 10 days
    c. 3 days
    d. 24 hours

4. To avoid discriminatory advertising, ads

    a. should be limited to information about the property itself.
    b. must include HUD's fair housing logo.
    c. should include anti-discrimination language.
    d. should state the specific audience the ad is targeting.

5. When a licensee is advertising on the Internet, what must be included on every viewable webpage of the site?

    a. The licensee's designation (salesperson, broker)
    b. The licensee's phone number
    c. The name and address of the firm
    d. The name and phone number of the firm

6. A licensee's website must be updated within _____ days of any information becoming outdated.

    a. 5
    b. 10
    c. 20
    d. 30

7. When using a trade name in advertising, the firm's name must be shown

    a. at the bottom of each printed document.
    b. on all office signs.
    c. above any properties the firm is advertising.
    d. below and smaller than the name of the advertising affiliated licensee.

8. The CAN-SPAM Act

    a. regulates telemarketing phone calls.
    b. requires an "opt out" option to stop receiving a sender's email messages.
    c. allows consumers to place their phone numbers on a Do-Not-Call list.
    d. allows unsolicited email commercial messages to wireless devices.

==

Answer Key:

Unit Six: Advertising Regulations

1. c. take steps to stop the advertising.
2. d. do not include the firm's name.
3. b. 10 days
4. a. should be limited to information about the property itself.
5. d. The name and phone number of the firm
6. d. 30
7. b. on all office signs.
8. b. requires an "opt out" option to stop receiving a sender's email messages.

UNIT 7:

GENERAL OFFICE RULES AND POLICIES

Unit Seven Learning Objectives: When the student has completed this unit, he or she will be able to:

- Explain the benefit of having written company policies and rules and identify topics that should be included as policies and rules.
- Describe what topics should be included in the company procedures.

GENERAL OFFICE RULES AND POLICIES

The broker or qualifying broker is responsible for establishing, implementing, and continuing procedures for all business areas and providing all licensed personnel with written policies, rules, and procedures as instructions under which they are expected to operate. An effective way to do that is by developing a policy manual that will set rules and boundaries under which staff and brokers can operate and will reflect the company's culture.

The written instructions or manual should also include ministerial acts performed by both licensees and unlicensed personnel.

Policies and rules

In addition to following real estate laws and rules, each managing broker most likely has his or her own philosophy on how the firm's business should be conducted. Therefore, the managing broker needs to make sure that all brokerage employees and contractors understand the company philosophy.

A well-managed brokerage relies on written policies and rules to keep the business running smoothly and professionally. Written and uniformly enforced rules let everyone in the firm know what to expect before problems arise. The company policies and rules should include the following:

- Personnel policies and rules – dress code, desk space and whether it will be shared, the purpose and schedules for floor time, cooperation among brokers and staff, telephone procedures, expense reimbursement, dispute prevention and resolution, office rules violations, causes of and procedures for termination, and so forth.
- Agency and independent contractor relationships – in addition to the legal mandates for these relationships, company rules should include how the managing broker wants the relationships to be handled within his or her own firm.
- Use and limitations of unlicensed personal assistants – lists of types of activities the assistants are allowed to perform and those that are prohibited without a license.
- Office policy regarding dual agency – development and enforcement of an office brokerage relationship policy that is provided to all affiliated licensees, with rules specifically permitting or rejecting disclosed dual agency.
- Disclosure of agency relationships by licensees in residential real estate transactions – a repeat of disclosure laws and rules as well as a copy of the form to be used.
- Designated agency relationships – the company's policy on assigning different affiliated licensees as agents to exclusively represent opposing brokerage clients in the same transaction and ensuring that each client is represented in compliance with BRRETA requirements.

- Ethical standards – the company's ethical standards, possibly referring to USPAP for ethical standards of the real estate profession as a whole as well as company rules for how these standards are to be practiced.
- Rules for continuing education, sales meeting participation, and property tours – although CE is covered within the state's license law and regulations, repeating the requirements within the company's rules would serve as a reminder to licensees.
- New or changed local, State, and federal real estate laws and regulations – policies for the distribution and dissemination of information on changes and updates within the laws.
- Marketing of the firm and business entities – the managing broker's policy for when to market the firm and related business entities and rules on how the marketing is to be performed.
- Advertisement requirements for real estate transactions – including who is responsible for and legally allowed to write advertisement content and place the ads, as well as what media the company permits to be used for advertising, who pays for advertising and signs, what is to be included or avoided in advertising, how the firm's name is to be displayed on signs and in ads, when and where signs are to be placed, and how the company's trade name (if applicable) is to be used.
- HUD poster – a standard HUD poster is to be displayed in every office to affirm the broker's compliance with fair housing laws in selling, renting, advertising, and financing residential properties. Failure to display the poster may be construed as discrimination.
- Responsibilities of the managing broker – policies on what responsibilities the managing broker has to employees and brokers, covering the level of supervision the managing broker will exercise over staff and brokers, licensing requirements, the managing broker's policy on enforcing rules and laws, application and transfer request procedures and signing, and so forth.
- Technology rules – for such areas as virus protection requirements, personal use of company email programs, use of personal technology devices, social networking language and potential liability issues, sharing equipment and password access, cell phone use, types of allowed devices, data storage and backup, regularly updated information on email and telephone scams.

Procedures

In addition to the company policies and rules, the managing broker should have documented procedures for staff and licensees to follow when conducting the business of the broker's firm. To provide the written policies, rules, and procedures, the managing broker may decide to cover all of these areas in one combined manual or in separate manuals which are updated as needed. Regardless of the form, written procedures should spell out how to handle every aspect of the company's business that agents, brokers, and unlicensed staff need to know:

- Responsibilities of staff and brokers – because each employee and contractor will have an employee agreement that includes the details of expectations of that individual, written procedures should cover general responsibilities such as following and staying up to date on all real estate and license laws, adhering to office policies, fiduciary duties to clients, maintaining appropriate insurance coverage such as Errors and Omissions, responsibilities if terminated, and so forth.
- Proper and legal handling of deposit monies and other funds – the legal requirements for handling trust funds and accounts as well as the broker's procedures for following those requirements.
- Compliance with federal, state, and local fair housing laws and regulations – reminders of the laws as well as procedures to include advertising requirements and prohibitions, sample ads, and suggestions for handling situations that could result in a fair housing violation.
- Dealing with MLS-related matters – to include what is to be listed and procedures for doing so.
- Contracts, leases, and brokerage agreements – the managing broker's preferred procedures for completing these agreements and who needs to approve them.

- Branch office licensing – procedures should include the requirement for branch office licensing and how to obtain the license.
- The sale or lease of a licensee's real property and the licensee's purchase or lease of real property for personal use – procedures for meeting the related requirements, restrictions, limitations, and legally required disclosures as well as the broker's rules on how the licensee is to handle the sale, lease, or purchase, including copies of disclosure forms to be used.
- Unauthorized practice of law by a licensee – a list of activities that constitute unauthorized practice of law and ways in which to avoid the violation.
- Listings and open houses – the company's procedures for showing properties and conducting open houses as well as safety measures to keep brokers safe during showings; also include the company's procedures for procuring listings and what types of listings to seek, what contracts and forms the company uses for listings and agreements including disclosures, working with cooperating brokers and out-of-state brokers, entertaining clients and who pays for the entertainment, allowable means for prospecting for clients and listings, how commissions and referral fees are handled, offers and counteroffers, escrow monies, and closings.
- Legalities – reiteration of certain laws, such as covering discriminatory practices and how to avoid them to prevent liability issues, what constitutes sexual harassment, how to avoid it, and what to do in case it happens. Procedures for incorporating fair housing, equal opportunity, RESPA, Do Not Call, and CAN SPAM laws into every-day conduct.

Adherence to the company policies, rules, and procedures reduces the risk that an individual will inadvertently commit an unlawful act. Whenever changes are made to the policies, rules, and procedures, each agent should be given written updates and be required to sign the documentation as evidence that the agent has examined it.

SNAPSHOT REVIEW: UNIT SEVEN

GENERAL OFFICE RULES AND POLICIES

GENERAL OFFICE RULES AND POLICIES

- managing brokers should develop written policies, rules, and procedures to provide to employees and contractors
- to include personnel policies, relationships, responsibilities, ethical standards, technology, marketing, law compliance, advertising, listings, and so forth
- reduces risk of law violations and should be updated with changes

==

Check Your Understanding Quiz:

Unit Seven: General Office Rules and Policies

Carefully read each question and provide your best answer based on what you learned in this unit. Then check your answers against the Answer Key which immediately follows the quiz questions.

1. To present the company's philosophy and spell out how to handle every aspect of the company's business, a broker should

    a. display posters in the office area.
    b. conduct training sessions.
    c. hold daily staff meetings.
    d. develop written policies, rules, and procedures.

2. Which of the following would not be appropriate to include in a company's written policies?

    a. The terms of an employment contract
    b. The company dress code
    c. The office philosophy on fiduciary duties
    d. Requirements to upgrade smart phones when new phone technology emerges

3. What is the purpose of written company policies and rules?

    a. To replace continuing education courses
    b. To serve as employment agreements
    c. To assure all employees and contractors understand the company philosophy
    d. To eliminate the need for a managing broker

4. Which of the following would cover the company's philosophy on assigning different affiliated licensees as agents to exclusively represent opposing brokerage clients in the same transaction and ensuring that each client is represented in compliance with BRRETA requirements?

    a. Disclosure of agency relationships
    b. Designated agency relationships
    c. Office policy regarding dual agency
    d. Ethical standards

5. Which of the following would not be included in a company rule on use of technology?

    a. Social networking language
    b. Sharing password access
    c. Telephone scams
    d. What media the company permits to be used for advertising

6. Which of the following would not be included in the procedures for staff and broker responsibilities?

   a. An employee agreement that includes the details of expectations of that individual
   b. How to follow and stay up to date on all real estate and license laws
   c. Maintaining appropriate insurance coverage
   d. A licensee's responsibilities if terminated

7. Which of the following would be most helpful in the procedures for avoiding unauthorized practice of law?

   a. A list of affiliated attorneys
   b. A copy of every form and contract the company uses
   c. A list of activities that constitute unauthorized practice of law
   d. An application to a local law school

8. When should managing brokers update and redistribute the company's written policies, rules, and procedures?

   a. When a new employee or contractor joins the firm
   b. When a new managing broker is assigned to the firm
   c. When changes are made
   d. When the firm adds an additional branch office

==

Answer Key:

Unit Seven: General Office Rules and Policies

1. d. develop written policies, rules, and procedures.
2. a. The terms of an employment contract
3. c. To assure all employees and contractors understand the company philosophy
4. b. Designated agency relationships
5. d. What media the company permits to be used for advertising
6. a. An employee agreement that includes the details of expectations of that individual
7. c. A list of activities that constitute unauthorized practice of law
8. c. When changes are made

UNIT 8:

TRUST ACCOUNTS AND HANDLING TRUST FUNDS

Unit Eight Learning Objectives: When the student has completed this unit, he or she will be able to:

- Explain the need for trust accounts and requirements for setting up and maintaining the accounts, including deposits and disbursement of the funds and monthly account reconciliation.
- Describe the Commission's role in approving and examining trust accounts.
- Identify trust fund handling requirements and prohibitions mandated by state law.

TRUST ACCOUNTS

Trust or Escrow Accounts (§ 43-40-20 and Rule 520-1-.08)

Brokers who accept, or whose affiliated licensees accept, any trust funds, including down payments, earnest money deposits, security deposits, rents, or association fees, regarding real estate brokerage transactions must maintain a separate, federally insured account at a financial institution located in Georgia. The account must be designated as a trust or escrow account. All applicable funds received by the broker or affiliated licensees on behalf of a principal or any other person must be deposited into that account.

A broker may maintain more than one trust account if the Commission is notified and provided with the required information.

The trust or escrow account must be registered with the Commission and cannot be subject to attachment or garnishment. Each broker who is required to maintain a trust or escrow account must notify the Commission of the name of the bank in which the trust account is maintained and the number of the account.

A broker who does not accept trust funds is not required to maintain a designated trust account. However, if a broker receives trust funds in a real estate transaction, the broker must open a designated trust or escrow account within one business day of the receipt of the trust funds.

Affiliated licensees must place all cash, checks, or other items of value received by the licensee in a real estate transaction into the custody of the licensee's broker as soon after receipt as practicably possible.

A broker is not entitled to any part of the earnest money, security deposit, or other trust funds paid to the broker in a real estate transaction as part or all of the broker's commission or fee until the transaction has been consummated or terminated.

Unless otherwise agreed in writing by the parties, the broker holding cash or checks must promptly deposit the funds in a federally insured checking account designated by the bank as a trust account and registered with the Commission, and the broker must make arrangements for the safekeeping of any items of value received other than cash or checks. The funds must be deposited within three business days of contract acceptance. If the broker deposits any funds into an interest-bearing trust account, the broker must obtain the written agreement of the parties indicating to whom the broker will pay any earned interest. The agreement must be obtained prior to depositing those funds into the interest-bearing account.

Depositing of trust funds when licensee is a principal. A licensee who is selling, leasing, or exchanging property owned by the licensee must place all cash, checks, or other items of value received by the licensee, and all security deposits received on property owned by the licensee, into the custody of the broker holding the licensee's license or in a trust account approved by the broker as soon after receipt as is practicably possible. Funds must be deposited into trust account within three business days of contract acceptance.

Nonresident Broker Trust Account. The Commission may allow a nonresident broker who accepts trust funds in real estate transactions to maintain the trust account in a bank in the nonresident broker's state of residence, if the Commission is authorized to examine the account when the Commission chooses, and the licensee meets all trust account rules established by the Commission.

Affiliated Licensees Receiving Funds. If the broker approves an affiliated licensee holding funds in a designated trust account owned by the licensee, the broker must assure that the bank designates the account as a trust account. The broker must also notify the Commission of the name of the bank in which the account is maintained, the number of the account, and the name of the licensee who owns the account. The licensee who owns the account must maintain records on the account as are required for broker's trust accounts, and must comply with the Rules and Regulations applicable to maintaining trust accounts. The licensee who owns the account must provide his or her broker a written reconciliation statement at least quarterly comparing the licensee's total trust liability with the reconciled bank balance of the licensee's trust account.

Broker's funds in a trust account. A broker may maintain the broker's own funds in a designated trust or escrow account only when they are clearly identified as the broker's deposit and only for certain purposes. If the bank has a minimum balance that must be maintained in order to keep the account open, the broker may maintain that amount in the account, but the amount must be designated as the broker's funds.

If the bank requires a service charge to be paid for the account, the broker may maintain a reasonable amount to cover that service charge, if identified as the broker's funds. The broker may also maintain in the account an amount to cover other occasional bank charges and costs of maintaining the account, including the cost of blank checks, deposit slips and any charges for returned checks.

A broker may allow commissions due to the broker that are being paid from funds of others and held in a trust or escrow account to remain in the account if the broker's accounting system for the trust fund designates those commissions as the broker's funds and properly accounts for them, and the broker removes from the account each month any of the broker's funds that exceed the minimum amount necessary to cover money belonging to others and bank charges.

Only checks made payable to the broker may be used to withdraw funds designated as the broker's funds from the trust or escrow account.

Accounting Requirements for Trust or Escrow Funds

Every broker required to maintain a trust account must maintain an accounting system that provides details of each deposit, including the names of the parties to the transactions, date and amount of deposits, property identification, and amount, date, and to whom each check drawn on the account is paid.

Licensees may meet accounting requirements with either manual or electronic accounting systems. However, it must include all items required by law and sound business practices, be readily accessible, be in an easily understandable format, and be available to an authorized Commission representative.

Disbursements

A broker who fails to disburse trust funds from the broker's trust or escrow account according to the terms of the contract will be considered by the Commission to have demonstrated incompetence in safeguarding the interest of the public.

The broker may disburse at the closing of a transaction or upon securing a written agreement signed by all parties having an interest in the trust funds that is separate from the contract directing the broker to hold the funds.

Funds may be disbursed by the broker when

- receiving a court order from a court of competent jurisdiction,
- when filing of an interpleader action, or
- upon a reasonable interpretation of the contract directing the broker to deposit the funds.

A broker may not disburse funds from a designated trust account until the broker is certain that the bank has credited the funds to the broker's trust account. When a broker disburses funds without the agreement of all parties to the contract, the broker must immediately notify all parties in writing.

A broker who claims any earnest money or other money paid to the broker regarding a real estate transaction as part or all of the broker's commission or fee will be considered to be in compliance if, in a lease or rental, possession has been delivered to the tenant, or in a lease/purchase, the transaction has closed or the date of closing stated in the sales contract and any extension have passed.

The broker is also in compliance if disbursing in a sales transaction when the transaction has closed or the date of closing stated in the contract and any extension have passed. Disbursement may also be made if the broker has obtained a written agreement, separate from the sales contract or lease agreement, signed by all parties having an interest in the transaction stating that the broker is entitled to the commission.

As indicated, the broker is not entitled to any part of earnest money, security deposit, or other trust funds as broker's commission or fee until the transaction has been consummated or terminated.

The total of all checks written against each deposit should reflect a zero balance in the designated escrow or trust account relating to the closing of each transaction, except when part of the deposit is transferred to the broker's name as commission payment. The total of the transfer and all checks written against that deposit should show a zero balance.

If a licensee who owns a designated trust account files for bankruptcy, he or she must immediately notify the Commission in writing of the filing of that petition. If a qualifying broker or the firm that a licensee serves as qualifying broker files for bankruptcy, the qualifying broker must immediately notify the Commission in writing.

Trust accounts for property management or association management

Brokers who manage real property or manage community associations may maintain designated rental or assessment trust or escrow accounts separate from their other trust or escrow accounts. If security deposits are kept in a designated rental trust or escrow account, they must be clearly identified and credited to the tenant, and there must always be a balance in the account equal to the total of all the security deposits.

A licensee who manages rental property owned by the licensee must deposit any security deposits collected in connection with his or her property in a designated trust account and may not post a bond in lieu of maintaining the deposits in the trust account.

Examination of trust accounts by the Commission

Each broker who is required to maintain a designated trust or escrow account must provide authorization for the Commission to have the account examined by an authorized representative of the Commission during each renewal period or at another time if the Commission directs with reasonable cause.

When contacted by the Commission's staff regarding the Commission conducting an examination of a trust account, a broker may choose to provide the Commission with a report of the broker's trust account from a Certified Public Accountant in lieu of an examination by the Commission. The report must be in the format provided by the Commission. The Commission is not required to accept the report and may conduct its own examination.

Copies of accounting system entries for trust or escrow accounts, bank deposits, bank statements, receipts and other documents related to the account must be available to authorized agents of the Commission upon reasonable request and at a reasonable cost to the Commission.

Renewal trust account examination. The Commission will examine each broker's trust account(s) during each renewal period. When renewing a broker's license, the broker must provide the Commission a summary of the broker's trust account on a form prepared by or approved by the Commission if that summary appears complete and includes no irregularities. In lieu of an examination, the Commission may accept a written report on the broker's trust account from a Certified Public Accountant. The report of the Certified Public Accountant must also be on the form provided by the Commission verifying that the broker's trust accounts are maintained in accordance with License Law and the Rules and Regulations.

Monthly reconciliation of trust accounts

A broker who is required to maintain a trust or escrow account must prepare, at least monthly, a written reconciliation statement comparing the broker's total trust liability with the reconciled bank balance of the broker's trust account. The broker's trust liability is the total of all deposits received, required by contract to be deposited, and being held by the broker at any time.

The minimum information to be included in the monthly reconciliation statement is

- the date the reconciliation was performed,
- the date used to reconcile the balances,
- the name of the bank and the account number,
- account balance and date,
- any deposits in transit,
- the amounts of any outstanding checks,
- an itemized list of the broker's outstanding trust liability showing the amount and source of funds received and not disbursed,
- other items required to reconcile the bank account balance with the balance in the broker's checkbook and with the amount of the broker's trust liability.

The broker must review the monthly reconciliation statement and retain copies in the broker's files for three years. Note that the IRS may require longer records retention periods.

If the trust liability and bank balances do not agree, the reconciliation statement must contain an explanation for the difference and any corrective action taken regarding any shortages or overages in the account.

Abandoned funds in a trust account. When a real estate licensee believes that a person whose funds have been placed in the trust account has abandoned those funds, the licensee may not disburse those funds unless the licensee's written authorization to hold the funds requires that disbursement, and the

71

licensee has complied with the requirements of the Disposition of Unclaimed Property Act or other ordered requirements.

Trust account requirements for non-broker licensee owned property [§43-40-20(h)]

Real estate licensees who are not brokers may open a trust account to deposit trust funds received on properties the licensee owns if his or her broker approves the account and if the licensee provides the broker with regular accounting reports accounting for the funds. The Commission considers a property "owned by a licensee" if the deed for the property reflects only the name of the licensee, or reflects only the name of a business entity of which the licensee is the sole owner, member, or stockholder.

If a licensee owns any interest in a property that is less than one hundred percent and receives any trust funds on the property, the licensee must deposit those funds into the trust account of the firm.

Trust fund disbursements. When a broker makes a disputed disbursement of funds, the broker must immediately notify all parties in writing. All refunds of earnest money must be paid by check or credited at the closing of transaction.

HANDLING TRUST FUNDS

State laws prescribe how licensees must handle any escrow or earnest money deposits they receive. Usually, the law allows the broker to hold an earnest money check uncashed until the offer is accepted, provided the buyer gives written permission and the seller is informed.
Typical trust fund handling requirements include:

- the broker named as trustee of the account
- a federally-insured bank or recognized depository located in the state
- an account that is not interest-bearing if the financial institution ever requires prior written notice for withdrawals
- maintenance of records in a particular accounting format
- separate records kept for each beneficiary, property, or transaction
- records of funds received and paid out regularly reconciled with bank statements
- withdrawals only by the broker-trustee or other specifically authorized person

Commingling and conversion. Mixing of personal or company funds with client funds is grounds for the revocation or suspension of a real estate license. Depositing client funds in a personal or business account, or using them for any purpose other than the client's business, is also grounds for suspension or revocation of a license. It is important for the broker to remove commissions, fees or other income earned by the broker from a trust account within the period specified by law to avoid committing an act of commingling.

SNAPSHOT REVIEW: UNIT EIGHT

TRUST ACCOUNTS AND HANDLING TRUST FUNDS

TRUST ACCOUNTS

- required by broker if handling funds of others; account info to Commission; deposit within 3 business days; nonresident broker account allowed; funds disbursed in accordance with law; affiliated licensees may have trust account with broker's permission; monthly reconciliation required; Commission examinations required; accounting system required

- also required for brokers who manage property or community associations

HANDLING TRUST FUNDS

- Broker as trustee; records maintenance and separation per beneficiary; commingling and conversion of trust funds prohibited

===

Check Your Understanding Quiz:

Unit Eight: Trust Accounts and Handling Trust Funds

Carefully read each question and provide your best answer based on what you learned in this unit. Then check your answers against the Answer Key which immediately follows the quiz questions.

1. Which of the following is not required for trust accounts?

    a. Licensees must maintain their own trust accounts for earnest money received.
    b. Trust accounts must be maintained in a financial institution within Georgia.
    c. Brokers who accept down payments or security deposits must maintain a trust account.
    d. A trust account must be registered with the Commission.

2. If a broker does not maintain a trust account but then receives funds related to a real estate transaction, the broker must open a designated account within _____ of receiving the funds.

    a. 1 business day
    b. 5 days
    c. 5 business days
    d. 10 days

3. What must a licensee do when he receives transaction-related funds?

    a. Immediately deposit the funds into his trust account.
    b. Hold the funds for 5 days before depositing them into the trust account.
    c. Turn the funds over to his affiliated broker for deposit into the broker's trust account.
    d. Licensees are not permitted to accept trust funds related to a transaction.

4. Which of the following statements is false?

    a. Nonresident brokers may accept trust funds related to transactions in Georgia.
    b. Nonresident brokers who receive trust funds in Georgia must turn the funds over to a Georgia broker for deposit into the Georgia broker's trust account.
    c. Nonresident brokers must allow the Georgia Commission to examine their trust accounts.
    d. Nonresident brokers may maintain trust accounts in their own state of residence.

5. When a broker meets the requirements for maintaining his own funds in a designated trust account, how may the broker withdraw his own funds?

    a. Only by having them electronically transferred to the broker's business or personal account
    b. Only by using a debit card related to the trust account
    c. Only by using checks made payable to the broker
    d. Only by having the client withdraw the funds and provide them to the broker

6. Which of the following statements are false?

   a. Brokers are required to maintain an accounting system which contains details of each deposit.
   b. Brokers may use either a manual or electronic accounting system.
   c. Accounting systems must include all items required by law and sound business practices.
   d. The broker's accounting system is confidential and not available for Commission inspection.

7. If a qualifying broker or licensee maintains a trust account and files for bankruptcy, the broker or licensee must

   a. notify the Commission.
   b. notify clients whose funds were being held in the trust account.
   c. include the trust funds in the bankruptcy filing.
   d. make arrangements to repay all trust funds to the original providers of the funds.

8. Which of the following statements is true?

   a. In lieu of examining a broker's trust account, the Commission is required to accept a CPA's report of the account.
   b. A broker is required to prepare an annual written reconciliation statement for his or her trust account.
   c. Brokers must retain copies of trust account reconciliation statements for 3 years.
   d. Licensees may maintain a trust account for funds received on the licensee's own property if the broker approves the account and the licensee submits monthly accounting reports to the Commission.

9. All refunds of earnest money must be paid by check or

   a. certified check.
   b. cash.
   c. credited at closing.
   d. electronic transfer.

10. Commingling is

   a. combining multiple clients' funds in one trust account.
   b. mixing the broker's personal funds with a client's funds in a trust account.
   c. mixing the broker's personal and business funds in the same account.
   d. allowing licensees to deposit funds into the broker's designated trust account.

Answer Key:

Unit Eight: Trust Accounts and Handling Trust Funds

1. a.   Licensees must maintain their own trust accounts for earnest money received.
2. a.   1 business day
3. c.   Turn the funds over to his affiliated broker for deposit into the broker's trust account.
4. b.   Nonresident brokers who receive trust funds in Georgia must turn the funds over to a Georgia broker for deposit into the Georgia broker's trust account.
5. c.   Only by using checks made payable to the broker
6. d.   The broker's accounting system is confidential and not available for Commission inspection.
7. a.   notify the Commission.
8. c.   Brokers must retain copies of trust account reconciliation statements for 3 years.
9. c.   credited at closing.
10. b.   mixing the broker's personal funds with a client's funds in a trust account.

SECTION III: MANAGING THE TRANSACTION

Unit 9: The Listing and Selling Process

Unit 10: Brokerage Relationships in Real Estate Transactions Act (BRRETA) Relationships

Unit 11: Property and Environmental Disclosures

Unit 12: Financial Qualification

Unit 13: Pricing Residential Property

Unit 14: The Sales Contract

Unit 15: Offers and Counter Offers, Acceptance, Document Handling

Unit 16: Pre-Closing and Closing Activities, TILA/RESPA Integrated Disclosure Rule (TRID)

Unit 17: Homeowners and Flood Insurance Requirements

Unit 18: Foreclosures and Short Sales

UNIT 9:

THE LISTING AND SELLING PROCESS

Unit Nine Learning Objectives: When the student has completed this unit, he or she will be able to:

- Describe the process and activities performed for obtaining listings, including prospecting and pricing, as well as negotiating the listing agreement.
- Explain the role of a Comparative Market Analysis in the listing process.
- Identify and explain the steps in selling a listed property: creating a marketing plan, selling the prospect, and obtaining offers; and the related critical skills.
- Describe Multiple Listing Services and their role in selling a listing.

THE LISTING PROCESS

Effecting a transaction. The core activity of real estate brokerage is the business of procuring a buyer, seller, tenant, or property on behalf of a client for the purpose of completing a transaction. If successful, the broker receives a commission according to the provisions of a listing agreement. A broker's compensation for effecting a transaction is usually a negotiated percentage of the purchase price.

A client hires a broker by executing a listing agreement which is a contract that establishes an agency relationship. Once hired, the broker or agent implements a marketing plan to procure the other principal party for the transaction. The broker then plays an important role in pre-closing activities to ensure successful closing of the transaction.

To serve clients and locate customers, a broker must become expert in local real estate market conditions. A fundamental part of maintaining market expertise is organizing and managing an information system.

Broker cooperation

In most cases, transactions require the assistance of a cooperating broker from another brokerage company acting as a subagent. Most listing agreements provide for brokerage cooperation in the multiple listing clause. A transaction involving a cooperating subagent is called **co**-brokerage. In a co-brokered transaction, the listing broker splits the commission with the "co-broker," typically on a 50-50 basis. A broker may cooperate with other brokers on either side of a transaction, either assisting a listing agent to locate a buyer or tenant, or assisting a buyer or tenant representative in locating a seller or landlord.

In the most common form of broker cooperation, an outside broker locates a buyer for the listing broker's seller. In such cases, the listing broker shares the commission with the cooperating "selling" broker on a pre-determined basis.

Obtaining listings

Listings are the traditional source of a broker's income. By obtaining a listing, a broker obtains a share of the commission generated whenever a cooperating broker finds a buyer. It is not so certain that working with a buyer will provide income. In the absence of an exclusive buyer representation agreement, a buyer may move from one agent to another without making any commitment. Agents can spend considerable time with a buyer and earn nothing. Hence the special value of a listing: it is likely to generate revenue.

Listing procedures

The marketing and self-promotional efforts of agents generate listings. New agents usually focus on becoming well known in a small geographical area and hope to encounter clients there who are willing to list with them. More experienced and better-known agents are able to rely to a greater extent on referrals in obtaining listings. New or experienced, an agent needs certain skills at each step in the process of obtaining a listing.

To generate business, as well as achieve the transactional objectives of clients, a broker must be proficient in four skill areas:

- obtaining a client listing
- marketing a listing
- facilitating the closing of a transaction
- managing market information

The following steps result in obtaining listings:

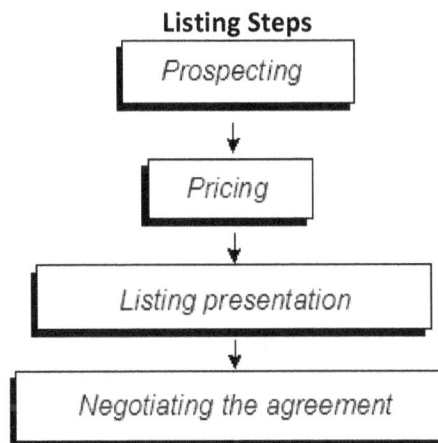

Listing Steps

Prospecting
↓
Pricing
↓
Listing presentation
↓
Negotiating the agreement

Prospecting

Prospecting is any activity designed to generate listing prospects: parties who intend to sell or lease property and who have not yet committed to a broker. Prospecting activities include mailing newsletters and flyers, selling directly and person-to-person, advertising, and selling indirectly via community involvement.

The goal of prospecting is to reach a potential seller or landlord, make that person aware of the agent's and brokerage's services, and obtain permission to discuss the benefits of listing, often in the form of a formal selling presentation.

Keep in mind that prospecting, or attempting to procure prospects (buyers, sellers, tenants, landlords), requires a real estate license. Acting as a referral agent in order to secure prospects is also an activity that can be performed only by a license, as is charging advance fees, other than advertising fees, when promoting the sale of a property by listing it in a publication designed for that purpose, or for referring property information to brokers.

Pricing

It is almost always necessary for an agent seeking a listing to suggest a listing price or price range for the property. It is important to make a careful estimate, because underpricing a property is not in the best interests of the seller, and overpricing it often prevents a transaction altogether.

The Comparative Market Analysis is one method of estimating value. In brief, an agent usually relies on an analysis of comparable properties which have recently sold in the same neighborhood. By making adjustments for the differences between the subject property and the comparables, the agent arrives at a general price range.

Agents must be careful to caution sellers that they are not appraisers, and that the suggested price range is not an expert opinion of market value. If a more precise estimate of market value is desired, the seller should hire a licensed appraiser.

Comparative Market Analysis (CMA). In preparing a Comparative Market Analysis, licensees should guard against using the terms "appraisal" and "value," which are reserved for the use of certified appraisers. Misuse of these terms could lead to a charge of misrepresenting oneself as an appraiser. In discussing listed properties with clients or customers, real estate licensees should be careful to use guarded terms such as "recommended listing price," "recommended purchase price,' and "recommended listing price range."

Agents should make every effort to help the sellers find a reasonable listing price based on the current market. If the CMA leads the seller to list at a price that is too high, the seller may blame the agent when the transaction fails because of an appraisal that comes in below the selling price. To minimize this risk, it is best to be conservative in the CMA and retain documentation that the seller went above the recommended price in spite of the agent's advice.

Listing presentation and negotiation of agreement

A listing presentation is an agent's opportunity to meet with a seller and present the merits of the agent's marketing plan, personal expertise, and company strengths. At the same time, an agent can explain the many phases and details of a real estate transaction and point out how the provisions of the listing agreement and the agent-principal relationship work to ensure a smooth transaction.

Listing agreement. Ultimately, the agent's aim in a presentation meeting is to have the principal execute a listing agreement. A listing agreement is a legally enforceable real estate agency agreement between a real estate broker and a client, authorizing the broker to perform a stated service for compensation. The agreement sets forth the various authorizations and duties, as well as requirements for compensation. A listing agreement establishes an agency for a specified transaction and has a stated expiration.

Once the agent has completed the listing agreement with the client, he or she must then submit the listing to the broker for approval and signing. This result will set in motion the process of marketing the property. In practice, it may take an agent many meetings with a prospect before the prospect signs an agreement.

Nature and accuracy of the listing agreement. In most states, including Georgia, a listing agreement is enforceable only if it is in writing. Most states, also including Georgia, forbid net listings because they violate the requirement that a valid listing agreement must specify a selling price and the agent's compensation. The licensee, in accordance with the duty of due diligence, must verify the accuracy of the statements in the listing regarding the property, the owner, and the owner's representations. Especially important facts for a broker or agent to verify are:

- material facts regarding the property condition
- ownership status
- the client's authority to act

An agent who does not act with a reasonable degree of due diligence in these matters may be exposed to liability if it turns out that the property is not as represented or the client cannot perform the contract as promised.

Before entering into a listing agreement, a licensee should explain that it is necessary to comply with fair housing laws and obtain the potential client's acknowledgment and agreement.

Authorizations and Permissions

Licensees should stay within the bounds of the authority granted by the agency agreement or must not do anything requiring permission without first getting that permission in writing. For instance, permission should be obtained before doing any of the following unless the listing agreement specifically grants the authority:

- post a sign on the property
- remove other signs
- show the property
- hand out the property condition disclosure
- distribute marketing materials
- advertise in various media
- use a multiple listing service
- cooperate with other licensees
- divide the commission or negotiate a commission split
- share final sales data with the MLS
- place a lock box on the property
- appoint subagents
- appoint a designated agent
- change agency status

THE SELLING PROCESS

Marketing listings

The process of marketing a listed property occurs in three broad steps, leading to the desired end of a completed sale contract. At each of these steps, there are critical skills an agent must master.

Skills and knowledge. Professionals in the brokerage business must have a broad range of real estate knowledge and skills. Agents must develop a thorough awareness of their local market and the properties within it. In addition, agents must develop a proficiency with the economics of real estate: prices, financing, closing costs, and so forth. Equally important are "people" skills: communicating with clients and responding to their needs.

```
┌─────────────────────────┐
│     Marketing Plan      │
└─────────────────────────┘
             │
             ▼
┌─────────────────────────┐
│   Selling the Prospect  │
└─────────────────────────┘
             │
             ▼
┌─────────────────────────┐
│     Obtaining Offers    │
└─────────────────────────┘
```

Marketing plan. After the broker formalizes the listing agreement, the sales agent initiates a marketing plan for the property. An ideal marketing plan is a cohesive combination of promotional and selling activities directed at potential customers. The best combination is one that aims to have maximum impact on the marketplace in relation to the time and money expended.

Selling the prospect. When marketing activities produce prospects, the agent's marketing role becomes more interpersonal. An agent must now:

- qualify prospects' plans, preferences, and financial capabilities
- show properties that meet the customer's needs
- elicit the buyer's reactions to properties
- report material results to the seller or listing agent

At the earliest appropriate time, an agent must make certain disclosures to a prospective customer. Depending on state laws, an agent may have to disclose the relevant agency relationship, the property's physical condition, and the possible presence of hazardous materials.

Obtaining offers. If a buyer is interested in purchasing a property, an agent obtains the buyer's offer of transaction terms, including price, down payment, desired closing date, and financing requirements.

An agent must be extremely careful at this point to abide by fiduciary obligations to the client, whoever that party may be. Discussions of price are particularly delicate: whether the client is buyer or seller, the agent's duty is to uphold the client's best interests. Thus, it is not acceptable to suggest to a customer what price the client will or will not accept. With pricing and other issues, it is always a good practice to understand what role the client wants the agent to assume in the offering phase of the transaction; in other words, exactly how far the agent may go in developing terms on the client's behalf.

When a buyer or tenant makes an offer, the agent *must* present it to the seller or landlord at the earliest possible moment. If the terms of the offer are unacceptable, the agent may assist the seller in developing a counteroffer, which the agent would subsequently submit to the customer or customer's agent. The offering and counteroffering process continues until a meeting of the minds results in a sale contract.

Multiple listing services and websites

The second prevalent form of broker cooperation is the multiple listing service, or MLS. A multiple listing service is an organization of brokers who have agreed to cooperate with member brokers in marketing listings. Members of the service also agree to enter all exclusive listings into the listing distribution network so that every member is promptly informed of new listings as they come on the market.

The listing agreement used by members of a multiple listing service discloses relevant procedures and policies so that all principal parties to the agreement are aware of the pooling of the listing. A broker who works on a transaction listed in the MLS has all the duties and responsibilities inherent in the laws of agency as the client's fiduciary agent. The listing agreement sets forth specific duties.

The posting and sharing of property listings and data among broker websites, firm websites, and MLS is one of the most effective marketing tools available to today's licensees. Broker cooperation assures sellers of maximum exposure for their properties, just as it assures buyers of seeing the widest possible range of listed properties.

To ensure fair use of MLS facilities, the National Association of REALTORS® has developed an Internet Data Exchange (IDX) policy that enables MLS members to display and use MLS data while respecting the rights of property owners and brokers to market their properties however they want.

Basically, persons who want to make use of MLS data have to share their own data as well. They can opt out of the sharing policy so that competitors cannot post their properties on competing websites, but then they cannot post competitors' properties on their own sites.

There are a number of websites that provide consumers with the capability to search through listings all over the country and even the world. Of course, it is always wise to recognize that information posted on the internet is not necessarily reliable and that the source of the information should be considered carefully.

SNAPSHOT REVIEW: UNIT NINE

THE LISTING AND SELLING PROCESS

THE LISTING PROCESS

Obtaining listings

- generate prospects; develop price range; complete listing presentation; negotiate execute and agreement

Listing steps

- prospecting, pricing, listing presentation, negotiating agreement
- CMAs for pricing
- listing authorities

THE SELLING PROCESS

Marketing listings

- necessary skills
- develop marketing plan; sell and qualify prospective buyers; complete necessary disclosures; obtain offers
- marketing on MLS

===

Check Your Understanding Quiz:

Unit Nine: The Listing and Selling Process

Carefully read each question and provide your best answer based on what you learned in this unit. Then check your answers against the Answer Key which immediately follows the quiz questions.

1. A property seller hires a broker by

    a. accepting a buyer's offer on the property.
    b. requesting that the broker hold an open house for the property.
    c. executing a listing agreement.
    d. having the broker sign an employment contract.

2. On what basis are cooperating subagents typically compensated?

    a. A percentage of the sale price agreed upon with the seller
    b. A commission split with the listing broker
    c. A fee paid by the buyer's broker
    d. A referral fee paid by the seller's broker

3. What should an agent have in place for the greatest assurance of receiving compensation for marketing efforts?

    a. A net listing agreement
    b. An exclusive listing agreement
    c. An exclusive right-to-sell agreement
    d. A cooperating broker agreement

4. Experienced, well known agents typically rely on what to generate listings?

    a. Conventions
    b. Referrals
    c. Newsletters
    d. Cold calling

5. Reaching a potential seller to make her aware of the broker's services is a goal of

    a. marketing.
    b. listing presentations.
    c. MLS.
    d. prospecting.

6. Which of the following activities requires a real estate license?

   a. Prospecting
   b. Referring property information to brokers
   c. Promoting the sale of property
   d. All of the above

7. The best means of obtaining a precise estimate of a property's market value is to

   a. perform a CMA.
   b. obtain an appraisal.
   c. submit an application to a mortgage lender.
   d. review property insurance coverage.

8. During the listing process, at what point does the agent explain the phases and details of a real estate transaction to a seller?

   a. Prospecting
   b. Pricing
   c. Listing presentation
   d. Listing agreement negotiation

9. Once a client signs a listing agreement, what is the agent's next step?

   a. Initiate the marketing plan
   b. File the agreement with the Commission
   c. Submit the agreement for the broker's approval
   d. Place signage on the property being listed

10. Before showing a property to prospective buyers, the agent must

    a. place a lock box on the property.
    b. post a sign on the property that includes the agent's name.
    c. obtain written permission.
    d. have an agency agreement with the owner.

11. Which of the following is a central foundation of marketing a listed property?

    a. Creating a marketing plan
    b. Executing the listing agreement
    c. Negotiating offers
    d. Extinguishing contingencies

12. The best marketing plans balance

    a. agent expertise with skills and knowledge.
    b. property condition with price.
    c. marketplace and culture.
    d. maximum marketplace impact with time and money spent.

13. When an unacceptable offer has been received, what should the seller's agent do?

    a. Refuse to show the offer to the seller
    b. Discuss a more acceptable price with the buyer
    c. Assist the seller in developing a counteroffer
    d. Reject the offer and find another potential buyer

14. An MLS promotes broker cooperation by

    a. providing free marketing services.
    b. eliminating duties owed by the law of agency.
    c. providing maximum exposure to other brokers' properties.
    d. requiring agency agreements between brokers.

15. Which of the following is a true statement?

    a. An MLS is an organization of licensees who are affiliated with the same broker.
    b. Members of an MLS agree to share exclusive listings with other member brokers.
    c. Use of an MLS limits exposure of a property for sale.
    d. A broker may enter a listing into an MLS whether the client agrees or not.

==

Answer Key:

Unit Nine: The Listing and Selling Process

1. **c.   executing a listing agreement.**
2. **b.   A commission split with the listing broker**
3. **c.   An exclusive right-to-sell agreement**
4. **b.   Referrals**
5. **d.   prospecting.**
6. **d.   All of the above**
7. **b.   obtain an appraisal.**
8. **c.   Listing presentation**
9. **c.   Submit the agreement for the broker's approval**
10. **c.   obtain written permission.**
11. **a.   Creating a marketing plan**
12. **d.   maximum marketplace impact with time and money spent.**
13. **c. Assist the seller in developing a counteroffer**
14. **c.   providing maximum exposure to other brokers' properties.**
15. **b.   Members of an MLS agree to share exclusive listings with other member brokers.**

UNIT 10:

BROKERAGE RELATIONSHIPS IN REAL ESTATE TRANSACTIONS ACT (BRRETA)

Unit Ten Learning Objectives: When the student has completed this unit, he or she will be able to:

- Describe the impact of BRRETA on a broker's relationship with sellers, landlords, buyers, and tenants.
- Identify the BRRETA disclosure requirements both to clients and other parties to a transaction.
- List the duties brokers have to sellers, landlords, buyers, and tenants under BRRETA.

BROKERAGE RELATIONSHIPS IN REAL ESTATE TRANSACTIONS ACT (BRRETA)

BRRETA governs real estate relationships. BRRETA (§ 10-6A) governs relationships between consumers, brokers and affiliated licensees. The Act is not intended to prescribe or affect contractual relationships between brokers and affiliated licensees. In other words, it does not specify whether an affiliated licensee must be an employee or an independent contractor, nor does it prescribe commission fee guidelines. It may serve as a basis for private rights of action and defenses by consumers and brokers.

Broker's legal relationship to customers or clients. A broker who performs brokerage services for a client or customer owes only duties and obligations that are outlined in BRRETA unless the parties have a written, signed agreement specifying additional duties.

Per BRRETA, the broker is NOT considered to have a fiduciary relationship with any party. The broker is responsible only for exercising reasonable care in carrying out duties specified in BRRETA, and for the client as delineated in the brokerage engagement. So, the only duties owed to the client are reasonable care and any duties specified in BRRETA and the brokerage agreement.

If a broker having a brokerage relationship with a customer or client enters into a new brokerage relationship with that customer or client, the broker must timely disclose the change to all brokers, customers or clients involved in the transaction.

Agency disclosure. Written agency disclosures must be made in a timely manner, but no later than when any party first makes an offer to purchase, sell, lease, or exchange real property.

BRRETA specified duties to clients and customers. BRRETA lists responsibilities to all clients engaged by the broker (seller, buyer, tenant, or landlord). These duties require the broker to perform the terms specified in the brokerage agreement with that client and to promote the interests of the client.

BRRETA further clarifies that a broker performing brokerage services for a client or customer owes that party only the specified duties and obligations, unless the parties expressly agree otherwise in writing. A broker is not considered to have a fiduciary relationship or fiduciary obligations to any party; he or she is responsible only for exercising reasonable care in the discharge of the specified duties indicated, and, in the case of a client, duties as specified in the brokerage engagement. Do keep in mind that promoting the best interests of the client includes protecting the client's confidential information.

Duties of brokers prior to entering into brokerage engagement relationships. All brokerage engagements must inform the prospective client of the types of agency relationship available through the broker. The prospective client must know what agency options are available. It is important for the prospective client to be made aware in the engagement form of any other brokerage relationships that would be in conflict with any interests of the prospective client that are known to the broker.

The engagement must also include the broker's compensation and whether the compensation will be shared with other brokers who may represent the other party to the transaction as that party's agent. The engagement must also inform the prospective client of the broker's obligation to keep client information confidential.

Compensation not related to agency. Who pays the broker's commission (or who promises to pay the commission) does not determine whether a brokerage relationship is created between the broker and the consumer. In other words, compensation does not create or determine agency.

Duties and responsibilities of the broker engaged by the seller or landlord. A broker who is engaged by the seller (represents the seller) has certain duties prescribed per BRRETA. The broker must perform the terms of the brokerage engagement with the seller, and must promote the best interests of the seller.

- Reasonable skill and care must be exercised by the broker in performing the duties prescribed in BRRETA or other applicable rules or regulations. This includes, but is not limited to, fair housing laws and contract law.
- The broker promotes the best interests of the seller by seeking a sale at the price and terms in the brokerage agreement or at the price and terms acceptable to the seller. The broker does not have an obligation to seek additional offers when the property is subject to an existing contract, unless the brokerage agreement states otherwise.
- Duties of the seller's broker includes timely presenting all offers to and from the seller, even when the property is subject to a contract. So, although the broker does not have an obligation to seek additional offers, he or she must present all offers that are made, even after the property is subject to a contract.
- The broker must also disclose to the seller any material facts of which the broker is aware regarding the transaction, and advise the seller to obtain expert advice in matters that are beyond the expertise of the broker. All monies and property belonging to the seller must be accounted for in a timely manner.
- The broker must keep confidential all confidential information received by the broker during the time of the engagement.

The broker representing the seller client may perform ministerial services to the buyer, and may show other properties to prospective buyers.

These same duties and responsibilities are also owed by a broker when engaged by a landlord.

Duties and responsibilities of a broker engaged by the buyer or tenant. A broker who is engaged by the buyer must perform the terms of the buyer brokerage agreement and promote the best interests of the buyer. He or she promotes the buyer's interests by attempting to locate a property at a price and terms acceptable to the buyer. The broker is not required to seek additional properties for the buyer client if the buyer is a party to an existing contract to purchase, unless the brokerage engagement states otherwise.

- The buyer's broker must timely present all offers to and from the buyer, even when the buyer is a party to a contract to purchase property, and must account for all money and property belonging to the buyer in a timely manner. If the buyer is currently under contract to purchase another property and is expressing a desire to terminate an existing contract, the buyer should be reminded that he or she is a party to a legal contract, and recommend the buyer seek legal counsel.
- All duties of the broker must be exercised with skill and care, and the broker must comply with all requirements of BRRETA and other applicable laws and rules.
- The broker must disclose any adverse material facts known to the broker regarding the transaction, and must advise the buyer to seek expert advice on matters outside the broker's expertise.
- Confidential information of the buyer must be kept confidential. As with any agency relationship, the duty of confidentiality goes beyond the termination of the agreement.
- The broker must comply with all requirements of BRRETA and other applicable laws and rules.

A broker engaged by the buyer may provide ministerial acts to the seller, and may show properties in which the buyer is interested to other prospective buyers.

These same duties and responsibilities are also owed by the broker when engaged by a tenant.

Required disclosures

Material facts disclosure by brokers engaged by seller or landlord. A broker engaged by a seller or landlord must make certain disclosures in a timely manner to all parties with whom the broker is working. These disclosures include all material facts pertaining to the physical condition of the property and improvements, including material defects in the property, environmental contamination, and facts required by law to be disclosed. The broker must also disclose material facts regarding existing adverse physical conditions in the immediate neighborhood within one mile of the property that could not be discovered by an inspection of the neighborhood or through review of available governmental documents and statistics.

The Act does not create any duty on the part of a broker to discover or seek to discover either adverse material facts pertaining to the physical condition of the property or existing adverse conditions in the immediate neighborhood.

Brokers are prohibited from giving prospective buyers or tenants false information. However, a broker is not liable to a buyer for providing the buyer false information if the broker did not have actual knowledge that the information was false and disclosed the source of the information to the buyer.

Disclosure responsibilities of the broker do not limit any obligation of a seller or landlord to disclose to prospective buyers or tenants all adverse material facts actually known by the seller pertaining to the physical condition of the property. Similarly, the broker disclosure requirements do not limit the obligation of prospective buyers and tenants to inspect and familiarize themselves with potentially adverse conditions related to the physical condition of the property and the neighborhood in which the property is located.

No cause of action will arise on behalf of any person against a broker for revealing information in compliance with BRRETA. Additionally, brokers are not liable for failure to disclose any matter other than those matters listed. Violations will not create liability on the part of the broker without a finding of fraud on the part of the broker.

Material facts disclosure by brokers engaged by buyer or tenant. A broker engaged by a buyer or tenant must make certain disclosures in a timely manner. It is important to note that the buyer's agent must disclose to the prospective seller all material facts known by the broker regarding the buyer's financial ability to perform on the terms of the contract. In residential transactions, the broker and buyer must both disclose whether or not the buyer intends to occupy the property as the principal residence.

When engaged by a tenant, the broker must disclose in a timely manner to a prospective landlord all adverse material facts known to the broker regarding the tenant's financial ability to perform the terms of the lease or letter of intent, or the tenant's intent to occupy the property as the principal residence.

A licensee may not knowingly provide false information to a seller or landlord. However, the licensee is not liable for providing false information if the licensee did not know that the information was false and disclosed the source of the information to the seller or landlord.

These disclosure requirements do not limit the prospective buyer or tenant's obligation to disclose to the prospective seller or landlord any known adverse material facts known by the buyer or tenant concerning his or her financial ability to perform on the terms of the contract.

Termination and duration of relationships

Brokerage relationships begin when a client engages the broker and continue until completion of performance of the engagement, or if the engagement is not completed, the expiration date agreed by the parties. If no expiration date is provided and no termination occurs, the relationship will end one year after initiation of the engagement.

After termination, the broker owes no further duties to the client, except accounting of all moneys and property of the client, and keeping confidential all confidential information of the client received during the engagement, unless the disclosure is required by law, it becomes public from a source other than the broker, or the client gives permission for the disclosure. Disclosure permission should be in writing.

Licensees should note that the duty of confidentiality continues after termination of the relationship, with no expiration of that duty.

Types of designated representation

Designated agency. The broker may assign different affiliated licensees as agents to exclusively represent opposing brokerage clients in the same transaction. The company policy must ensure that each client is represented in compliance with BRRETA requirements. If the broker appoints different designated agents to represent the two parties to the transaction, neither the broker, the affiliated licensees, nor the brokerage firm will be deemed to be dual agents.

Dual agency consent requirements. A dual agent is a broker who simultaneously has a brokerage relationship with both the seller and the buyer or both the landlord and the tenant in the same real estate transaction. He or she represents and owes certain duties to both clients. In order to act as a dual agent in Georgia, the licensee must have written consent of all clients.

Written disclosure of dual agency must be made to both parties in the transaction disclosing the parties for whom the firm will be acting as a dual agent and disclosing who will pay the commission. This disclosure must be made no later than when any party first makes an offer to purchase, sell, lease or exchange. Undisclosed dual agency is acting for both parties in the transaction without disclosing that fact to all parties. Undisclosed dual agency is a violation of License Law.

Transaction broker and performing ministerial acts. A transaction broker is a licensee who represents neither party to the transaction. He or she is not the agent of either party. Transaction brokers may provide assistance to consumers who are not represented by performing ministerial acts. Transaction brokers must timely disclose adverse material facts pertaining to the property's physical condition and pertaining to the immediate neighborhood within one mile known to broker and not discoverable by an inspection of the neighborhood or through the review of reasonably available governmental documents and statistics.

SNAPSHOT REVIEW: UNIT TEN

BROKERAGE RELATIONSHIPS IN REAL ESTATE TRANSACTIONS ACT (BRRETA) RELATIONSHIPS

BROKERAGE RELATIONSHIPS IN REAL ESTATE TRANSACTIONS

BRRETA

- Brokerage Relationships in Real Estate Transactions Act; defines relationships and required disclosures and duties.

Brokerage relationships

- agency not a fiduciary relationship; required duties of licensee: BRRETA specified duties and those in engagement; specific duties for agents engaged by buyer, seller, landlord and tenant

Required disclosures

- must disclose agency status no later than entering into contract, and disclose material facts; licensee to discloses client's financing terms

Termination and duration of relationships

- begin when client engages the broker, continue until performance; or if the engagement is not completed, expiration date agreed by parties or in amendment or authorized termination, whichever is earlier

Representation options

- designated agent, dual agent, transaction broker

Check Your Understanding Quiz:

Unit Ten: Brokerage Relationships in Real Estate Transactions Act (BRRETA) Relationships

Carefully read each question and provide your best answer based on what you learned in this unit. Then check your answers against the Answer Key which immediately follows the quiz questions.

1. What is the purpose of BRRETA?

    a. To prescribe commission fee guidelines for brokers and affiliated licensees
    b. To prescribe contractual relationships between brokers and affiliated licensees
    c. To govern relationships between consumers, brokers, and affiliated licensees
    d. To specify whether licensees must be an employee or an independent contractor

2. A licensee's duties to a client are provided

    a. exclusively by BRRETA.
    b. exclusively by the agency agreement.
    c. by the affiliated broker.
    d. by BRRETA and the agency agreement.

3. Agency disclosure must be made

    a. at first contact with any party.
    b. no later than a first offer.
    c. prior to showing a property.
    d. prior to performing ministerial acts for the party.

4. Which of the following statements is false?

    a. Compensation creates an agency relationship between a broker and a consumer.
    b. How an agent will be compensated must be included in the brokerage agreement.
    c. Prospective clients must be informed about available agency options.
    d. A brokerage engagement must include the broker's duty to keep client information confidential.

5. Which of the following statements is true?

    a. The broker must continue to seek additional offers even when the property is under contract.
    b. The broker should never advise a client to seek expert advice outside of the contracted firm.
    c. The broker representing the seller client may perform ministerial services to the buyer.
    d. The broker promotes the best interest of the seller by presenting only those offers that include the seller's asking price.

6. Brokers must disclose certain information about a property to all involved parties. Those disclosures include existing adverse physical conditions in the neighborhood within _____ of the property that could not be discovered by a neighborhood inspection.

    a. 500 feet
    b. viewing distance
    c. walking distance
    d. 1 mile

7. If no expiration date is included in a brokerage agreement and the engagement is not completed, when does the brokerage relationship end?

    a. Within 30 days of failure to complete the engagement
    b. One year after the initiation of the engagement
    c. When the client submits a written termination notice to the broker
    d. When the broker notifies the client that the relationship has ended

8. What is the most important aspect of a legal dual agency?

    a. Written consent of all clients
    b. Determination of who will pay the commission
    c. That two different agents from the same firm represent the two parties
    d. Disclosure of the parties for whom the firm will be acting

9. A dual agency must be disclosed to both parties

    a. prior to showing a property.
    b. no later than when any party first makes an offer on the property.
    c. prior to either party accepting an offer.
    d. at the initiation of the agreement.

10. A transaction broker

    a. is a dual agent who represents both parties to a transaction.
    b. always represents the seller.
    c. always represents the buyer.
    d. represents neither party to the transaction.

==

Answer Key:

Unit Ten: Brokerage Relationships in Real Estate Transactions Act (BRRETA) Relationships

1. c. To govern relationships between consumers, brokers, and affiliated licensees
2. d. by BRRETA and the agency agreement.
3. b. no later than a first offer.
4. a. Compensation creates an agency relationship between a broker and a consumer.
5. c. The broker representing the seller client may perform ministerial services to the buyer.
6. d. 1 mile
7. b. One year after the initiation of the engagement
8. a. Written consent of all clients
9. b. no later than when any party first makes an offer on the property.
10. d. represents neither party to the transaction.

UNIT 11:

PROPERTY AND ENVIRONMENTAL DISCLOSURES

Unit Eleven Learning Objectives: When the student has completed this unit, he or she will be able to:

- Identify what information an agent is required to disclose about a property, is not required to disclose, and is prohibited from disclosing.
- Explain stigmatized properties and the related disclosure and nondisclosure requirements.
- Explain the disclosure requirements of specified environmental hazards.

PROPERTY DISCLOSURES

Full disclosure. Proper disclosure primarily concerns disclosure of agency, property condition, and environmental hazards.

An agent has the duty to inform the client of all material facts and any known latent (hidden) defects, reports, and rumors that might affect the client's interests in the property transaction. A material fact is one that might affect the value or desirability of the property to a buyer if the buyer knew it.

In recent years, the disclosure standard has been raised to require an agent to disclose items that a practicing agent *should know,* whether the agent actually had the knowledge or not, and regardless of whether the disclosure furthers or impedes the progress of the transaction. The agent may be held liable for failing to disclose a material fact if a court rules that the typical agent in that area would detect and recognize the adverse condition.

The most obvious example of a "should have known" disclosure is a property defect, such as an inoperative central air conditioner, that the agent failed to notice. If the air conditioner becomes a problem, the agent may be held liable for failing to disclose a material fact if a court rules that the typical agent in that area would detect and recognize a faulty air conditioner.

Fair housing. Agents are prohibited from obtaining or disclosing information related to a customer's race, creed, color, religion, sex or national origin: anti-discrimination laws hold such information to be immaterial to the transaction.

Property condition disclosure

The residential property condition disclosure is the seller's written summary of the property's condition at the time of contracting for sale. This disclosure protects the buyer with a written list of any adverse material facts. It may also protect the seller and seller's agent because there is written evidence of what was disclosed to the buyer.

Seller's property condition disclosure. Most current listing forms require the seller to disclose the condition of the property to prospective buyers. New laws in most states allow buyers to cancel a sale contract if they have not received the seller's property condition disclosure before closing or occupancy or other deadline.

Some states' legislation requires owners of previously occupied single-family homes and buildings containing 1-4 dwelling units to provide the disclosure to prospective buyers if they are selling, exchanging, or optioning their property. Some exceptions and exemptions apply. When required, the disclosure must be transmitted to the prospective buyer no later than when the buyer makes an offer.

A typical form requires the seller to affirm whether or not problems exist in any of the listed features and systems of the property. In denying that a problem exists, the seller claims to have no knowledge of a defect. If a defect does in fact exist, the seller can be held liable for intentional misrepresentation. A third possible response to a property condition question is that of "no representation." Here, the seller makes no claim of knowledge as to whether a problem exists. With this answer, the seller is no longer held liable for a disclosure of any kind relating to a particular feature, whether a defect is known or otherwise.

Licensee's role. An agent who sees a "red flag" issue such as a potential structural or mechanical problem should advise the seller to seek expert advice. Red flags can seriously impact the value of the property and/or the cost of remediation. In addition to property condition per se, they may include such things as

- environmental concerns
- property anomalies, such as over-sized or peculiarly shaped lot
- neighborhood issues
- poor construction
- signs of flooding
- poor floorplan
- adjacent property features

Depending on the state, the licensee may have no further duty to disclose property condition after properly informing parties of their rights and obligations. However, the licensee may still be subject to legal action for

- deliberately distorting the facts (intentional misrepresentation)
- cheating any party (fraud)
- concealing or failing to disclose adverse facts which the licensee knew about or should have known about (intentional or unintentional misrepresentation)

Right of rescission. Once the seller has signed the form and delivered it to the buyer, the buyer must acknowledge receipt and knowledge of the property condition disclosures, along with other provisions set forth on the form. Sellers who fail to complete and deliver the property condition disclosure statement to buyers in a timely fashion effectively give the buyer a subsequent right under certain conditions to rescind the sale contract and re-claim their deposits. The buyer must follow certain procedures and meet certain deadlines in order to legitimately effect the cancellation. The buyer's right to cancel persists until closing or occupancy, whichever comes first.

Georgia property condition disclosure. However, some brokers request sellers to complete a disclosure. Although no specific form is required by law and whether or not a written disclosure is used, licensees must remember that the seller's agent must disclose material facts to all parties with whom the licensee is working. This BRRETA requirement includes material facts pertaining to the physical condition of the property and improvements located on the property including any environmental contamination and facts required by law to be disclosed which are actually known by the broker and could not be discovered by a reasonably diligent inspection of the property by the buyer.

Stigmatized property

Facts not considered to be material, and therefore not usually subject to required disclosure, include such items as property stigmatization. Licensees are not required to disclose if a property was occupied by someone infected with a virus or other disease highly unlikely to be transmitted through occupancy. (Keep in mind that federal fair housing laws prohibit sharing information regarding the occupant having AIDS or being HIV-positive. This information cannot be provided, ever.) Neither are they required to disclose if a property was the site of a homicide or other felony, or suicide or death by accidental or natural causes, or the fact that a known child molester lives in the immediate neighborhood. If a licensee is asked about these issues, the licensee must answer truthfully to the best of his or her knowledge unless disclosure is prohibited by law.

Licensees should note that disclosure by buyer agents to their clients regarding homicides, suicide, or felony is not prohibited; it is simply not required, unless they ask. When a licensee is representing a seller, disclosure of a fact that stigmatizes a property when the disclosure is not required by law could harm the negotiating position of the seller client. If the seller questions whether an occurrence should be legally disclosed, he or she should be advised to contact his or her attorney.

Some firms have a printed form advising buyers to seek other sources if they desire information on facts that stigmatize property, especially known child molesters in the area. The form provided by some firms lists local police or sheriff's office as a resource for this type of information. There is less liability and chance of the party receiving incorrect or incomplete information when that client or customer obtains the information from an official source.

ENVIRONMENTAL DISCLOSURES

Environmental issues

Health hazards occur within structures, on real estate parcels, and in the area surrounding real estate. They may occur naturally or as a result of human activity. Environmental laws regulate some, but not all, health hazards that affect real estate. Real estate agents, owners, and sellers have various responsibilities for detecting, disclosing, and remediating regulated hazards.

Licensee responsibilities & liabilities

Licensees are expected to be aware of environmental issues and to know where to look for professional help. They are not expected to have expert knowledge of environmental law nor of physical conditions in a property. Rather, they must treat potential environmental hazards in the same way that they treat other material facts about a property: disclosure. If a licensee knows the result of an inspection, this is a material fact to be disclosed. Disclosure of environmental issues on commercial and industrial properties is often not mandated. Where disclosure is not required, real estate licensees should suggest the use of a professional environmental audit.

It is advisable to have an attorney draft the appropriate disclosures to lessen the broker's liability should problems occur in the future.

In sum, for their own protection, licensees should be careful to:

- be aware of potential hazards
- disclose known material facts
- distribute the HUD booklet
- know where to seek professional help.

Lead-based paint disclosure

The Federal Lead-based Paint Act of 1992 requires sellers of houses built before 1978 to disclose known lead problems before accepting an offer to purchase. The licensee must tell the seller about this requirement, give the seller the proper disclosure form, and make sure that the buyer receives it.

The licensee must give the buyer or lessee a copy of the EPA-HUD-US Consumer Product Safety Commission booklet, "Protect Your Family from Lead in Your Home" and must inform the buyer or lessee if lead-based paint is present in the home.

Further, the 1996 lead-based paint regulation requires sellers or lessors of almost all residential properties built before 1978 to disclose known lead-based paint hazards and provide any relevant records available. The seller is not required to test for lead but must allow the buyer a ten-day period for lead inspection and risk assessment prior to purchasing the home. Only a licensed lead professional is permitted to deal with testing, removal or encapsulation. It is the real estate practitioner's responsibility to ensure compliance.

Georgia Lead Paint Protection Act of 1994. The Georgia Lead Paint Protection Act closely mirrors the federal Lead-Based Paint Hazard Reduction Act of 1992 which requires disclosure of any known lead-based paint hazards to purchasers and renters. It provides regulations for residential dwellings and child-occupied facilities built prior to 1978.

Other disclosures

The licensee must also make sure the seller discloses any other circumstances the situation and the law require, which may include:

- wood infestation inspection report
- soil test report
- subsurface sewage disposal system permit disclosure
- impact fees or adequate facilities taxes disclosure
- radon reports or treatments

Other environmental hazards that require disclosure include the following:

Illegal drug manufacturing. Any property suspected as having been a place for drug manufacturing should be investigated prior to being sold or leased, and the possible health hazards must be disclosed to the potential buyer or renter.

Leaking underground storage tanks. Potential buyers must be informed of the presence of a UST on the property and of the health and financial risks of purchasing a property that contains a UST.

Safe Drinking Water Act. Property sellers generally must disclose the source of drinking water for the property and the presence, type and location of any septic system on the property. A water supply other than a municipal one and any septic system other than a standard one should be tested.

Mold. The presence of mold in the home must be disclosed as a latent defect. Flooding and water damage must also be disclosed as both of those can lead to mold growth.

SNAPSHOT REVIEW: UNIT ELEVEN

PROPERTY AND ENVIRONMENTAL DISCLOSURES

PROPERTY DISCLOSURES

- seller and seller's agent must disclose adverse material facts and latent defects; agent must disclose facts concerning neighborhood within one mile of property
- seller discloses known problems; agent discloses known material facts known or should have known; failure to disclose grants right of rescission to buyer
- agent should advise seller of red flag issues detected; may include environmental concerns, property size and shape, neighborhood, construction quality, flooding, floorplan, adjacent property
- where required, re-seller of residential property must complete and deliver to buyer on or before offering; failure gives buyer right to rescind prior to closing or occupancy; agents must disclose material facts; buyers must acknowledge receipt

ENVIRONMENTAL DISCLOSURES

- licensees must be aware of issues, know where to find professional help, disclose
- typically include: lead-based paint, mold, water quality, drug manufacturing, underground tanks

Georgia Lead Paint Protection Act of 1994

- mirrors federal law requiring disclosure on residences built before 1978

Check Your Understanding Quiz:

Unit Eleven: Property and Environmental Disclosures

Carefully read each question and provide your best answer based on what you learned in this unit. Then check your answers against the Answer Key which immediately follows the quiz questions.

1. What answer might a seller give on a property condition disclosure form to avoid liability while not acknowledging whether or not a problem exists?

   a. No inspection
   b. No knowledge
   c. No representation
   d. No denial

2. What should a licensee do when spotting a "red flag" on the property?

   a. Order an inspection
   b. Advise the seller to seek expert advice
   c. Require the seller to complete a property condition disclosure with the red flag identified
   d. Require the seller to disclose the red flag item to the potential buyer

3. Which of the following may subject a licensee to legal action?

   a. Failing to disclose adverse facts
   b. Pointing out red flag items to the seller
   c. Failing to have the property inspected
   d. Refusing to disclose events that stigmatized a property

4. When a seller is required to provide a property condition statement to the buyer but fails to do so, the buyer has a right to cancel the sale contract

   a. until completion of an inspection.
   b. within 30 days of closing.
   c. until closing or occupancy, whichever happens first.
   d. within 10 business days of signing the contract.

5. In Georgia, sellers must provide buyers with a written property condition disclosure

   a. prior to accepting an offer.
   b. prior to closing.
   c. prior to the buyer occupying the property.
   d. Sellers are not required to provide property condition disclosures.

6. Which of the following statements is true?

   a. Buyer agents may disclose to their clients any factor that labels a property as stigmatized.
   b. Seller agents are required to disclose material facts such as the property being the site of a murder.
   c. Sellers must disclose any known child molesters who live in the immediate neighborhood.
   d. Seller agents are prohibited from disclosing factors that label a property as stigmatized even if the buyer asks directly.

7. If a seller asks his agent if he is legally required to disclose that a former occupant suffered from AIDS, what should the agent do?

   a. Explain fair housing laws to the seller
   b. Advise the seller to disclose the information as a material fact
   c. Advise the seller to contact his attorney
   d. Tell the seller that such information is never to be disclosed

8. What responsibility does an agent have regarding environmental hazards located on a property?

   a. The responsibility to disclose the hazard as a material fact
   b. The responsibility to advise the use of a professional environmental audit
   c. The responsibility to have expert knowledge of environmental law to determine the level of hazard
   d. The responsibility of remediating the hazard

9. What is the specific disclosure requirement for homes built before 1978?

   a. The source of drinking water
   b. Underground storage tanks
   c. Mold
   d. Lead-based paint

10. While sellers are not required to test properties for lead, they must allow the buyer _____ to have a lead inspection and risk assessment completed prior to purchasing the home.

   a. 30 days
   b. 20 days
   c. 10 days
   d. 5 days

Answer Key:

Unit Eleven: Property and Environmental Disclosures

1. c. No representation
2. b. Advise the seller to seek expert advice
3. a. Failing to disclose adverse facts
4. c. until closing or occupancy, whichever happens first.
5. d. Sellers are not required to provide property condition disclosures.
6. a. Buyer agents may disclose to their clients any factor that labels a property as stigmatized.
7. c. Advise the seller to contact his attorney
8. a. The responsibility to disclose the hazard as a material fact
9. d. Lead-based paint
10. c. 10 days

UNIT 12:

FINANCIAL QUALIFICATION

Unit Twelve Learning Objectives: When the student has completed this unit, he or she will be able to:

- Explain how a mortgage loan is qualified and the underwriting practices prohibited under the Equal Credit Opportunity Act.
- Explain the debt ratio and income ratio, the formulas used to determine each, and how they are each ratio is used to estimate an applicant's ability to fulfill a loan obligation.
- Explain a loan commitment and differentiate between the types of commitment; that is, a firm commitment, a lock-in commitment, a conditional commitment, and a take-out commitment.

FINANCIAL QUALIFICATION

To qualify for a mortgage loan, a borrower must meet the lender's qualifications in terms of *income, debt, cash, and net worth*. In addition, a borrower must demonstrate sufficient *creditworthiness* to be an acceptable risk.

Equal Credit Opportunity Act

The Equal Credit Opportunity Act (ECOA) requires a lender to evaluate a loan applicant on the basis of that applicant's own income and credit rating, unless the applicant requests the inclusion of another's income and credit rating in the application. In addition, ECOA has prohibited a number of practices in mortgage loan underwriting. Accordingly, a lender may not:

- discount or disregard income from part-time work, a spouse, child support, alimony, or separate maintenance. Further, the loan officer may not ask whether any of the applicant's income is derived from these sources.
- assume that income for a certain type of person will be reduced because of an employment interruption due to child-bearing or child-raising. The loan officer may not ask about the applicant's plans or behavior concerning child-bearing or birth control.
- refuse a loan solely on the basis that the security is located in a certain geographical area.
- ask applicants any question about their age, sex, religion, race or national origin, except as the law may require.
- require a spouse to sign any document unless the spouse's income is to be included in the qualifying income, or unless the spouse agrees to become contractually obligated, or the state requires the signature for some purpose such as clearing clouded title.

If a lender denies a request for a loan, or offers a loan under different terms than those requested by an applicant, the lender must give the applicant written notice providing specific reasons for the action.

Qualifying the borrower. The lender must rely on eight types of information to determine that the borrower has the ability to repay the loan:

1. current income or assets (excluding the value of the mortgaged property)
2. current employment status
3. credit history
4. monthly payment for the mortgage
5. monthly payments being made on other loans on the same property
6. monthly payments for other mortgage-related expenses
7. other debts
8. monthly debt payments compared to monthly income (debt-to-income ratio)

The lender cannot use a temporarily low rate (introductory or "teaser" rate) to determine qualification. For an adjustable rate mortgage (ARM), the highest rate the borrower might have to pay is generally to be used.

The "ability to repay" requirements are relaxed in certain circumstances where the borrower is attempting to refinance from a riskier loan (such as an interest-only loan) to a less risky one (such as a fixed-rate mortgage loan.

Qualified Mortgage. A Qualified Mortgage is one that meets the "ability-to-repay" requirements, has certain required features and is not allowed to have others. There are exceptions to these rules for certain kinds of small lenders. Issuing a Qualified Mortgage gives the lender certain legal protections in case the borrower fails to repay the loan.

Generally not allowed:

- an "interest-only" period--when interest, but not principal, is being repaid
- negative amortization—when principal increases over time
- balloon payment—larger than normal payment at the end of the loan term
- loan term longer than 30 years
- excessive upfront fees and points

Generally required:

- monthly debt no more than 43 % of monthly pre-tax income
- limits on points

Qualified Mortgages include loans that can be bought by Fannie Mae or Freddie Mac or insured by certain government agencies, such as the Department of Agriculture, even if the debt ratio is higher than 43 percent. Also, loans that are insured or guaranteed by the Department of Housing and Urban Development, including through the Federal Housing Administration, are qualified mortgages under rules issued by that agency.

Valuations. Before issuing a first mortgage loan, a lender must

- notify the borrower within three days of the loan application that a copy of any appraisal will be promptly provided
- provide the borrower with a free copy of any valuation used, including appraisal reports, automated valuation model reports, and broker's price opinions, promptly when completed and no later than three days before closing
- provide these copies even if the loan does not close

The lender may ask for the deadline to be waived so that the copies may be delivered at closing, and may charge a reasonable fee for obtaining the valuation.

Discovery and disclosure requirements. Creditors are required to provide applicants with free copies of all appraisals and other written valuations developed in connection with an application for a loan to be secured by a first lien on a dwelling and must notify applicants in writing that copies of appraisals will be provided to them promptly.

High cost loans. When the annual percentage rate (APR) or points and fees on a home loan, home equity loan, or home equity line of credit (HELOC) exceed certain limits, special consumer protections apply. The lender must provide information in advance that explains the costs, terms, and associated fees, and get a housing counselor to certify that the borrower has received counseling about the high-cost mortgage.

With high-cost mortgages, lenders are not allowed to add many kinds of fees and charges to the loan amount, namely:

- prepayment penalties for early loan payoff
- balloon payments
- late fees larger than 4 percent of the regular payment
- fees for payoff statements (statements of loan balance)
- loan modification fees

Income qualification

Lenders want to be assured that the borrower has adequate means to make all necessary periodic payments on the loan in addition to other housing expenses and debts such as credit card payments and car payments. Most lenders use two ratios to estimate an applicant's ability to fulfill a loan obligation: an *income ratio,* or *housing ratio*, and a *debt ratio*, or *housing plus debt ratio*. They also consider the stability of an applicant's income. Please note that the income and debt ratios in the discussion below do not necessarily reflect the latest ratios used by FHA, VA, or other lenders. Check for updates on the websites of those agencies.

Income ratio. The income ratio, or housing expense ratio, establishes borrowing capacity by limiting the percent of gross income a borrower may spend on housing costs. Housing costs include principal, interest, taxes, and homeowner's insurance, and may include monthly assessments, mortgage insurance, and utilities. The income ratio formula is:

Income Ratio

$$\frac{monthly\ housing\ expense}{monthly\ GROSS\ income} = income\ ratio$$

To identify the maximum monthly housing expense an income ratio allows, modify the formula as follows:

monthly gross income x income ratio = monthly housing expense

Most conventional lenders require that this ratio be *no greater than 25-28%*. In other words, a borrower's total housing expenses cannot exceed 28% of gross income. For an FHA-backed loan, the ratio is 31%. VA-guaranteed loans do not use this qualifying ratio.

For example, if a couple has combined monthly gross income of $12,000, and a lender's maximum income ratio is 28%, the couple's monthly housing expense cannot exceed $3,360:

$$\$12,000 \times 28\% = \$3,360$$

Debt ratio. The debt ratio considers all of the monthly obligations of the income ratio *plus any additional monthly payments the applicant must make for other debts*. The lender will look specifically at minimum monthly payments due on revolving credit debts and other consumer loans. The debt ratio formula is:

Debt Ratio

$$\frac{monthly\ housing\ expense + monthly\ debt\ obligations}{monthly\ GROSS\ income} = debt\ ratio$$

To identify the housing expenses plus debt a debt ratio allows, modify the formula as follows:

monthly gross income x debt ratio = monthly housing expense + monthly debt obligations

Most conventional lenders require that this debt ratio be *no greater than 36%*. For an FHA-backed loan, the debt ratio may not exceed 43%. The VA uses 41% and a variable "residual income" calculation. The FHA and VA include in the debt figure any obligation costing more than $100 per month and any debt with a remaining term exceeding six months.

Using the 36% debt ratio, the couple whose monthly income is $12,000 will be allowed to have monthly housing and debt obligations of $4,320:

$$\$12,000\ gross\ income \times 36\% = \$4,320\ expenses\ and\ debt$$

VA-guaranteed loans also require a borrower to meet certain qualifications based on net income after paying federal, state, and social security taxes, housing maintenance and utilities expenses. Such **residual income requirements** vary by family size, loan amount, and geographical region.

Income stability. A lender looks beyond income and debt ratios to assess an applicant's income stability. Important factors are:

- how long the applicant has been employed at the present job
- how frequently and for what reasons the applicant has changed jobs in the past
- how likely secondary income such as bonuses and overtime is to continue on a regular basis
- how educational level, training and skills, age, and type of occupation may affect the continuation of the present income level in the future.

Cash qualification

Since a lender lends only part of the purchase price of a property according to the lender's loan-to-value ratio, a lender will verify that a borrower has the cash resources to make the required down payment. If some of a borrower's cash for the down payment comes as a gift from a relative or friend, a lender may require a **gift letter** from the donor stating the amount of the gift and lack of any requirement to repay the gift. On the other hand, if someone is lending an applicant a portion of the down payment with a provision for repayment, a lender will consider this another debt obligation and adjust the debt ratio accordingly. This can lower the amount a lender is willing to lend.

Net worth

An applicant's **net worth** shows a lender the depth of the applicant's cash reserves, the value and liquidity of assets, and the extent to which assets exceed liabilities. These facts are important to a lender as an indication of the applicant's ability to sustain debt payment in the event of loss of employment.

Credit evaluation

Credit report and credit score. A lender must obtain a written credit report on any applicant who submits a completed loan application. The credit report will contain the applicant's history regarding:

- outstanding debts
- payment behavior (timeliness, collection problems)
- legal information of public record (lawsuits, judgments, bankruptcies, divorces, foreclosures, garnishments, repossessions, defaults)

Problems with payment behavior and legal actions are likely to cause a lender to deny the application, unless the applicant can provide an acceptable explanation of mitigating and temporary circumstances that caused the problem.

If a lender denies a loan on the basis of a credit report, the lender must disclose in writing that the applicant is entitled to a statement of reason from any creditor responsible for the negative report.

Since 1995, the Federal Home Loan Mortgage Corporation and the Federal National Mortgage Association have been encouraging lenders to use *credit scoring* to evaluate loan applicants. **Credit scoring** is a computer-based method of assigning a numerical value to an applicant's credit. The credit score is a statistical prediction of a borrower's likelihood of defaulting on a loan.

Loan commitment

When a lender's underwriters have qualified an applicant and the lender has decided to offer the loan, the lender gives the applicant a written notice of the agreement to lend under specific terms. This written promise is the **loan commitment**. The commitment may take a number of common forms, including *a firm commitment, a lock-in commitment, a conditional commitment, and a take-out commitment.*

A **firm commitment** is a straight forward offer to make a specific loan at a specific interest rate for a specific term. This kind of commitment is the one most commonly offered to home buyers.

A **"lock-in" commitment** is an offer to lend a specific amount for a specific term at a specific interest rate, *but the interest rate is subject to an expiration date*, for instance, sixty days. This guarantees that the lender will not raise the interest rate during the application and closing periods. The borrower may have to pay points or some other charge for the lock-in.

A **conditional commitment** offers to make a loan if certain provisions are met. This kind of commitment generally applies to construction loans. A typical condition for funding the loan is completion of a development phase.

A **take-out commitment** offers to make a loan that will "take out" another lender's loan, i.e., pay it off and replace it. The take-out loan is most often used to retire a construction loan. The take-out lender agrees to pay off the short-term construction loan by issuing a long-term permanent loan.

CLOSING A LOAN

Closing of a mortgage loan normally occurs with the closing of the real estate transaction. At the real estate closing, the lender typically has deposited the funded amount with an escrow agent, along with instructions for disbursing the funds.

The borrower deposits necessary funds with the escrow agent, executes final documents, and receives signed copies of all relevant documents.

Title to the mortgaged property is transferred and recorded according to legal procedures in effect at the time of closing. The borrower receives a package containing copies of all documents relevant to the transaction.

SNAPSHOT REVIEW: UNIT TWELVE

FINANCIAL QUALIFICATION

QUALIFYING FOR A MORTGAGE LOAN

Equal Credit Opportunity Act

- lender must evaluate applicant according to applicant's own income and credit information

Income qualification

- income ratio and debt ratio qualify borrower's income; income ratio applied to gross income determines housing expense maximum; debt ratio takes revolving debt into account

Cash qualification

- lender verifies applicant's sources of cash for down payment; extra cash enhances income qualification evaluation

Net worth

- extent to which applicant's assets exceed liabilities as a further source of reserves

Credit evaluation

- lender obtains credit reports to evaluate applicant's payment behavior

Loan commitment

- written pledge by lender to grant loan under specific terms; firm, lock-in, conditional, take-out

CLOSING A LOAN

- usually simultaneous with closing of real estate transaction; transfer of funds, signing of documents, escrow deposits

==

Check Your Understanding Quiz:

Unit Twelve: Financial Qualification

Carefully read each question and provide your best answer based on what you learned in this unit. Then check your answers against the Answer Key which immediately follows the quiz questions.

1. The Equal Credit Opportunity Act requires a lender to

   a. determine if a loan applicant's income is derived from alimony or child support.
   b. evaluate a loan applicant's own income and credit rating.
   c. assume a loan applicant's income will be reduced due to an employment interruption related to childbirth.
   d. disregard income from part-time work.

2. Under what circumstances are the "ability-to-repay" requirements on a mortgage loan relaxed?

   a. When payments are being made on other loans on the same property
   b. When the debt-to-income ratio is high
   c. When refinancing from a riskier loan to a less risky one
   d. When using an adjustable rate mortgage

3. A mortgage that meets the "ability-to-repay" requirements, has certain required features, and is not allowed to have others is a(n)

   a. adjustable rate mortgage.
   b. Qualified Mortgage.
   c. interest-only loan.
   d. negative amortization loan.

4. A balloon payment is when

   a. interest but not principal is being repaid.
   b. principal increases over time.
   c. a larger than normal payment is due at the end of the loan term.
   d. there are excessive upfront fees and points.

5. With a Qualified Mortgage, the borrower's monthly debt may not be more than _____ of monthly pre-tax income.

   a. 43%
   b. 29%
   c. 38%
   d. 52%

6. Before issuing a first mortgage loan, a lender must provide the borrower with a free copy of any valuation used

   a. no later than 3 days prior to closing.
   b. within 5 days after closing.
   c. within 2 business days of receiving the valuation.
   d. The lender is not required to provide a free copy of the valuation used.

7. With high-cost loans, lenders must

   a. add prepayment penalties for early payoff.
   b. include late fees of at least 5% of the regular loan payment.
   c. add loan modification fees to the loan.
   d. apply specific consumer protections.

8. Lenders use which of the following as ratios to estimate the loan applicant's ability to meet loan obligations?

   a. Stability ratio
   b. Expense ratio
   c. Housing ratio
   d. Housing minus debt ratio

9. If a couple has a monthly gross income of $10,000 and monthly housing expenses totaling $2,500, what is their income ratio?

   a. 25%
   b. $25,000
   c. $7,500
   d. 250%

10. If an individual has a monthly gross income of $7,000 and the FHA's maximum income ratio is 31% for an FHA-backed loan, the monthly housing expense cannot exceed

    a. $2,580
    b. $2,170
    c. $4,830
    d. $9,170

11. A debt ratio is determined by

    a. subtracting the monthly housing expense from the monthly gross income.
    b. adding the monthly housing expense to the monthly debt obligations.

c. multiplying the monthly gross income by the income ratio.
d. dividing the monthly housing expense plus the monthly debt obligations by the monthly gross income.

12. Most conventional mortgage lenders require that the debt ratio be _____ or less.

   a. 31%
   b. 24%
   c. 36%
   d. 42%

13. Using the debt ratio from the previous question, a borrower whose monthly income is $9,000 would be allowed to have monthly housing and debt obligations no greater than

   a. $2,790.
   b. $2,160.
   c. $3,240.
   d. $3,780.

14. A lender's offer to lend a specific amount for a specific term at a specific interest rate that is subject to an expiration date is a

   a. firm commitment.
   b. lock-in commitment.
   c. conditional commitment.
   d. take-out commitment.

15. A statistical prediction of a borrower's likelihood of defaulting on a loan is the

   a. loan commitment.
   b. net worth.
   c. income stability.
   d. credit score.

Answer Key:

Unit Twelve: Financial Qualification

1. **b.** evaluate a loan applicant's own income and credit rating.
2. **c.** When refinancing from a riskier loan to a less risky one
3. **b.** Qualified Mortgage.
4. **c.** a larger than normal payment is due at the end of the loan term.
5. **a.** 43%
6. **a.** no later than 3 days prior to closing.
7. **d.** apply specific consumer protections.
8. **c.** Housing ratio
9. **a.** 25%
10. **b.** $2,170
11. **d.** dividing the monthly housing expense plus the monthly debt obligations by the monthly gross income.
12. **c.** 36%
13. **c.** $3,240.
14. **b.** lock-in commitment.
15. **d.** credit score.

UNIT 13:

PRICING RESIDENTIAL PROPERTY

Unit Thirteen Learning Objectives: When the student has completed this unit, he or she will be able to:

- Define market value and market price.
- Explain how appraisals and comparative market analyses are used in pricing residential property.
- Describe the three approaches to determining a property's value and identify the steps within each approach.

VALUING RESIDENTIAL PROPERTY

The valuation of real property is one of the most fundamental activities in the real estate business. Its role is particularly critical in the transfer of real property since the value of a parcel establishes the general price range for the principal parties to negotiate.

MARKET VALUE

Market value is an estimate of the price at which a property will sell at a particular time. This type of value is the one generally sought in appraisals and used in brokers' estimates of value. Market value is an opinion of the price that a willing seller and willing buyer would probably agree on for a property at a given time if:

- the transaction is a cash transaction
- the property is exposed on the open market for a reasonable period
- buyer and seller have full information about market conditions and about potential uses
- there is no abnormal pressure on either party to complete the transaction
- buyer and seller are not related (it is an "arm's length" transaction)
- title is marketable and conveyable by the seller
- the price is a "normal consideration," that is, it does not include hidden influences such as special financing deals, concessions, terms, services, fees, credits, costs, or other types of consideration.

Another way of describing market value is that it is the highest price that a buyer would pay and the lowest price that the seller would accept for the property.

The market price, as opposed to market value, is what a property actually sells for. Market price should theoretically be the same as market value if all the conditions essential for market value were present. Market price, however, may not reflect the analysis of comparables and of investment value that an estimate of market value includes.

Appreciation is an increase in the market value of a parcel of land over time, usually resulting from a general rise in sale prices of real estate throughout a market area. Such an increase, whether actual or projected, is another investment benefit that contributes to real estate value.

Estimating market value

Appraisals. An appraisal is distinguished from other estimates of value in that it is an opinion of value supported by data and performed by a professional, disinterested third party. An appraisal helps in setting selling prices and rental rates, determining the level of insurance coverage, establishing investment values, and establishing the value of the real estate as collateral for a loan.

Appraisals use several systematic steps, including applying the three basic approaches to value to the subject: *the sales comparison approach, the cost approach, and the income capitalization approach.* Using multiple methods serves to guard against errors and to set a range of values for the final estimate.

Comparative market analysis (CMA). A broker's comparative market analysis may resemble an appraisal, but it differs from an appraisal in that it is not necessarily performed by a disinterested third party or licensed professional, and it generally uses only a limited form of one of the three appraisal approaches. In addition, the CMA is not subject to regulation, nor does it follow any particular professional standards.

A broker or salesperson who is attempting to establish a listing price or range of prices for a property uses a scaled-down version of the appraiser's sales comparison approach called a comparative market analysis, or CMA (also called a competitive market analysis). While the CMA serves a useful purpose in setting general price ranges, brokers and agents need to exercise caution in presenting a CMA as an appraisal, which it is not. Two important distinctions between the two are objectivity and comprehensiveness.

First, the broker is not unbiased: he or she is motivated by the desire to obtain a listing, which can lead one to distort the estimated price. Secondly, the broker's CMA is not comprehensive: the broker does not usually consider the full range of data about market conditions and comparable sales that the appraiser must consider and document. Therefore, the broker's opinion will be less reliable than the appraiser's opinion.

THE SALES COMPARISON APPROACH

The sales comparison approach, also known as the *market data approach*, is used for almost all properties. It also serves as the basis for a broker's opinion of value. It is based on the principle of substitution-- that a buyer will pay no more for the subject property than would be sufficient to purchase a comparable property-- and contribution-- that specific characteristics add value to a property. In other words, that a property is generally worth what other, similar properties are worth.

The sales comparison approach is widely used because it takes into account the subject property's specific amenities in relation to competing properties. In addition, because of the currency of its data, the approach incorporates present market realities.

The sales comparison approach is limited in that every property is unique. As a result, it is difficult to find good comparables, especially for special-purpose properties. In addition, the market must be active; otherwise, sale prices lack currency and reliability.

Steps in the approach

The sales comparison approach consists of comparing sale prices of recently sold properties that are comparable with the subject, and making dollar adjustments to the price of each comparable to account for competitive differences with the subject. After identifying the adjusted value of each comparable, the appraiser weights the reliability of each comparable and the factors underlying how the adjustments were made. The weighting yields a final value range based on the most reliable factors in the analysis.

To qualify as a comparable, a property must:

- resemble the subject in size, shape, design, utility and location
- have sold recently, generally within six months of the appraisal
- have sold in an arm's-length transaction

The time-of-sale criterion is important because transactions that occurred too far in the past will not reflect appreciation or recent changes in market conditions.

Adjustment criteria. The appraiser adjusts the sale prices of the comparables to account for competitive differences with the subject property. Adjustments are made to the comparables in the form of a value deduction or a value addition. The principal factors for comparison and adjustment are *time of sale, location, physical characteristics, and transaction characteristics (*such differences as mortgage loan terms, mortgage assumability, and owner financing).

Weighting comparables. Lastly, the appraiser performs a weighted analysis of the indicated values of each comparable. The appraiser must identify which comparable values are more indicative of the subject and which are less indicative. As a rule, *the fewer the total number of adjustments, the smaller the adjustment amounts, and the less the total adjustment amount, the more reliable the comparable.*

The comparable with the fewest adjustments tends to be most similar to the subject, hence the best indicator of value. If a comparable's total adjustments alter the indicated value only slightly, the comparable is a good indicator of value. If total adjustments create a large dollar amount between the sale price and the adjusted value, the comparable is a poorer indicator of value.

THE COST APPROACH

The cost approach is most often used for recently built properties where the actual costs of development and construction are known. It is also used for special-purpose buildings which cannot be valued by the other methods because of lack of comparable sales or income data. The cost approach generally aims to estimate either the *reproduction cost* or the *replacement cost* of the subject property.

A cornerstone of the cost approach is the concept of **depreciation**. Depreciation is the *loss of value in an improvement over time*. Since land is assumed to retain its value indefinitely, depreciation only applies to the improved portion of real property.

Steps in the approach

The cost approach consists of estimating the value of the land "as if vacant;" estimating the cost of improvements; estimating and deducting accrued depreciation; and adding the estimated land value to the estimated depreciated cost of the improvements.

To estimate land value, the appraiser uses the sales comparison method: find properties which are comparable to the subject property in terms of land and adjust the sale prices of the comparables to account for competitive differences with the subject property.

Estimating the cost of improvements includes determining the **reproduction cost** (the cost of constructing, at current prices, a *precise duplicate* of the subject improvements) and **replacement cost** (the cost of constructing, at current prices and using current materials and methods, a *functional equivalent* of the subject improvements).

Estimating and deducting accrued depreciation involves using the **straight-line** method, also called the **economic age-life method**, which assumes that depreciation occurs at a steady rate over the economic life of the structure. Therefore, a property suffers the same incremental loss of value each year. The **economic life** is the period during which the structure is expected to remain useful in its original use. The cost of the structure is divided by the number of years of economic life to determine an annual amount for depreciation. The straight-line method is primarily relevant to depreciation from physical deterioration.

The sum of accrued depreciation from all sources is then subtracted from the estimated cost of reproducing or replacing the structure. This produces an estimate of the current value of the improvements. To complete the cost approach, the estimated value of the land "as if vacant" is added to the estimated value of the depreciated reproduction or replacement cost of the improvements.

THE INCOME CAPITALIZATION APPROACH

The income capitalization approach, or income approach, is used for income properties and sometimes for other properties in a rental market where the appraiser can find rental data. The approach is based on the principle of anticipation: the expected future income stream of a property underlies what an investor will pay for the property.

The strength of the income approach is that it is used by investors themselves to determine how much they should pay for a property. Thus, in the right circumstances, it provides a good basis for estimating market value. However, the approach is limited in two ways. First, it is difficult to determine an appropriate capitalization rate. Secondly, the income approach relies on market information about income and expenses, and it can be difficult to find such information.

Steps in the approach

The income capitalization method consists of estimating annual net operating income from the subject property, then applying a capitalization rate to the income. This produces a principal amount that the investor would pay for the property.

Estimate potential gross income. Potential gross income is the scheduled rent of the subject plus income from miscellaneous sources such as vending machines and telephones. Scheduled rent is the total rent a property will produce if fully leased at the established rental rates.

Estimate effective gross income. Effective gross income is potential gross income minus an allowance for vacancy and credit losses. Vacancy loss refers to an amount of income lost because of unrented space. Credit loss refers to an amount lost because of tenants' failure to pay rent for any reason.

Estimate net operating income. Net operating income is effective gross income minus total operating expenses. Operating expenses include fixed expenses and variable expenses. Fixed expenses are those that are incurred whether the property is occupied or vacant. Variable expenses are those that relate to actual operation of the building.

Select a capitalization rate. The capitalization rate is an estimate of the *rate of return* an investor will demand on the investment of capital in a property. The judgment and market knowledge of the appraiser play an essential role in the selection of an appropriate rate for the subject property.

Apply the capitalization rate. An appraiser now obtains an indication of value from the income capitalization method by dividing the estimated net operating income for the subject by the selected capitalization rate.

SNAPSHOT REVIEW: UNIT THIRTEEN

PRICING RESIDENTIAL PROPERTY

VALUING RESIDENTIAL PROPERTY

Market value

- price willing buyer and seller would agree on given: cash transaction, exposure, information, no pressure, arm's length, marketable title, no hidden influences

Estimating market value

- appraisal - a professional's opinion of value, supported by data, regulated, following professional standards; used in real estate decision-making
- CMA – broker's opinion of value for listing price

SALES COMPARISON APPROACH

- most commonly used; relies on principles of substitution and contribution

Steps in the approach

- compare sale prices, adjust comparables to account for differences with subject

Qualifying as comparables

- must be physically similar, in subject's vicinity, recently sold in arm's length sale

Adjusting comparables

- deduct from comp if better than subject; add to comp if worse than subject

Weighting adjustments

- best indicator has fewest and smallest adjustments, least net adjustment from the sale price

COST APPROACH

- most often used for recently built properties and special-purpose buildings

Types of cost estimated

- reproduction and replacement

Depreciation

- loss of value from deterioration, or functional or economic obsolescence

Steps in the approach

- land value plus depreciated reproduction or replacement cost of improvements

INCOME APPROACH

- used for income properties and in a rental market with available rental data

Steps in the approach

- estimate potential gross income, estimate effective gross income, estimate net operating income, select capitalization rate, apply capitalization rate

==

Check Your Understanding Quiz:

Unit Thirteen: Pricing Residential Property

Carefully read each question and provide your best answer based on what you learned in this unit. Then check your answers against the Answer Key which immediately follows the quiz questions.

1. An estimate of the price at which a property will sell at a particular time is

   a. an appraisal.
   b. a broker's comparative market analysis.
   c. the market value.
   d. the listing price.

2. An increase in the market value of a parcel of land over time is called

   a. depreciation.
   b. appreciation.
   c. inflation.
   d. investment.

3. Which of the following is a difference between appraisals and comparative market analyses?

   a. Appraisals are estimates of a property's value.
   b. Appraisals help set the selling price.
   c. Appraisals are performed by a disinterested third party.
   d. Appraisals use aspects of sales comparison approach to determine value.

4. The sales comparison approach is based on the principle of

   a. substitution and contribution.
   b. comparison and replacement.
   c. comparison and substitution.
   d. reproduction and replacement.

5. Which of the following is a limitation of the sales comparison approach?

   a. Too many comparables
   b. An inactive market
   c. Reliable sale prices
   d. Ineffective for currency of sale prices

6. Which of the following is a factor used when adjusting the sale price of comparables?

   a. Number of comparables
   b. Demands of buyer
   c. Expertise of broker
   d. Time of sale

7. When using the sales comparison approach, a comparable is considered a good indicator of value if

   a. it is located near the subject property.
   b. it has recently sold.
   c. its total adjustments only slightly alter the indicated value.
   d. its total adjustments create a large dollar amount between the sale price and the adjusted value.

8. Which approach is most often used for recently built properties?

   a. The cost approach
   b. The sales comparison approach
   c. The income approach
   d. The income capitalization approach

9. _____ involves the cost of constructing a precise duplicate of the subject improvements at current prices.

   a. Straight-line method
   b. Reproduction
   c. Replacement
   d. Economic life

10. Selecting and applying a capitalization rate are steps in which approach?

   a. Income approach
   b. Cost approach
   c. Sales comparison approach
   d. Market data approach

==

Answer Key:

Unit Thirteen: Pricing Residential Property

1. c.   the market value.
2. b.   appreciation.
3. c.   Appraisals are performed by a disinterested third party.
4. a.   substitution and contribution.
5. b.   An inactive market
6. d.   Time of sale
7. c.   its total adjustments only slightly alter the indicated value.
8. a.   The cost approach
9. b.   Reproduction
10. a.   Income approach

UNIT 14:

TRANSACTION CONTRACTS:
THE LISTING AND THE SALES CONTRACTS

Unit Fourteen Learning Objectives: When the student has completed this unit, he or she will be able to:

- Explain the different types of listing agreements and their impact on the sale or lease of property.
- Define numerous legal characteristics of sales contracts, including validity; who may complete; contingencies; default; contract creation; and blank contracts

THE LISTING AGREEMENT

A listing agreement is a legally enforceable real estate agency agreement between a real estate broker and a client, authorizing the broker to perform a stated service for compensation. The unique characteristic of a listing agreement is that it is governed both by agency law and by contract law.

Agency law

The cornerstones of agency law in the context of a listing agreement are the definition of the roles of parties involved, the fiduciary duties of the agent, and the agent's scope of authority.

Contract law

Bilateral or unilateral agreement. Listings may be bilateral or unilateral, depending on the type of listing and the wording of the agreement. An open listing is a unilateral agreement in that the seller promises to pay a commission to any agent who produces a buyer but no agent promises or is obligated to take any action. On the other hand, most exclusive listings are bilateral agreements because of wording that promises the due diligence of the agent to procure a buyer in return for the seller's promise to pay a commission if a buyer is produced.

Validity. A listing agreement must meet the requirements for a valid contract to be enforceable.

Listing termination. A listing, like any contract, may terminate for any of the following causes: performance, infeasibility, mutual agreement, rescission, revocation, abandonment, lapse of time, invalidity, breach, incapacitation or death of either party, involuntary title transfer, and destruction of the property.

Legal form. The Statute of Frauds in Georgia requires a contract to sell or lease property to be in writing and will not be enforced otherwise. In practice, a written agreement sets forth the various authorizations and duties, as well as requirements for compensation. A listing agreement establishes an agency for a specified transaction and has a stated expiration. An express listing authorizes the broker to pursue certain actions for the client. Clients and agents may also create an *implied agency listing* based on substantive actions rather than on an express agreement. For example, if a seller allows a broker to undertake certain activities toward effecting a transaction without a specific authorization, but with full knowledge and consent, an implied agency may have been created.

Assignment. Since a listing agreement is a personal service contract, it is *not assignable*. In particular, a broker cannot assign a listing to another broker.

Types of listing agreement

A broker may represent any principal party of a transaction: seller, landlord, buyer, tenant. An **owner listing agreement** authorizes a broker to represent an owner or landlord. There are three main types of owner listing agreement: *exclusive right-to-sell (or lease)*; *exclusive agency*; and *open listing*. Another type of listing, rarely used today and illegal in many states, is a *net listing*.

Exclusive right-to-sell (or lease). This is the most widely used owner agreement. Under the terms of this listing, a seller contracts exclusively with a single broker to procure a buyer or effect a sale transaction. If a buyer is procured during the listing period, the broker is entitled to a commission, *regardless of who is procuring cause*. Thus, if anyone-the owner, another broker-- sells the property, the owner must pay the listing broker the contracted commission. The *exclusive right-to-lease* is a similar contract for a leasing transaction. Under the terms of this listing, the owner or landlord must pay the listing broker a commission if anyone procures a tenant for the named premises. The exclusive listing gives the listing broker the greatest assurance of receiving compensation for marketing efforts.

The listing includes **clauses** regarding all legal owners of the property, the broker and his or her authorization, the property description, personal property and fixtures included in the sale, the listing price, listing term, agent's duties and compensation, required disclosures, and other related clauses as well as signatures of the owners and broker.

Exclusive agency. An exclusive agency listing authorizes a single broker to sell the property and earn a commission, but *leaves the owner the right to sell the property without the broker's assistance*, in which case no commission is owed. Thus, if any party other than the owner is procuring cause in a completed sale of the property, including another broker, the contracted broker has earned the commission. This arrangement may also be used in a leasing transaction. An exclusive agency listing generally must have an expiration date.

Open listing. An open listing is a *non-exclusive* authorization to sell or lease a property. The owner may offer such agreements to any number of brokers in the marketplace. With an open listing, the broker who is the first to perform under the terms of the listing is the sole party entitled to a commission. Performance usually consists of being the procuring cause in the finding of a ready, willing, and able customer. If the transaction occurs without a procuring broker, no commissions are payable. Open listings are rare in residential brokerage. Brokers generally shy away from them because they offer no assurance of compensation for marketing efforts. In addition, open listings cause commission disputes. In most states, open listings do not require a stated expiration date. Rather, they expire after a "reasonable" period of time as locally defined.

Net listing. A net listing is one in which an owner sets a minimum acceptable amount to be received from the transaction and allows the broker to have any amount received in excess as a commission, assuming the broker has earned a commission according to the other terms of the agreement. The owner's "net" may or may not account for closing costs. Net listings are generally regarded as unprofessional today because they create a conflict of interest for brokers who encourage the owner to put the lowest possible acceptable price in the listing, regardless of market value, to increase the broker's commission. Net listings are illegal in Georgia because the broker may violate the fiduciary duty of placing the client's interest above the broker's interest.

A **buyer agency** or **tenant representation agreement** authorizes a broker to represent a buyer or tenant. The most commonly used form is an *exclusive right-to-represent* agreement, the equivalent of an exclusive right-to-sell. However, exclusive agency and open types of agreement may be also used to secure a relationship on this side of a transaction. Generally, buyer and tenant representation agreements are subject to the same laws and regulations as those applying to owner listings.

Duties of the Agent. At the formation of the relationship, the buyer agent has the duty to explain how buyer or tenant agency relationships work. During the listing term, the buyer or tenant agent's principal duties are to diligently locate a property that meets the principal's requirements. In addition, the agent must comply with his or her state agency-disclosure laws which may differ from those of traditional listing agents.

A buyer or tenant agreement includes *clauses* regarding the representation of exclusivity, agent compensation, and acknowledgement of the agent working with other buyers or tenants.

Transaction brokerage agreements may be exclusive or non-exclusive and contain provisions for identifying the parties and property, the agent's authority, a non-agency declaration, broker duties and compensation, buyer and seller duties, agreement term, and signatures.

THE SALES CONTRACT

A real estate sale contract is a binding and enforceable agreement wherein a buyer, the **vendee**, agrees to buy an identified parcel of real estate, and a seller, the **vendor**, agrees to sell it under certain terms and conditions. It is the document that is at the center of the transaction.

A sample of the Georgia sale contract can be found online at F201 01.01.19.pdf or Microsoft Word - Purchase and Sale Contract 01152012.doc (wikiform.org).

Legal characteristics of sales contracts

Executory contract. A sale contract is executory: the signatories have yet to perform their respective obligations and promises. Upon closing, the sale contract is fully performed and no longer exists as a binding agreement.

Signatures. All owners of the property should sign the sale contract. If the sellers are married, both spouses should sign to ensure that both spouses release homestead rights to the buyer at closing.

Enforceability criteria. To be enforceable, a contract for the sale of real estate must:

- be validly created (mutual consent, consideration, legal purpose, competent parties, voluntary)
- be in writing
- identify the principal parties
- clearly identify the property, preferably by legal description
- contain a purchase price
- be signed by the principal parties

Assignment. Either party to a sale transaction can assign the sale contract to another party, subject to the provisions and conditions contained in the agreement.

Who may complete a sales contract? A broker or agent may assist a buyer and seller in completing an offer to purchase, provided the broker represents the client faithfully and does not charge a separate fee for the assistance. Brokers are to use a standard contract form promulgated by state agencies or real estate boards, as such forms contain generally accepted language. This relieves the broker of the dangers of practicing law, an act for which the broker is not licensed.

Signing blank contracts. Licensees are prohibited from having a party sign a contract with blanks to be completed later. Changes or deletions in a contract must be initialed or signed and dated. A licensee should advise a party who is unsure regarding any legal issue or language to use to contact an attorney.

Contract creation

Offer and acceptance. A contract of sale is created by full and unequivocal acceptance of an offer. Offer and acceptance may come from either buyer or seller.

Equitable title. A sale contract gives the buyer an interest in the property that is called equitable title. If the seller defaults and the buyer can show good faith performance, the buyer can sue for specific performance to compel the seller to transfer legal title upon payment of the contract price.

Contract contingencies

A sale contract often contains contingencies, i.e., conditions that must be met before the contract is enforceable. The most common contingency concerns financing. A buyer makes an offer contingent upon securing financing for the property under certain terms on or before a certain date. If unable to secure the specified loan commitment, the buyer may cancel the contract and recover the deposit. A loan commitment eliminates the contingency, and the buyer must proceed with the purchase.

To avoid problems, the statement of a contingency should be explicit and clear, have an expiration date, and expressly require diligence in the effort to fulfill the requirement.

SALE CONTRACT PROVISIONS

Sale contracts can vary significantly in length and thoroughness. They also vary according to the type of sale transaction they describe, such as residential, commercial, foreclosure, new construction, land, or exchange. As the most common sale transaction is a residential sale, a Residential Contract of Sale is the type with which a licensee should first become familiar.

Primary provisions of a typical residential sale contract

Parties, consideration, and property. One or more clauses will identify the parties, the property, and the basic consideration, which is the sale of the property in return for a purchase price. There must be at least two parties to a sale contract: one cannot convey property to oneself. All parties must be identified, be of legal age, and have the capacity to contract.

Primary provisions. The contract will also include provisions regarding the property's legal description, the price and terms, fixtures and personal property included in the sale a financing contingency, how earnest money and escrow will be handled, closing and possession dates, closing costs, the type and conditions of the deed to be used for conveying the property, evidence of property ownership, default remedies, who pays the broker, and the seller's warrant of no liens.

Secondary provisions. Secondary provisions that may be included in the sale contract include inspections and action based on the findings, disclosure of a homeowners' association and related assessments, a survey, disclosure of environmental hazards, the seller's warrant of no undisclosed building code or zoning violations, loans that become due upon the property's sale, tenants' rights, FHA or VA financing contingency, flood plain disclosure, resolution disputes, C.L.U.E. claims history report, any applicable addenda to the sale contract, and other provisions as deemed appropriate.

SNAPSHOT REVIEW: UNIT FOURTEEN

TRANSACTION CONTRACTS: THE LISTING AND THE SALES CONTRACTS

THE LISTING AGREEMENT

- governed both by agency law and by contract law
- can be either bilateral or unilateral based on type of listing
- must meet validity requirements; must be in writing
- multiple termination causes

Types of listing agreements

- **owner listings** – exclusive right-to-sell (or lease), exclusive agency, and open listing; net listings illegal in GA
- **buyer agency or tenant representation** – broker represents buyer or tenant; exclusive right-to-represent most common agreement; equivalent to exclusive right-to-sell; includes agent duties
- **transaction brokerage** – exclusive or non-exclusive

THE SALES CONTRACT
Legal characteristics

- binding, bilateral contract for purchase and sale; enforceable; executory, or to be fulfilled; expires upon closing; must be in writing; contain valuable consideration; identify property; be signed by all; be a valid contract

Contract creation

- by unqualified acceptance of an offer; gives buyer equitable title, power to force specific performance

Contract contingencies

- conditions that must be met for the contract to be enforceable

SALE CONTRACT PROVISIONS

Primary provisions

- parties, consideration, legal description, price and terms, loan approval, earnest money, escrow, closing and possession dates, conveyed interest, type of deed, title evidence, property condition warranty, closing costs, damage and destruction, default, broker's representation, commission, seller's representations

Secondary provisions

- inspections, owner's association disclosure, survey, environmental hazards, compliance with laws, due-on-sale, seller financing disclosure, rental property tenant's rights, FHA or VA financing condition, flood plain and flood insurance, condominium assessments, foreign seller withholding, tax-deferred exchange, merger of agreements, notices, time of the essence, fax transmission, survival, dispute resolution, addenda

==

Check Your Understanding Quiz:

Unit Fourteen: Transaction Contracts:
The Listing and The Sales Contracts

Carefully read each question and provide your best answer based on what you learned in this unit. Then check your answers against the Answer Key which immediately follows the quiz questions.

1. At what point is a sales contract considered fully performed?

    a. When signed by all owners of the property
    b. When filled out by the involved parties
    c. When the transaction closes
    d. When the offer is fully and unequivocally accepted

2. Which of the following statements is false regarding the enforceability of a sales contract?

    a. It must be in writing.
    b. It must include a closing date.
    c. It must include a purchase price.
    d. It must be signed by the principal parties.

3. A sale contract gives the buyer equitable title. What is equitable title?

    a. An interest in the property
    b. The deed to the property
    c. Ownership of the property equal to that of the seller
    d. A recordable title

4. A condition that must be met before the sale contract is performed is a(n)

    a. primary provision.
    b. assignment.
    c. secondary provision.
    d. contingency.

5. The most common sale transaction is a

    a. residential contract of sale.
    b. commercial contract of sale
    c. contract for sale of new construction.
    d. foreclosure contract of sale.

6. Which of the following is a primary provision in a typical residential sale contract?

   a. Title evidence
   b. Inspection
   c. Environmental hazards
   d. C.L.U.E. Report

7. There must be at least _____ party(ies) to a sale contract.

   a. 1
   b. 2
   c. 3
   d. 4

8. A sale contract's statement of a contingency should not

   a. be explicit.
   b. include an expiration date.
   c. be very broad.
   d. expressly require diligence in the effort to fulfill the requirement.

9. Which of the following would be considered a secondary provision of a sale contract?

   a. Compliance with zoning laws
   b. Type of deed
   c. Seller's representations
   d. Broker's commission

10. A C.L.U.E. Report shows

   a. the buyer's credit history.
   b. disputes resolved through arbitration.
   c. insurance claims history.
   d. agreements between the parties that are not expressed in the contract.

===

Answer Key:

Unit Fourteen: Transaction Contracts:
The Listing and The Sales Contracts

1. c. When the transaction closes
2. b. It must include a closing date.
3. a. An interest in the property
4. d. contingency.
5. a. residential contract of sale.
6. a. Title evidence
7. b. 2
8. c. be very broad.
9. a. Compliance with zoning laws
10. c. insurance claims history.

UNIT 15:

OFFERS AND COUNTER OFFERS, ACCEPTANCE, DOCUMENT HANDLING

Unit Fifteen Learning Objectives: When the student has completed this unit, he or she will be able to:

- Explain the offer and acceptance process, including counteroffers and multiple offers.
- Identify how offers are revoked or terminated.
- Explain transaction document delivery and maintenance requirements.

OFFER, COUNTEROFFER, AND ACCEPTANCE

The first stage of the conventional transfer of real estate ownership is the negotiating period where buyers and sellers exchange offers in an effort to agree to all transfer terms that will appear in the sale contract.

Offer

An **offer** is a proposal to enter into a binding contract under certain terms, submitted by an offeror to an offeree.

An offer expresses the offeror's intention to enter into a contract with an offeree to perform the terms of the agreement in exchange for the offeree's performance. In a real estate sale or lease contract, the offer must clearly contain all intended terms of the contract in writing and be communicated to the offeree.

Expiration date. A licensee may be punished for using any real estate listing agreement form, sales contract form, or offer to purchase form that lacks a definite expiration or termination date. If an offer contains an expiration date *and* the phrase "time is of the essence," the offer expires at exactly the time specified on the date specified. In the absence of a stated time period, the offeree has a "reasonable" time to accept an offer.

Financing disclosure. When writing offers, licensees are required to include financing terms if a financing contingency exists. Sellers must be made aware of financing terms.

Broker duties

If a buyer is interested in purchasing a property, an agent obtains the buyer's offer of transaction terms, including price, down payment, desired closing date, and financing requirements. An agent must be extremely careful at this point to abide by statutory obligations to the client, whoever that party may be. Discussions of price are particularly delicate: whether the client is buyer or seller, the agent's duty is to uphold the client's best interests. Thus, it is not acceptable to suggest to a customer what price the client will or will not accept. With pricing and other issues, it is always a good practice to understand what role the client wants the agent to assume in the offering phase of the transaction; in other words, exactly how far the agent may go in developing terms on the client's behalf.

Duties include timely presenting all offers to and from the seller, even when the property is subject to a contract. When a buyer or tenant makes an offer, the agent must present it to the seller or landlord at the earliest possible moment. The broker does not have an obligation to seek additional offers when the property is subject to an existing contract, unless the brokerage agreement states otherwise. So, although the broker does not have an obligation to seek additional offers, he or she must present all offers that are made, even after the property is subject to a contract.

Multiple offers

Multiple offer situations are common in seller's markets. If a listing is priced well, in good condition and in a hot area, then it will sell quickly and may result in a bidding war. Multiple offers can be difficult to organize, but one strategy is to call for a "highest and best" offer from all of the agents. This will save time from going back and forth with each agent and ensure that the offers are the strongest option a buyer is willing to make.

Once all of the new offers are in, organizing the important terms in an Excel sheet is a helpful way to present the offers to the sellers.

The important terms to organize are as follows:

- purchase price
- earnest money deposit
- financing type (cash, conventional, FHA, VA, USDA)
- down payment amount
- length of inspection period
- closing date
- incentives (are the buyer's asking for any closing cost assistance?)
- miscellaneous additional terms

Acceptance

Offer and acceptance. The mutual consent, also known as *meeting of the minds,* required for a valid contract is reached through the process of offer and acceptance. Mutual consent requires that a contract involve a clear and definite offer and an intentional, unqualified acceptance of the offer.

The **offeror** proposes contract terms in an **offer** to the **offeree**. An offer gives the offeree the power of accepting. For an acceptance to be valid, the offeree must manifestly and unequivocally accept all terms of the offer without change, and so indicate by signing the offer, preferably with a date of signing.

If the offeree accepts all terms without amendment, the offer becomes a contract. In effect, the parties must agree to the terms without equivocation.

A contract of sale is created by full and unequivocal acceptance of an offer. The exact point at which the offer becomes a contract is when the offeree gives the offeror notice of the acceptance. The acceptance must be communicated to the offeror. If the communication of acceptance is by mail, the offer is considered to be communicated as soon as it is placed in the mail.

Broker duties. An agent's foremost duty following acceptance of an offer is to submit the contract and the earnest money to the employing broker without delay. Most states impose deadlines for this requirement, usually within twenty-four hours from the agent's receipt of the deposit.

Broker violations. A listing broker may not tell a buyer that the seller will accept an offer regardless of its terms. Telling the offeror that the offer *is* accepted would be an even more serious breach of the agreement.

Under agency law, a client is liable for actions the broker performs that are within the scope of authority granted by the listing agreement. However, a client is *not liable* for acts of the broker which go beyond the stated or implied scope of authority. A broker who exceeds the scope of authority in the listing agreement risks forfeiting compensation and perhaps even greater liabilities.

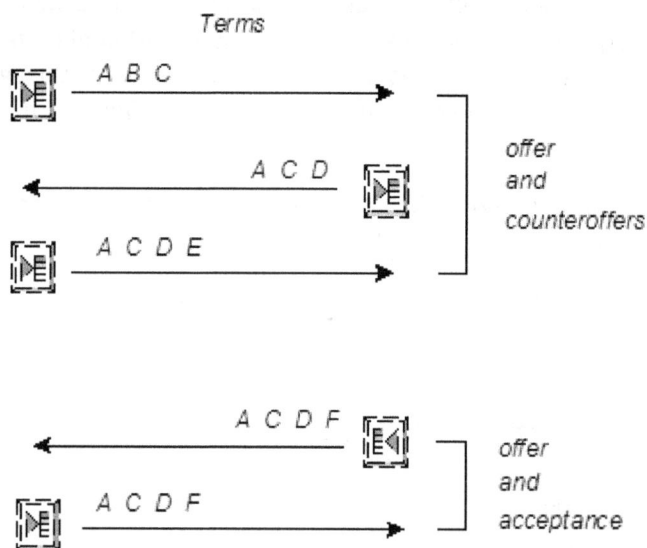

Counteroffers

Offer and acceptance may come from either buyer or seller. The offeree must accept the offer without making any changes whatsoever to any of the terms of an offer. If the terms of the offer are unacceptable, the agent may assist the seller in developing a new offer, or counteroffer, which the agent would subsequently submit to the buyer or buyer's agent. Any change automatically terminates the offer and creates a counteroffer.

At this point, the offeree becomes the offeror, and the new offeree gains the right of acceptance. If accepted, the counteroffer becomes a valid contract provided all other requirements are met.

For example, a seller (offeree) changes the expiration date of a buyer's (offeror's) offer by one day, signs the offer and returns it to the buyer. The single amendment extinguishes the buyer's offer, and the buyer is no longer bound by any agreement. The seller's amended offer is a counteroffer which now gives the buyer the right of acceptance. The seller has become the offeror and the buyer the offeree. If the buyer accepts the counteroffer, the counteroffer becomes a binding contract.

 The offering and counteroffering process continues until a meeting of the minds results in a sale contract.

Revocation of an offer

An offer may be revoked, or withdrawn, at any time before the offeree has communicated acceptance. The revocation extinguishes the offer and the offeree's right to accept it.

For example, a buyer has offered to purchase a house for the listed price. Three hours later, a family death radically changes the buyer's plans. She immediately calls the seller and revokes the offer, stating she is no longer interested in the house. Since the seller had not communicated acceptance of the offer to the buyer, the offer is legally cancelled.

If the offeree has paid consideration to the offeror to leave an offer open, and the offeror accepts, an option has been created which cancels the offeror's right to revoke the offer over the period of the option.

Termination of an offer

Any of the following actions or circumstances can terminate an offer:

- acceptance: the offeree accepts the offer, converting it to a contract
- rejection: the offeree rejects the offer
- revocation: the offeror withdraws the offer before acceptance
- lapse of time: the offer expires
- counteroffer: the offeree changes the offer
- death or insanity of either party

DOCUMENT HANDLING

Document delivery. Licensees must provide copies of any document used in the transaction to the individuals signing the documents. If an offer is accepted and signed by all parties, copies must be distributed to each of the parties and to each brokerage firm involved in the transaction. Failing to deliver, within a reasonable time, a completed copy of the offer to buy or sell to the purchasers and sellers is a violation.

Maintaining transaction records. Transaction documents must be maintained for a minimum of three years and must be made available to the Commission upon reasonable request. These documents must be maintained by any broker identified in the sales contract, brokerage agreement, closing statement, lease, or other document related to the transaction. They must also be maintained by any company that participates in negotiating the transaction. Required records that firms are required to keep typically include:

- listing agreements
- offers
- contracts
- closing statements
- agency agreements
- disclosure documents
- correspondence and other communication records

Records may be maintained in any record storage system that utilizes paper, film, electronic, or other media if the licensee can produce true copies and if copies can be made available to the Commission's authorized representative upon reasonable request.

SNAPSHOT REVIEW: UNIT FIFTEEN

OFFERS AND COUNTER OFFERS, ACCEPTANCE, DOCUMENT HANDLING

OFFERS, COUNTER OFFERS, AND ACCEPTANCE

- **offer and acceptance** – A process that creates a contract. Acceptance is the offeree's unequivocal, manifest agreement to the terms of an offer.
- offer becomes a contract when the acceptance has been communicated to the offeror
- ERSTH

Counteroffer

- any offer in response to an offer or any altered original offer; nullifies original offer
- created when changes are made to offer

Revocation of an offer

- offeror may revoke offer prior to communication of acceptance by offeree

Termination of an offer

- acceptance; rejection; revocation; expiration; counteroffer; death or insanity

DOCUMENT HANDLING

- deliver document copies to signing parties and to involved brokerages
- maintain records three years by broker listed in document and company participating in transaction
- maintain in record storage system allowing licensee to produce true copies and allowing Commission's access upon request

==

Check Your Understanding Quiz:

Unit Fifteen: Offers and Counter Offers, Acceptance, Document Handling

Carefully read each question and provide your best answer based on what you learned in this unit. Then check your answers against the Answer Key which immediately follows the quiz questions.

1. A prospective homebuyer submits a signed offer to buy a house with the condition that the seller vacates the property on a certain date. The seller disagrees, changes the vacate date, then signs and returns the document to the buyer. At this point, the seller has

    a. accepted the offer.
    b. created a counteroffer.
    c. rejected the offer.
    d. created a sales contract.

2. A seller agrees to all terms of a buyer's offer, signs the offer, and has it delivered back to the buyer. At this point, the seller has

    a. altered the offer.
    b. created a counteroffer.
    c. rejected the offer.
    d. created a sales contract.

3. Which of the following statements is true?

    a. If a seller has accepted one buyer's offer, the seller's agent must not accept any other offers.
    b. If a seller has accepted one buyer's offer, the seller's agent is still obligated to seek other offers.
    c. When multiple offers have been received, the seller's agent must only present the offer with the highest purchase price.
    d. When a seller accepts a buyer's offer, the seller's agent must immediately submit the resulting contract and earnest money to the agent's affiliated broker.

4. When handling offers, licensees perform certain acts. Which of the following is a legal act agents may perform?

    a. Presenting additional offers to the client even after the property is subject to a contract
    b. Telling a buyer that the seller client will or will not accept a specific price
    c. Suggesting to a buyer what price to offer to the seller client
    d. Telling a buyer that the seller client will accept the offer regardless of its terms

5. When a seller makes changes to a buyer's offer,

    a. the buyer's offer is automatically terminated.
    b. the seller is creating a counteroffer.
    c. the offeree becomes the offeror.
    d. All of the above

6. At what point in the offer and acceptance process is it too late for the buyer to revoke an offer?

    a. As soon as the offer is presented to the seller
    b. After 5 business days from the date of the offer
    c. When the seller notifies the buyer that the offer has been accepted
    d. When the seller presents a counteroffer to the buyer

7. Mutual consent is reached

    a. when one party counteroffers the other party's offer.
    b. through the offer and acceptance process.
    c. by one party presenting an offer to the other party.
    d. when the offeree becomes the offeror.

8. A buyer submits an offer to a seller. Two hours later, the buyer finds a better house, calls the first seller, and withdraws the offer. Which of the following is true?

    a. The buyer may not revoke the offer in such a short period of time.
    b. The seller may sue the buyer for specific performance.
    c. The seller may still accept the offer and prohibit the buyer from revoking.
    d. The original offer is legally revoked.

9. An offer is terminated when

    a. the offeree changes the offer.
    b. the offeree accepts the offer.
    c. the offeror withdraws the offer prior to acceptance.
    d. All of the above

10. Any document used in a real estate transaction must be kept for at least

    a. 3 years.
    b. 60 days.
    c. 5 years.
    d. 18 months.

===

Answer Key:

Unit Fifteen: Offers and Counter Offers, Acceptance, Document Handling

1. b. created a counteroffer.
2. d. created a sales contract.
3. d. When a seller accepts a buyer's offer, the seller's agent must immediately submit the resulting contract and earnest money to the agent's affiliated broker.
4. a. Presenting additional offers to the client even after the property is subject to a contract
5. d. All of the above
6. c. When the seller notifies the buyer that the offer has been accepted
7. b. through the offer and acceptance process.
8. d. The original offer is legally revoked.
9. d. All of the above
10. a. 3 years.

UNIT 16:

PRE-CLOSING AND CLOSING ACTIVITIES, TILA/RESPA INTEGRATED DISCLOSURE RULE (TRID)

Unit Sixteen Learning Objectives: When the student has completed this unit, he or she will be able to:

- Explain the activities that lead up to a real estate transfer closing, to include the responsibilities of the involved parties, contract contingencies, and preparations.
- Summarize the closing process to include the attorney's required role, the lender requirements, and the process of transferring the property title.
- Identify and explain the disclosure requirements of RESPA and the Truth-In-Lending Act.
- Demonstrate expense and income prorating.
- Identify taxes related to real estate transfers and explain how they are determined.

PRE-CLOSING AND CLOSING ACTIVITIES

The Sales and Purchase Contract of a given transaction sets forth the duties, schedules, and responsibilities of each contracting party. The contract assumes that both parties are satisfied with the binding terms of the contract. The contract is legally enforceable only when all validity criteria of the contract have been satisfied, and the buyer and seller have signed the contract.

Salesperson responsibilities

The salesperson is responsible for assisting in negotiating the contract and ensuring that the contract is completed properly. If the salesperson receives an escrow deposit, it needs to be delivered to the broker by the end of the next business day if the broker is to hold the deposit. If a closing agent is involved, the deposit and a copy of the contract should be delivered to such closing agent as soon as possible.

The salesperson's responsibility is to ensure all contingencies in the contract are met and completed in the timeframe laid out in the contract. If a contingency is not completed on time, the contract becomes voidable by the other party unless both parties sign an extension, and a new completion date is established.

The salesperson should also go over all the required disclosures and ensure each party understands what they must pay. Each party should estimate how much money they will need to bring to closing or how much they will receive from the closing.

Broker responsibilities

The broker is required to ensure the salesperson has properly completed the sales contract. If the broker holds the escrow deposit, he or she should ensure it is deposited in a trust account within three days of receiving it from the salesperson. Typically, a broker will only become involved in the negotiation or execution of a contract if the salesperson runs into problems.

The broker or salesperson usually continues to provide pre-closing services between the signing of the sale contract and the closing. This includes making arrangements for pre-closing activities such as inspections, surveys, appraisals, and repairs and generally taking steps to ensure that the closing can proceed as scheduled.

The broker or associate is expected to explain and verify entries on the closing documents as well as attend the closing with the buyer or seller. The broker or associate is also responsible for delivering the escrow check to the closing agent.

Inspections

Most closings are contingent on the property meeting certain condition criteria. Meeting property condition requirements is one of the most important steps in the closing process. This is the only way the buyer can ensure that there are no major problems with the property. If something major is found, the contract may need to be renegotiated; or depending on how the contract is written, the buyers may be able to void the contract and get their escrow deposit back. It is important that, even with an "As-Is" contract, timely property inspections are completed in order to determine what issues exist and what the costs are to complete any repairs. The home inspector will check the home's structure and all systems on the property, such as plumbing, electric, HVAC, etc. Most inspectors give the buyers and their agent a detailed and photo-supported explanation of what they found in the home inspection.

Loan approval

A buyer who plans to finance the home purchase must obtain a mortgage loan before completing the purchase transaction. The contract usually sets out the buyer's timeframe for their loan and how long they have to get loan approval.

Most transactions allow for the contract to be contingent on the buyer's obtaining conventional or FHA financing for the purchase. Since loan approval is typically a contingency within the purchase contract, the seller should be notified when the approval is obtained or denied.

Problems with getting financing through the bank's underwriters are the number one reason why delays in closing may occur. The salesperson should ensure that the parties have allowed enough time to get the loan approved when setting the closing date. If they cannot meet the documented closing date because the financing has not been approved, the contract must be extended or terminated by the seller.

The salesperson should use care when completing the contract's financing section and include the exact amount of money the buyer needs to close the deal and the maximum amount of interest the buyer is willing to pay. If the financing section is completed properly, the buyer can get out of the contract and get their escrow deposit back if the contract terms cannot be met.

Other contingencies

The purchase contract usually contains several different contingencies to the purchase. The most typical contingencies include the following:

- the buyer obtaining financing
- the buyer performing a home inspection and, if needed, a "wood-destroying organism" inspection
- the seller's disclosure of all known material facts that can affect the home's value
- the seller's completing any agreed-upon repairs
- the buyer's right to cancel the contract based on the results of the inspection

- the home appraising for the sales price or higher
- the title search being completed with the result being unclouded, marketable title
- a survey that clears any encumbrances not already identified

Final preparations to closing

All buyers should complete a final walk-through inspection on the day of closing. This ensures all fixtures and personal property listed on the contract remain with the property and that no damage was done to the property when the seller moved out.

The buyer should also review the Closing Disclosure Statement (CD) with their salesperson to ensure all CD charges are in accord with charges indicated in the Sales Contract. The buyer should then wire-transfer the final amount due to the closing agent.

Care should be taken when wiring the purchase funds, as mortgage fraud has become an increasingly prevalent occurrence. For example, one common fraud tactic is to send the buyer a phony email from what appears to be the title company. The email states that the routing number and account number on the first email has changed due to banking errors. It then gives new routing numbers and account numbers to wire the money to. Often, the new numbers will be to a country where the money cannot be traced or recovered.

CLOSING ESSENTIALS

The settlement process

The closing process consists of the buyer and the seller verifying that each has fulfilled the terms of the sale contract. If they have, then at closing, the mortgage loan, if any, is closed and those funds transferred to the title company. All expenses are apportioned and paid; the consideration is exchanged for the title; all final documents are signed; and arrangements are made to record the transaction according to local laws.

Title transfer and closing

While the process of buying property is basically the same in all US states, local law does have an impact. In Georgia, the closing must be conducted by a licensed GA real estate attorney who is effectively a real estate specialist. Furthermore, this attorney must be physically present at the closing, and according to a Georgia Supreme Court order, "in control of the closing process from beginning to end." The attorney who handles the real estate closing represents the lender and not the buyer or the seller. Even though the closing attorney represents the lender, he or she has a responsibility to complete the closing efficiently and accurately in the interests of all parties involved.

One important step at closing is the voluntarily delivery and acceptance of the deed. In order to close, the seller must produce evidence of marketable title, as evidenced by title insurance, and the opinion of title or an affidavit of title. A clean, marketable title generally is a title without liens or claims on title that must be settled. The seller may also be asked to execute an affidavit of title stating that, since the date of the original title search, the seller has incurred no new liens, judgments, unpaid bills for repairs or improvements, no unrecorded deeds or contracts, no bankruptcies or divorces that would after the title, or any other defects the seller is aware of.

Attorney's role. Among other things, it is the Georgia real estate closing attorney's responsibility to:

- Ensure all documents are completed correctly
- Ensure deeds, affidavits, and all other documents are delivered to the right people

- Prepare the settlement or closing statement
- Disburse money in terms of the closing statement

Georgia law also requires the closing attorney to prepare a detailed statement that shows all disbursements and receipts from the buyer and the seller; and this must be given to both parties, and possibly the broker if there is one involved. Normally, the closing attorney explains the contents of the documentation to the buyer and seller at the closing, before everything is signed and sealed.

Lender's requirements at closing. Before approving the loan, the lender will qualify the loan applicant and the property held as collateral for the loan. The collateral must not be endangered by

- defects in the title
- by liens that would take priority over the principal mortgage lien, such as property taxes
- by physical damage to the property if not repaired

To safeguard the property collateral, the lender typically requires

- a survey
- a property inspection
- hazard insurance
- a title insurance policy
- a reserve account for hazard insurance and property taxes
- if applicable, private mortgage insurance where there is insufficient equity in the down payment.

In some cases, the lender may also require occupancy certificates to verify that any new construction performed complies with local building codes.

TILA/RESPA INTEGRATED DISCLOSURE RULE (TRID)

Effective October 3, 2015, a Truth-in-Lending Act/ Real Estate Settlement Procedures Act (TILA/RESPA) developed the Integrated Disclosure Rule (TRID). This rule integrated the disclosure requirements of RESPA and the Truth-In-Lending Act. It also replaced the Good Faith Estimate form and the HUD-1 Uniform Settlement Statement with the new Loan Estimate form and the Closing Disclosure form, respectively.

This act's main purpose was to make the loan processes and costs more transparent to the consumer. Both documents clearly outline all the charges and expenses of the buyer's loan and the total amount the buyer will pay the lender over the life of the loan.

Information booklet. A lender subject to RESPA must give loan applicants the Consumer Financial Protection Bureau (CFPB) booklet, "Your Home Loan Toolkit," within three days of receiving a loan application. This booklet describes loans, closing costs, and the Closing Disclosure form.

Lender disclosures. At the time of loan application or within three business days of application, a lender must give the applicant a Loan Estimate (H-24) of likely settlement costs. This estimate is usually based on comparable transactions completed in the area. The terms stated in the subsequent Closing Disclosure must agree with those of the Loan Estimate within pre-set limits.

Mortgage servicing. The lender must disclose to the buyer whether the lender intends to service the loan or convey it to another loan-service organization for servicing. This disclosure must also be accompanied by information as to how the buyer can resolve complaints.

Escrow disclosures. Loan servicers must provide borrowers with an annual escrow statement that summarizes all inflow and outflows in the prior 12-month period. The statement must also disclose shortfalls or overages in the account and how the discrepancies will be resolved.

Section 10 of RESPA limits the amounts lenders can require borrowers to place in escrow to pay taxes, hazard insurance, and other property-related expenses. The limitation applies to the initial deposits and deposits made over the course of the loan's terms. If the amount being held in the account is $50 or more at the end of the year, then the money must be returned to the buyer.

Referrals and kickback disclosures. RESPA prohibits the payment of fees as part of a real estate settlement when no services are rendered. This includes kickbacks or referral fees from any party directly involved in the closing, including the title company, real estate agents, lender, surveyor, attorney, or the appraiser.

H-25 disclosures of settlement costs

Under CFPB rules, a lender must use the Closing Disclosure (H-25) to disclose settlement costs to the buyer. This form covers all costs that the buyer will have to pay at closing, whether to the lender or other parties. Use of this form enforces RESPA's prohibition against a lender's requiring a buyer to deposit an excessive amount in the tax and insurance escrow account or to use a particular title company for title insurance. The consumer must receive the completed form not later than three business days before closing. The consumer also has the right to inspect a revised form one business day before closing.

H-25 form. The Closing Disclosure (CD) is a 5-page document where pages 1, 4, and 5 will change depending on the type of loan the buyer is getting. Real estate agents are generally concerned with pages 2 and 3. The following information is based on a 30-year fixed rate amortized mortgage:

- Page 1 has four sections: general information about the lender and borrower, the property, and the type of loan, it states the projected payments and what is included in those payments, and the Costs at Closing.
- Page 2 has four columns. It shows the expenses incurred by the buyer and seller. It also differentiates the expenses being paid during the closing process and those paid before closing.
- Page 3 has two sections, one for calculating cash to close, the other to summarize the buyer and seller's transaction. It also compares the loan estimate costs to the actual costs. It also gives the final number for the closing, the amount of money the buyer must transfer to close, and how much the seller will get at closing.
- Page 4 provides additional loan information such as escrow accounts, late payments, etc.
- Page 5 provides additional calculations, disclosures, and contact information for the individual involved in the closing.

Prorations

A proration is an expense or an income item where the buyer and seller pay or receive their pro rata share based on how much of the benefit of the payment (tax) or income (rent) they respectively enjoy. Take taxes for example. If a seller and buyer close two-thirds of the way through the year, the seller must pay taxes for that 2/3 period where he owned the property, and the buyer must pay for one-third where she owned the property. Since the taxes are paid in arrears, the buyer will receive the entire bill. To avoid the problem, the tax expense is simply apportioned to the parties at closing – and, specifically, the seller gets a charge and the buyer gets a credit for two-thirds of the tax bill that the buyer will receive at the end of the year.

To calculate a proration properly, an agent must understand who owns the day of closing. If the day of closing belongs to the buyer, the buyer pays all expenses of the day of closing and earns all income of the day of closing. If the seller owns the day of closing, this must be added to the contract in the notes section.

For example, An apartment rents for $900 per month. The owner decides to sell the unit. The day of closing is April 14th. What proration would occur on the Closing Disclosure Statement? Assume the day of closing belongs to the buyer.

> $900 ÷ 30 days in April = $30 rent earned per day
> $30 x 17 buyer days = $510
> Credit buyer $510, Debit seller $510

Since we know the day of closing, we use the **365-day method** of proration. The seller collects the rent on the 1st of the month, so the seller owes the buyer the rent for the days the buyer owns the house. The day of closing belongs to the buyer, so we count that day in our numbers.

The other proration method is the **360-day method**. This method assumes that every month has 30 days in it, including February. This method is used if the closing date is unknown or the agent estimates the closing cost for the buyer or seller.

It is important to understand how items are paid. Some items such as property taxes and utilities are paid in arrears. At the closing time, the seller has incurred the expense, but the expenses have not been billed or paid yet. The buyer will have to pay the bill sometime after closing. If an item is paid in arrears, the proration will be a credit to the buyer and a debit to the seller. The seller must pay the buyer for the time they owned the house. Example 2 shows property taxes that are paid in arrears.

Some items such as rent which the seller has already received, or HOA fees that the seller has already paid are known as advance fees. So, the buyer reimburses the seller for the time the buyer owns the home. If an item is paid in advance, the proration will be a credit to the seller and a debit to the buyer. The previous example shows rent that was paid in advance.

Example: The annual property taxes on a property piece are estimated to run $2,236 for the current year. The date of closing is May 16th, and the day of closing belonging to the buyer. What would be the proration on the Closing Disclosure for the property taxes?

> $2236 ÷ 365 = $6.13
> J31 + F28 + M31 + A30 +M15 = 135 seller days
> 135 days x $6.13 per day = $827.55
> Credit buyer $827.55, Debit seller $827.55

Taxes due at closing

State taxes on the deed. Most states impose a **transfer tax** when real estate is conveyed. The tax is usually paid when the deed is recorded, often in the form of **documentary stamps** purchased from the recorder where the deed is recorded. The stamps must be attached to deeds and conveyances before they are recorded.

Tax rates are specific to each state. Methods of stating the transfer tax due include quoting the tax as a percentage of the taxable consideration and as a dollar rate per $100.00 of total selling price. If the number of 100's is not a whole number, it must be rounded up to the next 100. For instance, if a property sells for $350,120 and the tax rate is $.55 per $100.00 "or any fraction thereof," the tax stamps will cost:

350,120 ÷ 100.00	=	3,501.20
3,501.20 *rounded up*	=	3,502
3,502 x $.55	=	$1,926.10

State taxes on the mortgage. Some states also impose a tax on instruments that contain promises to pay money, such as mortgages, notes, and contracts. Such taxes may be paid by the purchase of documentary stamps from the agency which will record the instrument. In addition, some states impose a further tax on the mortgage as an item of intangible personal property.

Taxes on the mortgage are typically paid by the buyer/borrower.

SNAPSHOT REVIEW: UNIT SIXTEEN

PRE-CLOSING AND CLOSING ACTIVITIES, TILA/RESPA INTEGRATED DISCLOSURE RULE (TRID)

PRE-CLOSING AND CLOSING ACTIVITIES

Salesperson responsibilities

- ensuring contingencies are cleared in a timely manner and schedule the inspection

Broker responsibilities

- ensuring the escrow deposit is handled legally

Inspections

- home inspector hired to inspect property; usually one of the major contingencies to be fulfilled

Loan approval

- contract states when buyer must submit the loan application and deadline for getting loan approval - agent's responsibility to ensure these dates are met or the contract becomes voidable by seller

Other contingencies

- survey, appraisal, financing terms, material facts disclosures, right to cancel

CLOSING ESSENTIALS

The settlement process

- agents confirm all parties have fulfilled the terms of the contract
- principals exchange consideration stated in the contract, sign all the required documentation

Title transfer and closing

- seller required to give a marketable title at closing; remove all liens or encumbrances necessary to deliver marketable title

- **Attorney's role –** handle closing, ensure proper documents, prepare closing statement, disburse money
- **Lender's requirements at closing –** provide all the documentation to close the loan and ensure funds are released upon signing, verifying paperwork, safeguard collateral

RESPA / TRID SYNOPSIS

Information booklet

- lender must provide borrower with the Consumer Financial Protection Bureau booklet

Lender disclosures

- must provide the H-24 Loan Estimate within three days of the loan application being completed

Mortgage servicing

- lender must let the borrower know who will be servicing the loan

Escrow disclosures

- Loan servicers must provide annual escrow statements to the borrowers

Referrals and kickback disclosures

- RESPA prohibits referral fees and kickbacks paid to anyone directly involved in the closure

H-25 disclosures of settlement costs

- lender must use CFPB's H-25 Closing Disclosure Statement to list settlement charges each party is paying

PRORATIONS

- income or expenses incurred by the buyer or the seller in advance or arrears; 365-day and 360-day methods used

TAXES AT CLOSING

- state-imposed transfer tax; documentary stamps; state-specific tax rates
- state-imposed tax on mortgage; documentary stamps; paid by buyer/borrower

==

Check Your Understanding Quiz:

Unit Sixteen: Pre-Closing and Closing Activities, TILA/RESPA Integrated Disclosure Rule (TRID)

Carefully read each question and provide your best answer based on what you learned in this unit. Then check your answers against the Answer Key which immediately follows the quiz questions.

1. The duties, schedules, and responsibilities of each party to a real estate transaction are set forth in the

   a. listing agreement.
   b. offer.
   c. sales contract.
   d. closing statement.

2. Which of the following items are paid in arrears?

   a. Taxes
   b. Rent
   c. Interest
   d. Surveys

3. A prorated expense that is paid in arrears is

   a. a debit to the buyer and seller.
   b. a credit to the buyer and a debit to the seller.
   c. a credit to the buyer and seller.
   d. a debit to the buyer and a credit to the seller.

4. The Loan Estimate must be given to the borrower within _____ of completing the loan application.

   a. 3 business days
   b. 10 calendar days
   c. 15 business days
   d. 30 days

5. In Georgia, who does the closing attorney represent?

   a. The buyer
   b. The lender
   c. The seller
   d. The broker

6. If a sale contract indicates that the day of closing is "the buyer's day," this means that

    a. the seller must pay prorated expenses inclusive of the day of closing.
    b. the buyer pays all expenses of the day of closing and earns all income of the day of closing.
    c. the buyer is free from paying expenses for that day.
    d. the seller must pay the buyer's portion of prorated expenses instead of the seller's portion.

7. Documentary stamps are used to

    a. document the procedures employed to close a transaction.
    b. document the payment of a transfer tax.
    c. certify that a transaction was recorded.
    d. mail closing documents to principal parties after closing.

8. Assume a seller at closing must pay transfer taxes at the rate of $1.00 for every $500 of purchase price, or fraction thereof. If the sale price is $450,500, how much tax must the seller pay?

    a. $90
    b. $900
    c. $901
    d. $90.10

9. If a seller paid $675 for transfer taxes at closing, and the rate was $1.00 for every $400 or fraction thereof of the sale price, what was the sale price?

    a. $270,500
    b. $2,700,000
    c. $270,000
    d. $27,400

10. Form H-25 is used for

    a. requiring a buyer to purchase title insurance.
    b. reporting property inspection findings.
    c. recording transfer taxes.
    d. disclosing settlement costs to the buyer.

11. If the amount being held in an escrow account for taxes and hazard insurance is $75 at the end of the year,

    a. the money must be returned to the buyer.
    b. interest must be paid on the $75 balance.
    c. that balance is rolled over to the next year.
    d. the escrow holder must recalculate the required escrow funds for the following year.

12. The purpose of TRID is to

    a. make the mortgage loan processes and costs more transparent to the consumer.
    b. itemize the costs both buyers and sellers will pay at closing.
    c. disclose transfer taxes.
    d. explain required escrow disclosures.

13. In Georgia, closings must be conducted by

    a. a title company.
    b. the broker.
    c. a GA real estate attorney.
    d. the lender.

14. In order to close a sale transaction, the seller must

    a. vacate the property.
    b. produce a marketable title.
    c. repair problems found in the property inspection.
    d. release any funds held in the escrow account.

15. What is the most common reason why closings are delayed?

    a. Inspection reports showing problems
    b. The buyer failing to obtain financing
    c. Either party attempting to renegotiate the contract
    d. Errors in the Closing Disclosure form H-25

===

Answer Key:

Unit Sixteen: Pre-Closing and Closing Activities, TILA/RESPA Integrated Disclosure Rule (TRID)

1. **c.** sales contract.
2. **a.** Taxes
3. **b.** a credit to the buyer and a debit to the seller.
4. **a.** 3 business days
5. **b.** The lender
6. **b.** the buyer pays all expenses of the day of closing and earns all income of the day of closing.
7. **b.** document the payment of a transfer tax.
8. **c.** $901
9. **c.** $270,000
10. **d.** disclosing settlement costs to the buyer.
11. **a.** the money must be returned to the buyer.
12. **a.** make the mortgage loan processes and costs more transparent to the consumer.
13. **c.** a GA real estate attorney.
14. **b.** produce a marketable title.
15. **b.** The buyer failing to obtain financing

UNIT 17:

INSURANCE REQUIREMENTS: HOMEOWNERS AND FLOOD

Unit Seventeen Learning Objectives: When the student has completed this unit, he or she will be able to:

- Explain the features and types of coverage in homeowner insurance policies.
- Identify the six major policies that cover homeowners, renters, and condominium or cooperative owners and explain the nuances of each.
- Describe flood hazard zones and the federal requirements for insurance coverage for structures within flood zones.

HOMEOWNERS INSURANCE REQUIREMENTS

Homeowners' insurance covers the home itself, personal property or contents of the home, and liability for injury others may suffer on the insured property.

Standard policy features

Content. The content of a policy explains in detail what is covered and to what extent. If the policy does not include a specific peril or threat, then a loss caused by that peril will not be covered.

Declarations. The declarations page includes the basic details of the policy, effective dates, deductibles, endorsements, and the name of any mortgagee. It also states the insurance rating of the property as determined by the property description.

Coverage

Each policy contains certain types of coverage. The coverages can be basic or comprehensive, providing more extensive coverage. The main types of coverage and those most commonly included in homeowners' policies are as follows.

Dwelling coverage. This pays for damage to the home itself and any structures or fixtures attached to the home. Coverage would include attached garages, plumbing, electrical systems, HVAC systems, and so forth. This is the most basic and common coverage and typically includes fire, windstorm, hail, tornadoes, vandalism, smoke, etc. It may not cover hurricanes, earthquakes, or mold unless specifically added.

Other structures coverage. This pays for damage to structures not attached to the home. These include unattached garages, fences, sheds, pool houses, or any other structure located on the property but not attached to the home.

Personal property coverage. This pays for the loss of personal belongings that are not considered to be the home itself. Examples include furniture, appliances, clothing, computers, televisions, home décor, books, and so forth. This coverage typically includes damage, loss, and theft of the personal property, whether or not it is actually on the property. For example, if the homeowner is traveling and loses a laptop computer during the trip, the personal property coverage on the owner's policy would pay for the laptop.

Loss of use coverage. This pays some expenses to live elsewhere after the home has been damaged or destroyed by a covered peril. Again, if the peril is not covered, the policy will not pay for loss of use.

Liability coverage. This pays if the homeowner is sued and found to be responsible for someone being injured on the owner's property. Liability insurance would cover the financial penalty imposed by the injured visitor's lawsuit. Liability also covers damage to someone else's property caused by the policyholder's negligence.

Medical payment coverage. This pays the medical bills if someone is hurt on the homeowner's property. Also, if the homeowner owns a dog that injures someone, the medical payments coverage would pay for the resulting medical bills. However, some insurance companies exclude dogs altogether or exclude certain breeds of dogs that they deem to be dangerous breeds.

Exclusions. It is worth mentioning again that numerous perils are typically excluded. These include hurricanes, earthquakes, and mold. However, for an increased premium, these perils can be added to the policy. Some types of coverage are always excluded from homeowners' policies, for example, flood. Separate flood policies are purchased through federal insurance programs.

Endorsements. An endorsement (or rider) provides coverage for property or perils not covered in the original policy. An example of an endorsement would be coverage for expensive jewelry.

Conditions. A condition is a specific requirement for coverage in a policy. For example, a car may be covered only when it is parked in the garage.

The 80% rule. Homeowner policies should insure the home for at least 80% of the home's replacement cost. With this coverage, the insurance company will pay losses in full up to the face amount of the policy, minus the deductible. For example, if the total coverage amount is $300,000 and the deductible is $500, a total loss of the home would pay $299,500.

However, if the home is not insured for 80% of the replacement cost, the loss would be paid based on the actual cash value of the property. This coverage amount would be based on depreciation and the home's age. For example, the recovery from a total loss of the same $300,000 home may be considerably less than the cost to replace the home if the home is 10 years old. A 10-year depreciation amount would be figured into the loss, and the company would pay the loss based on that factor.

Deductibles

Most policies include a deductible, which is a stated amount of money the policy holder must pay before the insurance benefits commence. The deductible amount will be determined by the premium amount – the lower the deductible, the higher the premium. The typical deductible on a homeowner's policy is $500 to $1,000.

Homeowners' policies

Homeowners' insurance policies are based on the Homeowners 2000 Program which made revisions to forms and endorsements in 2010. Under HO 2000, there are six major policies that cover homeowners, renters, and condominium or cooperative owners. Mobile homes or house trailers can only be covered by other insurance policies.

HO-1 is the basis for most homeowners' policies. It provides coverage for losses from the following perils:

- theft
- lightning, wind, and hail
- fire and smoke
- theft and vandalism
- explosion
- civil damage and riots
- war and terrorism
- damage from vehicles and aircraft
- glass breakage
- damage to property being removed in an emergency situation such as fire

In addition, the **HO-1** policy includes liability coverage for

- personal injury – resulting from negligence on the part of the insured
- medical payments – for injuries occurring to guests or resident employees of the insured
- physical damage – caused by the insured to the property of others

HO-2, also known as a peril policy, covers items in addition to those included in the HO-1 policy. These items include electric current, accidental discharge of water, weight of ice and snow, falling objects and building collapse. In a peril policy, if the item is not listed, it is not covered.

HO-3 is a more comprehensive all-risk policy that differs from the HO-2 in that it covers all perils unless they are listed in the policy.

HO-4 is a policy is for renters. Individuals renting or leasing an apartment or a house may carry a renters' insurance policy. This policy covers damage or loss of the renter's personal property by any peril covered in the policy as well as damage to the property or injuries to other people in the rented unit. Renters' insurance is similar to homeowners' insurance except it does not cover the actual dwelling. The landlord still needs to carry homeowners' insurance to cover the dwelling itself.

HO-5 policies have the most comprehensive coverage of all the homeowners' policies. It includes coverage for structures, personal property, and loss of use.

HO-6 policies are specific to condominiums and cooperatives. This policy type does not cover the structure itself but does cover semi-permanent structures such as cabinets, carpeting, wallpaper, etc. It also covers personal property. The condominium association or cooperative would carry coverage for the actual structure.

HO-7 policies provide an extended form of real and personal property coverage designed specifically for very expensive houses.

HO-8 policies are for older homes with replacement costs higher than the home's market value. This policy type pays to repair or replace damaged property with cheaper common construction materials and methods, referred to as functional replacement.

Owner-placed insurance

A property owner should consider the following when seeking homeowner's insurance coverage:

- the size and value of the property
- the potential for an increase or decrease in the property's value
- the value of the items contained in the home
- the age of the items in the home and how much depreciation will impact their coverage if they need replacing
- the area where the property is located and what weather conditions may threaten the home
- what type of structure is being insured
- whether the property is rented or owner occupied
- the lender's coverage requirements
- the cost and terms of the policy

Lender-placed insurance

Most lenders will place homeowner's insurance on a home if the owner has let the insurance lapse. Premiums for lender-placed, or forced-place, insurance are considerably higher than those for insurance an owner would buy. The coverage is also typically much less and limited to the structure itself. The lender will usually add the amount of the premium payment to the mortgage payments and require the homeowner to pay the higher amount. The lender will do this until the homeowner obtains a policy on his or her own.

FLOOD INSURANCE REQUIREMENTS

National Flood Insurance Act insurance requirement

Federal law requires that borrowers seeking to finance real estate through federally related loans obtain flood insurance if the property is located in a designated flood-hazard area. Flood insurance, which is a separate policy, cannot be purchased directly from the NFIP but must be purchased through the same companies that provide regular homeowners' insurance. The Department of Housing and Urban Development administers a program to subsidize flood insurance for borrowers in communities that have entered the program and complied with its construction standards. The Army Corps of Engineers has prepared flood-zone maps for the entire country.

Flood hazard. Flood zones as designated by FEMA are areas that border rivers and streams where flooding is a concern. Designated flood hazard zones are subject to restrictions on the location, type, and elevation of all improvements to the land (residential, agricultural, commercial, and industrial). Flood maps generally show a community's flood zones, floodplain boundaries, and Base Flood Elevation. This information, when examined together, determines the risk of flooding.

Flood hazards will change over time. The flow of water and how it drains can change due to natural or manmade causes. New land use and community development, natural forces such as climate change, terrain changes, and wildfires all can impact the risk of flooding.

If an entire structure is above the 100-year flood plain, it has a 1% annual chance of flooding, and the requirement for flood insurance may be waived. The zone it is located in is called the Special Flood Hazard Area (SFHA), also known as the **1% annual chance flood** zone. Properties located in low- to moderate-risk flood hazard areas such as the SFHA are not federally mandated to be covered by flood insurance; however, a lender may still require it. As flood hazard area maps are revised and properties move from low- to high-risk areas, flood insurance becomes a requirement.

Residents in a high-risk flood zone who have received federal disaster assistance in the form of grants from FEMA or low-interest disaster loans from the U.S. Small Business Administration (SBA) following a

Presidential Disaster Declaration must maintain flood insurance in order to be considered for any future federal disaster aid.

Cost of insurance. Charges for flood insurance are based on the following:

- flood zone classification (this determines the risk of flooding)
- age of the building and number of floors
- occupancy as well as contents and their location
- location of the lowest floor of the building in relation to the base flood elevation
- amount of coverage
- deductibles

Disclosure. Brokers have the responsibility to disclose if any portion of a property is located in a flood hazard area, as this is a material fact. Buyers should be advised to consult FEMA flood maps and/or check with the local planning office to determine the precise location of any flood zones and restrictions.

SNAPSHOT REVIEW: UNIT SEVENTEEN

INSURANCE REQUIREMENTS: HOMEOWNERS AND FLOOD

HOMEOWNERS INSURANCE REQUIREMENTS

- protects assets and complies with lender requirements

Standard policy features

Content

- explains what is covered, and to what extent; exclusions; basic details in declarations page

Coverage

- dwelling coverage protects home and attached structures or fixtures
- other structures coverage protects unattached structures such as fences and sheds
- personal property coverage protects personal belongings and contents of home even when not located on the property
- loss of use coverage pays some expenses to live away from the home during repairs from covered perils
- liability coverage protects homeowner when sued for injuries to others
- medical payment coverage pays medical bills for someone injured on homeowner's property
- exclusions of some perils such as earthquakes are typical; must be added at increased premium; flood is always excluded and requires separate policy

Deductibles

- when purchasing insurance, must consider deductible amount, replacement cost, or actual cash value, all of which impact premium amount

Homeowners' policies

- HO-1 is basic policy; HO-2, HO-3, and HO-5 are most common for modern homes; HO-2 has least coverage; HO-5 has most comprehensive coverage; all include structure and personal property
- HO-6 for condominiums and cooperatives; covers semi-permanent structures such as cabinets and personal property
- HO-8 for older or unique homes with replacement costs higher than property market value
- HO-4 for renters covers personal property and liability; HO-7 for extended coverage of expensive homes

Owner-placed insurance

- homeowner should consider size, age, location, type, and value of property and contents and terms of policy

Lender-placed insurance

- lender-placed more expensive than owner-placed

FLOOD INSURANCE REQUIREMENTS

NFIP requirements

- NFIP requires flood insurance for federally related mortgage loans if property located in designated flood-hazard area; separate policy from homeowner policy
- required if the homeowners have received federal disaster grants or loans and want to be considered for federal disaster aid in the future

Flood hazard

- Zones designated by FEMA; change over time; required insurance waived if structure above the 100-year flood plain

Cost of insurance

- based on: flood zone, age and height, occupancy, contents, location, amount, deductibles

Disclosure

- location of a property in a flood zone is a material fact to be disclosed

==

Check Your Understanding Quiz:

Unit Seventeen: Insurance Requirements: Homeowners and Flood

Carefully read each question and provide your best answer based on what you learned in this unit. Then check your answers against the Answer Key which immediately follows the quiz questions.

1. What type of insurance coverage would pay for damage to a single-family home's kitchen cabinets from fire?

    a. Dwelling
    b. Other structures
    c. Personal property
    d. Liability

2. While traveling in Europe, Sarah's cell phone was stolen. What insurance coverage must Sarah have to cover the loss of her phone?

    a. Dwelling
    b. Other structures
    c. Personal property
    d. Travel

3. John has a homeowner's insurance policy that covers dogs but excludes German Shepherd dogs. John's neighbor was teasing the dog in John's driveway and was subsequently bitten, requiring stitches. Who is liable for the neighbor's medical bill?

    a. John's homeowner's insurance, because it does cover dogs
    b. John, because his dog breed was excluded from the policy
    c. John's neighbor, because he was teasing the dog
    d. John's neighbor's homeowner's insurance, because it also covers dogs

4. Sue carries a homeowner insurance policy that insures her home for at least 80% of the replacement cost. Her policy has a $1,000 deductible with a total coverage amount of $400,000. If Sue's house is completely destroyed by fire, how much will her policy pay given that the home is 10 years old.

    a. $400,000
    b. $320,000
    c. $399,000
    d. The actual cash value of the home based on depreciation determined by the home's age.

5. Steve has just signed a lease on an apartment and would like to insure his personal property against loss or damage. Which type of policy does Steve need?

   a. HO-1
   b. HO-6
   c. HO-7
   d. HO-4

6. What type of home does an HO-8 policy cover?

   a. Condominium
   b. Older home with replacement cost higher than the home's market value
   c. Very expensive home
   d. Rental home

7. Which type of homeowner policy has the most comprehensive coverage of all of the policies?

   a. HO-1
   b. HO-8
   c. HO-5
   d. HO-2

8. Which of the following does not need to be a consideration when purchasing an HO-4 policy?

   a. The value of the items contained in the home
   b. The cost and terms of the policy
   c. The lender's coverage requirements
   d. The age of the items in the home and how much depreciation will impact their coverage if they need replacing

9. Who designates flood zones?

   a. Insurance companies
   b. FEMA
   c. HUD
   d. Army Corps of Engineers

10. Which of the following is true?

    a. If an entire structure is above the 100-year flood plain, it must be covered by flood insurance.
    b. Brokers are not required to disclose if any portion of a property is located in a flood hazard area.
    c. Residents in high-risk flood zones who received federal disaster assistance from FEMA must carry flood insurance.
    d. Lenders may not require flood insurance for properties located in a special flood hazard area.

Answer Key:

Unit Seventeen: Insurance Requirements: Homeowners and Flood

1. a.   Dwelling
2. c.   Personal property
3. b.   John, because his dog breed was excluded from the policy
4. c. $399,000
5. d.   HO-4
6. b.   Older home with replacement cost higher than the home's market value
7. c.   HO-5
8. c.   The lender's coverage requirements
9. b.   FEMA
10. c.   Residents in high-risk flood zones who received federal disaster assistance from FEMA must carry flood insurance.

UNIT 18:

FORECLOSURES AND SHORT SALES

Unit Eighteen Learning Objectives: When the student has completed this unit, he or she will be able to:

- Identify the three types of foreclosure and explain when each is used.
- Describe the process involved with the use of each type of foreclosure.
- Explain when short sales transpire and the transaction benchmarks of the sale.
- Describe the roles of each party to a short sale: seller, buyer, listing agent, buyer's agent, and lender.

FORECLOSURES

Lien Enforcement

All liens can be enforced by the sale or other transfer of title of the secured property, whether by court action, operation of law, or through powers granted in the original loan agreement. The enforcement proceedings are referred to as foreclosure.

A property owner who fails to fulfill loan obligations or pay taxes may lose an estate through foreclosure, which extinguishes all prior interests in a property, including a leasehold.

State law governs the foreclosure process. Broadly, a statutory or court-ordered sale enforces a general lien, including a judgment lien. A lawsuit or loan provision authorizing the sale or direct transfer of the attached property enforces a specific lien, such as a mortgage. Real estate tax liens are enforced through **tax foreclosure sales**, or **tax sales**.

The defaulting borrower may also offer the lender a **deed in lieu of foreclosure** to avoid the foreclosure process, but the lender does not have to accept it. Finally, there is the option of a **short sale**, which also avoids foreclosure but must be agreed to by the lender and borrower.

FORECLOSURE

Three types of foreclosure process enforce mortgage liens:

- judicial foreclosure
- non-judicial foreclosure
- strict foreclosure

Foreclosure Processes

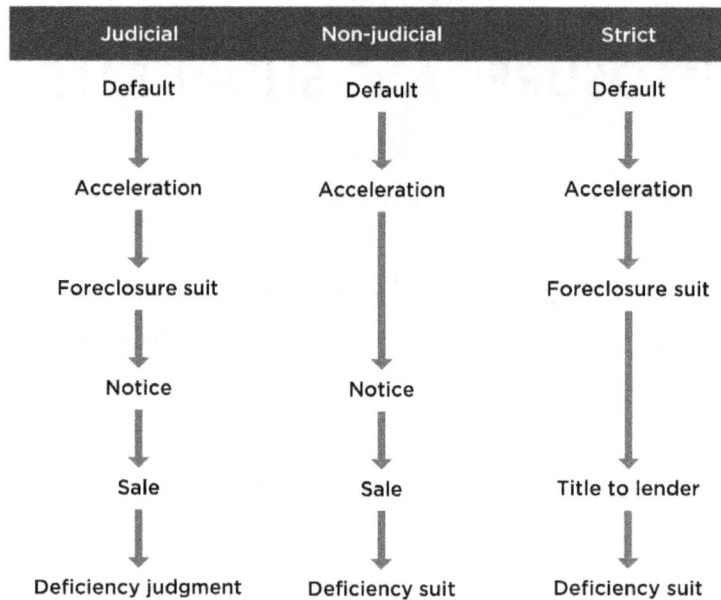

Judicial	Non-judicial	Strict
Default	Default	Default
↓	↓	↓
Acceleration	Acceleration	Acceleration
↓	↓	↓
Foreclosure suit		Foreclosure suit
↓	↓	↓
Notice	Notice	
↓	↓	↓
Sale	Sale	Title to lender
↓	↓	↓
Deficiency judgment	Deficiency suit	Deficiency suit

Judicial foreclosure

Judicial foreclosure occurs in states (such as Georgia) that use a two-party mortgage document (borrower and lender) that does not contain a "power of sale" provision. Lacking this provision, a lender must file a **foreclosure suit** and undertake a court proceeding to enforce the lien.

Acceleration and filing. If a borrower has failed to meet loan obligations in spite of proper notice and applicable grace periods, the lender can **accelerate** the loan, or declare that the loan balance and all other sums due on the loan are payable immediately.

If the borrower does not pay off the loan in full, the lender then files a foreclosure suit, naming the borrower as defendant. The suit asks the court to:

- terminate the defendant's interests in the property
- order the property sold publicly to the highest bidder
- order the proceeds applied to the debt

Lis Pendens. In the foreclosure suit, a **lis pendens** gives public notice that the mortgaged property may soon have a judgment issued against it. This notice enables other lienholders to join in the suit against the defendant.

Writ of execution. If the defendant fails to meet the demands of the suit during a prescribed period, the court orders the termination of interests of any and all parties in the property, and orders the property to be sold. The court's **writ of execution** authorizes an official, such as the county sheriff, to seize and sell the foreclosed property.

Public sale and sale proceeds. After public notice of the sale, the property is auctioned to the highest bidder. The new owner receives title free and clear of all previous liens, whether the lienholders have been paid or not. Proceeds of the sale are applied to payment of liens according to priority. After payment of real estate taxes, lienholders' claims and costs of the sale, any remaining funds go to the mortgagor (borrower).

Deficiency judgment. If the sale does not yield sufficient funds to cover the amounts owed, the mortgagee may ask the court for a deficiency judgment. This enables the lender to attach and foreclose a judgment lien on other real or personal property the borrower owns.

Right of redemption. The borrower's right of redemption, also called equity of redemption, is the right to *reclaim a property* that has been foreclosed by paying off amounts owed to creditors, including interest and costs. Redemption is possible within a **redemption period**. Some states allow redemption during the foreclosure proceeding at any time "until the gavel drops" at the sale. Other states have statutory periods of up to a year following the sale for the owner of a foreclosed property to redeem the estate.

Georgia has an *equitable right of redemption* in foreclosure proceedings. This means that the owner has a right to redeem the mortgaged real property prior to the foreclosure sale. Georgia owners do not have a statutory right of redemption after the sale.

Non-judicial foreclosure

When there is a "power of sale" provision in the mortgage or trust deed document, a non-judicial foreclosure can force the sale of the liened property *without a foreclosure suit*. The "power of sale" clause in effect enables the mortgagee to order a public sale without court decree.

Foreclosure process. On default, the foreclosing mortgagee records and delivers notice to the borrower and other lienholders. After the proper period, a "notice of sale" is published, the sale is conducted, and all liens are extinguished. The highest bidder then receives unencumbered title to the property.

Deficiency suit. The lender does not obtain a deficiency judgment or lien in a non-judicial foreclosure action. The lender instead must file a new deficiency suit against the borrower.

Re-instatement and redemption. During the notice of default and notice of sale periods, the borrower may pay the lender and terminate the proceedings. Exact re-instatement periods vary from state to state. There is no redemption right in non-judicial foreclosure.

Strict foreclosure

Strict foreclosure is a court proceeding that gives the lender title directly, by court order, instead of giving cash proceeds from a public sale.

On default, the lender gives the borrower official notice. After a prescribed period, the lender files suit in court, whereupon the court establishes a period within which the defaulting party must repay the amounts owed. If the defaulter does not repay the funds, the court orders transfer of full, legal title to the lender.

Deed in lieu of foreclosure

A defaulting borrower who faces foreclosure may avoid court actions and costs by voluntarily deeding the property to the mortgagee. This is accomplished with a deed in lieu of foreclosure which transfers legal title to the lienholder. The transfer, however, does not terminate any existing liens on the property.

SHORT SALES

Short sale transaction benchmarks

A **short sale** is what must transpire whenever a property owner attempting to convey his or her property owes more than resale value and loan pay-off amount. In the short sale transaction, the seller agrees to let the lender dictate or approve the terms of the transaction in exchange for the lender's promise to release the owner from the mortgage lien and to convey marketable title to the buyer.

The lender, however, may or may not agree to accept the deficient price as a satisfactory loan payoff and may require the seller to make up deficient amounts by way of a deficiency judgment. In other instances, there may be tax consequences for the seller if the lender agrees to grant an increment of loan forgiveness – which can amount to taxable income for the seller. To avoid the deficiency charge in the short sale, the seller must make sure that the agreements include a full release of the underlying debt and a statement that it was fully satisfied.

The parties to a short sale are the buyer, the seller, their agents and the lender. The lender is a third-party contingency who must approve the sale. The process of a short sale generally unfolds as follows.

Short sale transaction benchmarks

1. The borrower-sellers or their agents contact the lender to discuss the short sale option.
2. If willing, the lender sets the required terms of the short sale.
3. For an updated valuation estimate, the real estate agent provides the lender with a Broker's Price Opinion (BPO).
4. Subsequently, the agent lists the property for sale at the highest possible price that the market will bear.
5. The agent places the listing into the MLS with a special note to the brokerage community stating that the lender will consider a short sale.
6. At some point, a buyer takes an interest in the property and submits an offer.
7. After negotiating price and terms, the owner and buyer agree to the terms of a contract
8. The lender is then brought into the proceedings to evaluate and (hopefully) approve the final terms of the short sale.
9. The closing date is established, the pre-closing period is completed, and ideally, the transaction closes.
10. The final terms may or may not include a deficiency proceeding to recover unacceptable shortfalls in the sales proceeds.

The success of a short sale transaction depends on the collaboration of the seller, buyer, agents, and all lenders involved (1st, 2nd, 3rd position lienholders). Each party has a specific role to ensure the transaction can go smoothly.

Seller's role in the short sale

To get the transaction off to a good start, the seller must accurately identify exactly how much is owed on the property. The lenders can certainly provide this information. It is vital that the seller be upfront with all parties about every property-secured loan they have, as well as any equipment they are leasing (water softeners, solar panels, adjunct power systems, etc., all of which will have to be paid off with the sale of the home).

The seller should request payoff amounts from all lenders and provide this information to the listing agent so they can together create a net sheet. The net sheet will help the seller determine what they can afford to pay back to the various lenders once the closing costs are built in.

One common characteristic of a short sale is that the homeowner is experiencing some form of hardship that is putting pressure on the owners to sell in the short term as opposed to waiting until financial conditions improve. These circumstances should not be concealed. In order to get the short sale approved by the lender, the seller will need to provide documentation supporting the fact that they are experiencing financial hardship. Subsequently, to have a successful transaction under these adverse conditions, the seller's role will need to involve open and honest collaboration with the lender's representatives. In addition, the seller will need to understand that the short sale will require more time to complete than conventional conveyances.

Buyer's role in a short sale

Once the buyers decide to submit an offer for a short sale property, they can choose whether they would like to hire a short sale negotiator. Since short sales have become more commonplace in recent years, title companies and law firms have augmented their staffs with short sale specialists. These negotiators can be very beneficial to both principal parties – for the seller they can secure a top-dollar price, and for the buyer they can negotiate difficult agreements that might otherwise fail. The job of the short sale negotiator is to argue with the lenders and persuade them to approve the buyer's offer price.

Once a short sale is approved by all lenders, the buyer will go under contract. Since it is a short sale, the buyer should be prepared for a longer transaction and for additional paperwork. The buyer should also be aware that it is rare for any repairs or price accommodations for repairs to be accepted.

Above all, the buyer should be prepared for a very common outcome – that the short sale negotiations fail and the transaction falls apart. A consummated short sale is never a guaranteed proposition since the lenders can change their requirements at any point. Buyers (and sellers) must understand that the lender does not have to agree to lose money. While the risk of a defaulted loan is higher, lenders are under stockholder pressure to generate earnings, like everyone else. The lender can just wait it out until conditions improve. Such changes can result in lost time and not insignificant losses of money for the buyer.

Listing agent's role

One of the most important roles of a listing agent is to provide a net sheet for the sellers. They can either create their own net sheet or request one from a title company. When creating this net sheet, the listing agent should ask the seller to disclose all current mortgages. This net sheet will help the seller to better understand what position they are in.

The listing agent is responsible for generating a Broker's Price Opinion on the property. They do this by selecting the best comparable properties and adjusting them accordingly to determine an appropriate price. Once the agent completes the BPO, they will submit it, along with the seller's documentation of hardship, to the seller's lender. The lender will then review the information and either counter or accept the BPO. The review process could take weeks or months depending on the situation, the backlog in the market, and the number of lenders involved. Each lender will have to agree to collaborate with the short sale terms and parties. The more mortgagees involved, the longer it could take to approve the short sale.

Within the short sale transaction scenario, the seller can either wait for the official approval from the lender, or opt to list the property immediately. Here, the listing agent is responsible for submitting the listing into the MLS and marking it as a short sale. The listing agent should be upfront with all buyers whether the short sale is lender-approved or still under review. They must also be ready to explain the short sale process to all potential buyers as well as notify them that repair and price negotiations are unlikely.

It is also important to note that, as yet another negative characteristic of the short sale transaction, the real estate agent's commission might be lower than what practitioners typically charge for residential conveyances. Indeed, all parties must give and take in order to make short sales happen.

Buyer agent's role

The buyer's agent role in the short sale transaction – in addition to all the duties inherent in a conventional transaction -- is to inform the buyer of how the short sale process works and what they should expect. In particular, short sale properties are not always in the best condition, and most sellers cannot afford to make whatever repairs that might be identified as necessary by the inspection. Thus, the short sale is, in effect, an "as-is" conveyance, and buyers should be aware of the fact that the price may not be their last expense in completing their move.

The buyer's agent should also disclose to the buyer whether or not the listing already has an approved short sale price. If the price is not yet approved by the lender, then the process can take months of negotiating with the lender. The buyer should understand that this circumstance is much like a financing contingency that must be removed for the closing to take place.

Again, it is also important to note that a real estate agent's commission might be lower with the short sale compared to conventional transactions.

Lender's role

Each lender will have to collaborate with the sellers to agree on a short sale price.

They will also typically discuss the listing agent's BPO. If necessary, the lender will generate its own BPO to validate the listing agent's value estimate.

As an interesting possibility in the short sale transaction, one should realize that the final price going onto the market may not be less than market value. If the lender does not agree to a certain price, the seller might have to list it at market value – then see what happens. But from the buyer's perspective, the short sale is not necessarily a below-market bargain or fire sale.

If there are multiple lenders who are owed money in the transaction, it can become difficult to have them all agree on their smaller payoff amounts. This negotiation process can significantly expand the time required to consummate the short sale transaction.

Another important consideration from the lender's perspective is that, in fact, the common alternative to a short sale is a default and foreclosure, both of which can cost more than loan forgiveness amounts lost in the short sale. Thus, the lender has no real win-win outcomes, and the ultimate decision to approve the upside-down short sale price must be measured against indeterminable losses incurred by a default.

SNAPSHOT REVIEW: UNIT EIGHTEEN

FORECLOSURES AND SHORT SALES

Enforcement

- enforcement of mortgage lien by tax foreclosure sale, deed in lieu of foreclosure, or short sale

FORECLOSURE

- liquidation or transfer of collateral property by judicial, non-judicial, or strict foreclosure

Judicial foreclosure

- lawsuit and court-ordered public sale; deficiency judgments, redemption rights

Non-judicial foreclosure

- "power of sale" granted to lender; no suit; no deficiency judgment; equitable right but no statutory right of redemption

Strict foreclosure

- court orders legal transfer of title directly to lender without public sale

Deed in lieu of foreclosure

- defaulted borrower deeds property to lender to avoid foreclosure

SHORT SALES

Transaction benchmarks

- short sales necessary when seller owes more on mortgage than property is worth
- lender must agree to the short sale price and terms
- benchmarks: lender sets terms using BPOs; agent lists, markets; offers presented to lender for approval; lender decides; if positive, transaction is completed

Roles of seller, buyer, agents, lender

- seller typically enduring financial hardship; establishes relationship with listing agent; identifies all amounts owed; reviews net sheet to understand degree of deficiency
- buyer role is to appreciate difficulty of short sale; extended transaction time; limited negotiation flexibility; possibility of failure
- listing, buyer agent's roles are to facilitate communications with principals, MLS, and lenders; key action is to generate BPO to justify pricing; conduct negotiations for client
  lender's role is to approve the pricing package and the eventual buyer's offer

==

Check Your Understanding Quiz:

Unit Eighteen: Foreclosures and Short Sales

Carefully read each question and provide your best answer based on what you learned in this unit. Then check your answers against the Answer Key which immediately follows the quiz questions.

1. Foreclosure may be avoided through

   a. a promissory note.
   b. a deed in lieu of foreclosure.
   c. a redemption notice.
   d. a lis pendens.

2. The foreclosure process is governed by

   a. the Real Estate Commission.
   b. federal law.
   c. state law.
   d. the lending institute.

3. Judicial, non-judicial, and _____ are the three types of foreclosure processes.

   a. deed in lieu
   b. deficiency judgment
   c. equitable redemption
   d. strict

4. Foreclosure suits are used when

   a. the property owner owes more on the loan than the property's market value.
   b. public notice is given that the mortgaged property may soon have a judgment against it.
   c. the mortgage document does not include a power of sale provision.
   d. the property is seller financed.

5. A _____ authorizes an official to seize and sell the foreclosed property.

   a. lis pendens
   b. deficiency judgment
   c. right of redemption
   d. writ of execution

172

6. Georgia's equitable right of redemption gives property owners

    a. time to reclaim the property after a foreclosure sale.
    b. the right to redeem the property prior to the foreclosure sale.
    c. the right to approve the property buyer during a foreclosure sale.
    d. no rights since Georgia has no such thing.

7. In which foreclosure action does a lender not obtain a deficiency judgment?

    a. Non-judicial
    b. Judicial
    c. Strict
    d. All of the above

8. In which foreclosure action does the court order transfer of the property's legal title directly to the lender without a public sale?

    a. Non-judicial
    b. Judicial
    c. Strict
    d. None of the above

9. Which foreclosure act has no redemption right?

    a. Judicial
    b. Non-judicial
    c. Strict
    d. None of the above

10. What mortgage provision allows the mortgagee to order a public sale without a court decree?

    a. Right of redemption
    b. Equitable right of redemption
    c. Power of sale
    d. Acceleration

11. When a property owner sells the property in a short sale for less than what is owed on the mortgage loan, to avoid having to pay the lender the deficient amount, the seller needs the lender to agree to

    a. a full release of underlying debt.
    b. a deficiency judgment.
    c. a deed in lieu.
    d. the short sale itself.

12. In a short sale, who creates the net sheet?

    a. The lender
    b. The buyer and the buyer's agent
    c. The seller and the seller's agent
    d. The lender and the seller

13. What is the job of the short sale negotiator?

    a. To get the buyer the lowest possible purchase price for the property
    b. To persuade the lender to approve the buyer's offer price
    c. To persuade the seller to accept the buyer's offer
    d. To persuade the buyer to pay the seller's full asking price

14. Why might a lender prefer a short sale to a foreclosure on a particular property?

    a. The short sale is a quicker process.
    b. The foreclosure will release all liens on the property.
    c. The short sale will cost less than the foreclosure.
    d. The short sale requires the lender to forgive the loan amounts lost in the sale.

15. In a short sale, who determines the approved sale price?

    a. The lender
    b. The listing agent
    c. The broker
    d. The seller

===

Answer Key:

Unit Eighteen: Foreclosures and Short Sales

1. b. a deed in lieu of foreclosure.
2. c. state law.
3. d. strict
4. c. the mortgage document does not include a power of sale provision.
5. d. writ of execution
6. b. the right to redeem the property prior to the foreclosure sale.
7. a. Non-judicial
8. c. Strict
9. b. Non-judicial
10. c. Power of sale
11. a. a full release of underlying debt.
12. c. The seller and the seller's agent
13. b. To persuade the lender to approve the buyer's offer price
14. c. The short sale will cost less than the foreclosure.
15. a. The lender

SECTION IV: PROFESSIONAL PRACTICES

Unit 19: National Association of REALTORS® Code of Ethics

Unit 20: Risk Management

Unit 21: Safety Precautions

UNIT 19:

NATIONAL ASSOCIATION OF REALTORS® (NAR) CODE OF ETHICS

Unit Nineteen Learning Objectives: When the student has completed this unit, he or she will be able to:

- Summarize the role, general structure and organization of the Realtor® Code of Ethics.
- Describe the purpose and import of the Preamble for the Code of Ethics.
- Characterize the general import and practical applicability of Articles 1-9 of the Realtors® Code of Ethics.
- Explain the duties a Realtor® owes to the public and to other Realtors®.
- Summarize the overriding thesis of the Pathway to Professionalism.
- Identify the penalties for violating the Code of Ethics.

NAR'S CODE OF ETHICS

Historical abstract

In the early 1900s, real estate agents were given licenses by county judges, and often they were "peddlers" licenses. The 1900s was a time of land scams and speculation. In 1908, the National Association of Realtors® (NAR) formed to eliminate the notion of "Caveat emptor" or let the buyer beware. Their goal was to protect the public and promote homeownership in the United States.

In 1913, NAR introduced the Code of Ethics for Realtors® to follow in their dealings with their clients, the public, and other Realtors®. This document has been fluid and ever-changing over the years. Today, Realtors® have one of the strongest professional Code of Ethics in the United States.

The Code of Ethics also provides standard practices and procedures setting forth how Realtors® should react in their dealings with specific individuals and others in their field. The Code of Ethics, however, is not law. Rather, the Code of Ethics enhances local, state, or federal laws.

A quote in the 2020/2021 Code of Ethics and Arbitration Manual reads, "Because the Code is a living document and real estate is a dynamic business and profession, the law need never be its substitute. So long as the aspiration to better serve the public remains the underlying concept of the code, it must evolve and grow in significance and importance consonant with but independent of the law."

Structure of the Code of Ethics

The Code of Ethics has four sections:

I.   The Preamble
II. Duties to Clients and Customers (Articles 1 – 9)
III. Duties to the Public (Articles 10 – 14)
IV. Duties to Realtors® (Articles 15 – 17)

The Articles within the Code of Ethics define the broad statements about the licensee's behavior and duties. The **Standards of Practice**, within each Article, gives more specific guidance to the licensee. The Standards of Practice support and interpret the Articles.

In resolving ethics complaints, complainants are to cite only the Article(s) violated and not the Standard of Practice. It will be up to the Professional Standards Committee to give the specific Standard of Practice violated in their final report.

SECTION I –PREAMBLE

"Under all is the land."

This statement is a powerful start to NAR's Code of Ethics. It means that everything we do, are, or aspire to become, begins with the land beneath our feet. The quote shows the importance of the role each Realtor® holds in our society. Real estate impacts everything.

The Preamble of the Code of Ethics serves as a vision statement on how licensees should conduct themselves and represent their profession to the public. The Preamble calls for Realtors® to "maintain and improve the standards of their calling." It also states that it is the Realtor's responsibility to "act with integrity and honesty."

As of January 1, 2021, the Board of Directors of NAR changed the Preamble. It added that licensees should not dishonor the profession or do anything that will hurt the organization's public trust. The Board of Directors altered the Preamble wording to reflect the changes in Article 10 of the Code of Ethics.

SECTION II – DUTIES TO CLIENTS AND CUSTOMERS

Article 1

> *"When representing a buyer, seller, landlord, tenant, or other client as an agent, REALTORS® pledge themselves to protect and promote the interests of their client. This obligation to the client is primary, but it does not relieve REALTORS® of their obligation to treat all parties honestly. When serving a buyer, seller, landlord, tenant or other party in a non-agency capacity, REALTORS® remain obligated to treat all parties honestly."*

Central themes. Article 1 of the Code of Ethics promotes honesty as a critical virtue of any licensee. The 16 Standards of Practices within Article 1 describe the different duties a licensee may have and how they must act in specific situations. The basis of the Standards of Practices is the duties owed to our customers and clients based on Agency Law.

Article 1 Standards of Practice. The central thrust of Article 1 is reflected in its Standards of Practices 1.1 through 1.16. These are as follows:

SP 1.1 – Be careful to abide by the Code when you are representing yourself in a transaction.
SP 1.2 – The Code of Ethics applies to all transactions.
SP 1.3 – Do not mislead the owner as to the real market value of a piece of property.
SP 1.4 – Do not mislead the savings or benefits of utilizing the services of a Realtor®.
SP 1.5 – No dual agency. An agent cannot have a fiduciary relationship with both parties in a transaction.
SP 1.6 – Submit all offers and counteroffers promptly.

SP 1.7 – When working as the listing agent, present all offers until closing, unless waived in writing.

SP 1.8 – When working as the buyer's agent, present all offers until contract acceptance, unless waived in writing.

SP 1.9 – Maintain confidentiality even after termination of a relationship.

SP 1.10 – In property management, the licensee must comply with the management agreement and ensure their tenants' rights, safety, and health.

SP 1.11 – Use skill, care, and diligence in all transactions.

SP 1.12 – Disclose to sellers and landlords cooperation policy and compensation to all parties.

SP 1.13 – Disclose cooperation with other brokers.

SP 1.14 – Appraisal fees must not be based on the market value of the property.

SP 1.15 – Disclose any other offers already presented or any expected offers.

SP 1.16 – Do not enter the property without permission or authorization from the owner.

Article 1 illustration. A broker was preparing a CMA for a listing appointment. The broker knew the seller was interviewing several other brokers. He decided to increase the property's market value to show the seller how much more money they could earn from hiring him. The violation in this example is of Article 1, Standard Practice 1.3 and 1.4.

Article 2

> *"REALTORS® shall avoid exaggeration, misrepresentation, or concealment of pertinent facts relating to the property or the transaction. REALTORS® shall not, however, be obligated to discover latent defects in the property, to advise on matters outside the scope of their real estate license, or to disclose facts which are confidential under the scope of agency or non-agency relationships as defined by state law."*

Central theme. Article 2 of the Code of Ethics discusses the need for transparency in all transactions. While licensees are not required to seek out defects in the property, they must disclose any defects they know exists. This duty is necessary no matter the type of agency relationship the broker has established.

Article 2 Standards of Practice. Article 2 has five Standards of Practice:

SP 2.1 – A Realtor® must disclose any latent defects they know about or that are readily observable to a lay-person. They are not required to be experts in fields other than their own.

SP 2.2 – Moved to Standard of Practice 1.12

SP 2.3 – Moved to Standard of Practice 1.13

SP 2.4 – A Realtor® must not participate in doctoring the numbers on any contract.

SP 2.5 – Realtors® must not disclose non-material items not pertinent to the transaction.

Article 2 illustration. Susie is showing a potential buyer a house. The MLS stated that the roof was 25 years old and had a few leaks. During the showing, Susie's customer asked about the condition of the roof. Susie stated she was not aware of any problems. Susie has violated Article 2, Standard 2.1.

Article 3

> *"REALTORS® shall cooperate with other brokers except when cooperation is not in the client's best interest. The obligation to cooperate does not include the obligation to share commissions, fees, or to otherwise compensate another broker."*

Central theme. Article 3 promotes cooperation among brokers unless it is not in the client's best interest.

Article 3 Standards of Practice. Article 3 has eleven Standards of Practice as follows:

SP 3.1 – Realtors® must establish terms of cooperation.
SP 3.2 - Realtors® who change the compensation in a transaction must communicate it to other licensees.
SP 3.3 – Realtors® may change the cooperative compensation.
SP 3.4 – Realtors® must disclose variable rate commissions.
SP 3.5 – Realtors® must disclose all pertinent facts before and after the sale.
SP 3.6 - Realtors® should disclose any current accepted offers.
SP 3.7 – Realtors® must disclose their status when calling other Realtors® about a listed property.
SP 3.8 – Realtors® must not give false information about the availability of property to be shown.
SP 3.9 – Realtors® must not provide access to a listed property in any way other than what is agreed upon by the seller.
SP 3.10 – Realtor should share information on listed property and make the property available to other brokers.
SP 3.11 – Realtors® may not violate Fair Housing laws and refuse to show a piece of property to someone in a protected class.

Article 3 illustrated. Janet's seller told her that they did not want to sell their home to anyone who was not white. Janet told potential buyers who were not white that the house was no longer available or was not available to be shown. The violation in this example is of Article 3, Standards of Practice 3.8 and 3.11.

Article 4

> *"REALTORS® shall not acquire an interest in or buy or present offers from themselves, any member of their immediate families, their firms, or any member thereof, or any entities in which they have any ownership interest, any real property without making their true position known to the owner or the owner's agent or broker. In selling property, they own, or in which they have any interest, REALTORS® shall reveal their ownership or interest in writing to the purchaser or the purchaser's representative."*

Central theme. Article 4 requires Realtors® to disclose that they have a real estate license when buying or selling property for themselves. If they do not disclose this fact, then they have an unfair advantage over the average consumer. By telling them, the Realtor® is giving them a chance to obtain representation in the transaction. Thus, keeping it an arms-length transaction.

Article 4 Standard of Practice. The one Standard of Practice for Article 4 requires the Realtor® to reveal their ownership or interest in the property in writing before entering into any contract.

Article 4 illustrated. John has put in an offer to buy a house being sold by its owner. He put several contingencies in the offer that the every-day person buying real estate would not necessarily know to include. What John failed to include in the offer was the disclosure that he is a licensed real estate broker. John's failure to include the disclosure is a violation of Article 4.

Article 5

> *"REALTORS® shall not undertake to provide professional services concerning a property or its value where they have a present or contemplated interest unless such interest is specifically disclosed to all affected parties."*

Central theme. Article 5 requires Realtors® to disclose any conflict of interest before providing any professional services. The only time this would be allowed is with the written permission of all parties involved in providing the service.

Article 5 illustrated. ABC Realty shares office space with a lender and a title company. They recommend that all their buyers use these companies since they are in the same location, and it allows them to communicate with the lender and title company to ensure the closing goes smoothly. What the Realtor® did not disclose to their customers is the fact that family members own these companies. Consequently, ABC Realty has violated Article 5 by not disclosing the potential conflict of interest.

Article 6

"REALTORS® shall not accept any commission, rebate, or profit on expenditures made for their client, without the client's knowledge and consent.

When recommending real estate products or services (e.g., homeowner's insurance, warranty programs, mortgage financing, title insurance, etc.), REALTORS® shall disclose to the client or customer to whom the recommendation is made any financial benefits or fees, other than real estate referral fees, the REALTOR® or REALTOR®'s firm may receive as a direct result of such recommendation."

Central theme. Article 6 states a Realtor® may not accept any compensation in the form of a commission, rebate, kickback, etc., without the client's written consent. This requirement includes gifts from home inspectors, appliance companies, plumbers, etc.

Article 6 illustrated. A Realtor® hired Ace Home Inspection to inspect a home for a buyer. The Realtor did not tell the buyer that he received a $50 gift card for the referral. The Realtor® violates Article 6 of the Code of Ethics.

Article 7

"In a transaction, REALTORS® shall not accept compensation from more than one party, even if permitted by law, without disclosure to all parties and the informed consent of the REALTOR®'s client or clients."

Central theme. Article 7 states that a Realtor® cannot accept compensation from more than one person without disclosing the fact to all parties. The Realtor should also have that consent in writing.

Article 7 illustrated. A broker has a Buyer's Broker Agreement with a buyer. The agreement states that the broker will get a 3% commission on a home valued up to $350,000. The broker finds a home for $300,000 that the buyer likes, and they enter into a sales contract. The listing broker will pay the buyer's broker a 3% commission, but the broker does not disclose this to the buyer. Instead, the broker accepts both the listing broker's commission and the 3% commission from the buyer. This type of action would be a violation of Article 7 of the Code of Conduct. The broker may not receive compensation from more than one party in a transaction unless he has obtained written consent from all parties to the transaction.

Article 8

"REALTORS® shall keep in a special account in an appropriate financial institution, separated from their own funds, monies coming into their possession in trust for other persons, such as escrows, trust funds, clients' monies, and other like items."

Article 8 central themes. Article 8 addresses escrow funds and how to handle other people's money. A Broker must be careful not to commingle funds. Commingling is mixing their personal money with money held in trust for others. The only time commingling is legal is when a Broker puts up to $1,000 of personal funds for a Sales Escrow Account or $5,000 in a Tenant Escrow Account to stop the possibility of conversion.

Article 8 illustrated. Broker Sue decided to save banking fees by using one escrow account for her business funds and funds from other people, such as down payments and tenant deposits. By doing so, Sue has violated Article 8 by commingling her personal and business funds with funds belonging to other people.

Article 9

> *"REALTORS®, for the protection of all parties, shall assure whenever possible that all agreements related to real estate transactions including, but not limited to, listing and representation agreements, purchase contracts, and leases are in writing in clear and understandable language expressing the specific terms, conditions, obligations, and commitments of the parties. A copy of each agreement shall be furnished to each party to such agreements upon their signing or initialing."*

Central themes. Article 9 states Brokers must ensure all documents related to a real estate transaction be in clear, concise language. The contracts must also clearly represent the terms and conditions of the agreement between the parties. Georgia law requires that the broker keep all contracts and real estate related transaction documents for a minimum of three years.

Article 9 Standards of Practice. Article 9 has 2 Standards of Practice as follows:

SP 9.1 – Realtors® should use reasonable care to ensure extensions and amendments.
SP 9.2 – Realtors® should make a reasonable effort to explain the different parts of a contract to clients when working electronically.

Article 9 illustrated. Broker Jane is working with a buyer electronically. She sends the buyer an electronic contract and indicates where the buyer needs to sign. Jane does not review the Sales and Purchase Agreement with the buyer or go over any of the disclosures. Upon return of the contract, Jane does not send a copy to the buyer. Broker Jane violates Article 9 of the Code of Articles which requires brokers to explain contracts to clients when working electronically.

SECTION III – DUTIES TO THE PUBLIC

Article 10

> *"REALTORS® shall not deny equal professional services to any person for reasons of race, color, religion, sex, handicap, familial status, national origin, sexual orientation, or gender identity. REALTORS® shall not be parties to any plan or agreement to discriminate against a person or persons on the basis of race, color, religion, sex, handicap, familial status, national origin, sexual orientation, or gender identity."*

> *"REALTORS®, in their real estate employment practices, shall not discriminate against any person or persons on the basis of race, color, religion, sex, handicap, familial status, national origin, sexual orientation, or gender identity."*

Central theme. Article 10 of the Code of Ethics prohibits Realtors® from discrimination against the protected classes identified in the Code of Ethics. NAR has added protected classes to their Code of Ethics, making it stricter than the Federal Fair Housing Laws.

Article 10 Standards of Practice. Article 10 has 5 Standards of Practices as follows:

SP 10.1 – Realtors® may provide necessary demographic information of a neighborhood; however, they cannot provide information about the neighborhood's racial, religious, or ethnic composition.

SP 10.2 – Realtors® may gather demographic information; however, they must be careful how the information is used and distributed.

SP 10.3 – Realtors® should be cautious with any advertisement that indicates a neighborhood's racial or ethnic makeup or targets one of the protected classes.

SP 10.4 – Realtors® must follow fair employment practices of employees or independent contractors.

SP 10.5 – Realtors® may not use harassing speech, hate speech, epithets, or slurs against someone in one of the protected classes.

Amendments to SP 10.5. In November 2020, the NAR Board of Directors made changes to Standard Practice 10.5. After extensive research, the Professional Standards Committee recommended changes that effectively broadened the context of this standard. In the past, the Code of Ethics only covered Realtors'® activities during a real estate transaction. The applicability of the new Standard of Practice 10.5 covers all activities of a Realtor®.

Under the changes made in November 2020, a Realtor® can be found guilty of a Code of Ethics violation whether the infraction related to a transaction, or other membership-related context. Presently, any potential breach of Article 10 will be looked at individually to see if it is in violation of Article 10 or if it is someone expressing their First Amendment rights.

The new wording of Article 10, SP 10.5 became:

> "Realtors® must not use harassing speech, hate speech, epithets, or slurs" based upon an individual or group that falls under one of the protected classes."

Article 10 illustrated. A Realtor® created an advertisement using models and demographic information about a neighborhood's racial makeup. The purpose was primarily to steer specific individuals to a particular community. This action is a violation of Article 10, Standards of Practice 10.2 and 10.3.

Article 11

> *"The services which REALTORS® provide to their clients and customers shall conform to the standards of practice and competence which are reasonably expected in the specific real estate disciplines in which they engage; specifically, residential real estate brokerage, real property management, commercial and industrial real estate brokerage, land brokerage, real estate appraisal, real estate counseling, real estate syndication, real estate auction, and international real estate."*

> *"REALTORS® shall not undertake to provide specialized professional services concerning a type of property or service that is outside their field of competence unless they engage the assistance of one who is competent on such types of property or service, or unless the facts are fully disclosed to the client. Any persons engaged to provide such assistance shall be so identified to the client, and their contribution to the assignment should be set forth."*

Central theme. Realtors® should only work within real estate areas in which they have sufficient knowledge to protect their customer or client. One agent can't know everything about all areas of specialization within the industry.

Article 11 Standards of Practice. Article 11 has four Standards of Practice as follows:

SP 11.1 – When preparing an opinion of value on a piece of property, they must know that specific area of real estate and provide detailed information to the customer or client.
SP 11.2 – A Realtor® should perform only in an area that they have reasonable competence.
SP 11.3 – When providing consulting services or advice, they shall objectively present the material. The fee shall be contingent on the level of difficulty and the market value of the real property.
SP 11.4 – Competency required under Article 11 is based on the services agreed to by the customers or clients and follows the Code of Ethics and state law.

Article 11 illustrated. A Realtor® is asked to prepare an appraisal for a bank on a commercial building's short sale. The agent had no experience in doing an appraisal or in commercial real estate. If this agent does prepare the appraisal without having experience in appraisals and commercial real estate, the agent would be guilty of violating Article 11 Standards of Practice 11.1, 11.2, and 11.4.

Article 12

> *"REALTORS® shall be honest and truthful in their real estate communications and shall present a true picture in their advertising, marketing, and other representations. REALTORS® shall ensure that their status as real estate professionals is readily apparent in their advertising, marketing, and other representations and that the recipients of all real estate communications are, or have been, notified that those communications are from a real estate professional."*

Central theme. Realtors® should be honest in all their advertising and marketing.

Article 12 Standards of Practice. Article 12 has 13 Standards of Practices:

SP 12.1 – Realtors® who advertise something as free must disclose if they will receive any compensation and from whom they are going to receive the payment.
SP 12.2 – Deleted in January 2020.
SP 12.3 – Realtors® should use care if offering a prize or other compensation for real estate services. They must fully disclose the requirement to receive the compensation.
SP 12.4 – Realtors® should not advertise a property they are not authorized to market.
SP 12.5 – Realtors® must be careful not to practice Blind Advertising. The brokerage name must always appear in all advertising.
SP 12.6 – When selling their own property, a Realtor® must disclose their license status.
SP 12.7 – Only the brokers directly involved in a transaction may advertise that they sold or have a contract on the property with permission from the owner.
SP 12.8 – A Realtors® website should present current, accurate information, and they should keep the information current.
SP 12.9 – A Realtors® website shall disclose the brokerage's name and licensure state in a readily apparent manner.
SP 12.10 – Realtors® must advertise truthfully and give correct information and not be deceptive to the public in their URLs, websites, or the images they use.
SP 12.11 – Realtors® who intend to sell consumer information should disclose this wherever they gather the data.
SP 12.12 – Realtors® shall not use URL or domain names that may mislead the public.

SP 12.13 - Realtors® are only allowed to use designations, certifications, and other credentials they have earned and have maintained membership.

Article 12 illustrated. A Realtor® developed a website in which he promoted himself as the top producing agent in his area. He also stated that he had the following designations, Certified International Property Specialist (CIPS) and Graduate Realtor Institute (GRI). He had earned these designations but did not complete the required annual renewal for either one. He also did not put the name of his employing brokerage on his website. The Realtor® has violated Article 12 and Standards of Practices 12.5, 12.9, and 12.13.

Article 13

> *"REALTORS® shall not engage in activities that constitute the unauthorized practice of law and shall recommend that legal counsel be obtained when the interest of any party to the transaction requires it."*

Central theme. Realtors® must not represent themselves as attorneys nor give legal advice.

Article 13 illustrated. While filling out an offer to buy a piece of real property, Realtor® John was asked by his customer how they should take title to the property. John answered the question without telling his customer that they should seek legal advice. John, who is not an attorney, was practicing law by answering the question and, thus, was in violation of Article 13.

Article 14

> *"If charged with unethical practice or asked to present evidence or to cooperate in any other way, in any professional standards proceeding or investigation, REALTORS® shall place all pertinent facts before the proper tribunals of the Member Board or affiliated institute, society, or council in which membership is held and shall take no action to disrupt or obstruct such processes."*

Central theme. Realtors® must assist the Professional Standards Committee in any investigation or hearing. They must always present the truth and not interfere with the process.

Article 14 Standards of Practice. Article 14 has four Standards of Practice:

SP 14.1 – Only one board may hear any case of alleged violations of the Code of Ethics.
SP 14.2 – A Realtor® should not disclose any information they learned at an ethics hearing.
SP 14.3 – A Realtor® should not threaten or intimidate a witness or respondent in an ethics case.
SP 14.4 – A Realtor® should not mislead the investigation into an Ethics case, nor can they file multiple charges based on the same transaction.

Article 14 illustrated: Broker Alicia was named in a Code of Ethics violation. She denied the allegations. Trying to get the case canceled, Alicia threatened the person who filed the charges against her and refused to turn over information to the Professional Standards Committee. Alicia violated Article 14 Standards of Practices 14.3 and 14.4.

SECTION IV – DUTIES TO REALTORS®

The fourth section of NAR's Code of Ethics covers how Realtors® should behave when interacting with other Realtors®. Articles 15 to 17 and their Standards of Practices identify specific behavior and guidelines for dealing with other Realtors®. This section restates many of the same ideas expressed in Articles 1 through 14; however, it explicitly identifies the duties owed to NAR members.

Article 15

> " REALTORS® shall not knowingly or recklessly make false or misleading statements about other real estate professionals, their businesses, or their business practices."

Central theme. Article 15 of the Code of Ethics prohibits Realtors® from making a false or misleading statement about other real estate professionals, their own business, or their business practices.

Article 15 Standards of Practices: Article 15 three Standards of Practices as follows:

SP 15.1 – Realtors® may not file false or misleading statements about their business.
SP 15.2 – Realtors® may not make a false or misleading statement about other Realtor®. This Standard covers the false statements no matter what medium they are presented, i.e., digital, written, in person, etc.
SP 15.3 – Realtors® publish clarification if they discover a previous statement is false or misleading.

Article 15 illustrated: A Realtor® told everyone at her office that a broker from a competitive brokerage was not doing well financially. She even posted these statements on her Facebook page. She was trying to get agents from the other brokerage to join her company. She then boasted about how great her business was doing when, in fact, it was struggling. This broker violated Article 15, Standard of Practices 15.1 and 15.2 by making false and misleading statements about another Realtor®.

Article 16

> " REALTORS® shall not engage in any practice or take any action inconsistent with exclusive representation or exclusive brokerage relationship agreements that other REALTORS® have with clients."

Central theme. Realtors® must not try to steal away another broker's client. If they know someone is already working with a Realtor®, they must not try and get that client to come to them.

Article 16 Standards of Practice. Article 16 has 20 Standards of Practice as follows:

SP 16.1 – This Standard of Practice serves to set boundaries a Realtor® should not cross with respect to other practitioners. It is not trying to eliminate aggressive or innovative business practices.
SP 16.2 – A Realtor® may make general statements about their business and participate in marketing campaigns without infringing on other licensees' client relationships. Standard of Practice 16.2, however, outlines two unethical types of solicitation:
  1.) Telephone or personal solicitation of sellers identified by yard signs or through MLS information; and,
  2.) Mail or other written solicitation sent to customers or clients of other Realtors® that are not part of a mass marketing campaign.
SP 16.3 – A Realtor® may contact a client or customer of another Realtor® to offer different services than those the client is already under contract. Realtors® cannot use MLS information to target potential customers.
SP 16.4 & 16.5 – A Realtor® should not try to steal listings or represented buyers from another agent. The only time a Realtor® may contact another Realtors® client is to get specific information not available by the other agent or not listed in the MLS.

SP16.6 – If someone under contract with another Realtor® contacts a Realtor®, the Realtor® may discuss how they would work with the customer once their contract is up with the other real estate agent.

SP16.7 – The fact that a customer has worked with a specific Realtor® in the past does not prohibit another Realtor® from trying to get hired once any existing contract has expired. People do not have to return to the same Realtor® for every transaction they complete.

SP 16.8 – The fact that an exclusive agreement existed in the past does not prohibit another Realtor® from entering into a similar agreement once the first contact expires.

SP 16.9 – Before entering into an agreement with a client, a Realtor® must ensure that the client is not already in another contract with a different Realtor®.

SP 16.10 – A buyer's agent should disclose that the agreement exists between them when they begin to negotiate a contract.

SP 16.11 – For unlisted property, Realtors® must disclose any relationship between themselves and other customers. They should also request any desired compensation at the first meeting.

SP 16.12 – All contractual relationships should be disclosed before entering into a Purchase agreement.

SP 16.13 – Realtors® should communicate to the co-broking Realtor® and not the customer or client.

SP 16.14 – A Realtor® may enter into any representation but may not require them to pay compensation if the other party is contracted to pay compensation.

SP 16.15 – All monies and compensation must be paid broker to broker.

SP 16.16 – A Realtor® may not use the terms of an offer to modify the compensation terms already laid out.

SP16.17 – Realtors® shall not attempt to extend a listing broker's offer of cooperation without the listing broker's consent.

SP 16.18 – A Realtor® shall not use information obtained from another agent or the MLS to negotiate the client away from the firm.

SP 16.19 – Realtors® must have the owner's permission before placing signs on the property.

SP 16.20 – When a Realtor® leaves a brokerage, their listing stays with the brokerage. Agents are not allowed to entice customers to follow them to another agency.

Article 16 illustrated: A Realtor® is holding an open house. A couple comes in and begins looking around. They start asking the Realtor® questions and state they want to put an offer in on the house. The agent writes up an offer and presents it to the seller, who accepts it. Only after the offer is accepted does it come out that the buyers have a Buyer's Broker Agreement with another Realtor®. Because the seller's Realtor® did not ask if the buyers were under contract with another Realtor®, the Realtor® violated Article 16 under the Code of Ethics.

Article 17

" In the event of contractual disputes or specific non-contractual disputes as defined in Standard of Practice 17-4 between REALTORS® (principals) associated with different firms, arising out of their relationship as REALTORS®, the REALTORS® shall mediate the dispute if the Board requires its members to mediate. If the dispute is not resolved through mediation, or if mediation is not required, REALTORS® shall submit the dispute to arbitration in accordance with the policies of the Board rather than litigate the matter.

In the event clients of REALTORS® wish to mediate or arbitrate contractual disputes arising out of real estate transactions, REALTORS® shall mediate or arbitrate those disputes in accordance with the policies of the Board, provided the clients agree to be bound by any resulting agreement or award.

The obligation to participate in mediation and arbitration contemplated by this Article includes the obligation of REALTORS® (principals) to cause their firms to mediate and arbitrate and be bound by any resulting agreement or award."

Central theme. Realtors® should first commit to mediation if there are unsettled disputes. If mediation does not settle the conflicts, then the agents will move to binding arbitration.

Article 17 Standards of Practices: Article 17 has five Standards of Practices:

SP 17.1 – Realtors® who file litigation and refuse to withdraw in an arbitrable issue will constitute a refusal to arbitrate.

SP 17.2 – Parties to a dispute are not required to commit to mediation, but they are not relieved of the duty to arbitrate by not entering mediation.

SP 17.3 – Realtors®, when acting solely as principals, are not obligated to arbitrate disputes with other Realtors®.

SP 17.4 – This Standard of Practice lays out specific times when non-contractual disputes are subject to arbitration. Procuring cause disputes fall under this category.

SP 17.5 – The requirement to arbitrate includes disputes between Realtors® from different states. It also states which association will have jurisdiction over the disputes.

Article 17 illustrated. Realtor® Terry and Realtor® Brian are in a dispute over a particular real estate transaction. Brian refused to arbitrate and filed a law suit against Terry in a local court. Consequently, Brian has violated Article 17 by not keeping the dispute out of the legal system.

NAR DISPUTE RESOLUTION

Processing complaints

Anyone can file a complaint. It can be Realtor® vs. Realtor® or client/customer against Realtor®. Once filed with a local association of Realtors®, the complaint is then forwarded to the Grievance Committee to determine if there is a violation of the Code of Ethics and an arbitrational issue. If the Grievance Committee believes there is sufficient evidence of an ethics violation, a hearing will be scheduled with the Professional Standards Committee to hear the case and recommend the Board of Directors on outcome and punishment.

If there is a monetary issue, then the matter will be sent to the local Board's Ombudsman program to help the parties decide. If the Ombudsman does not settle the dispute, the parties will be offered the opportunity to enter mediation and then go on to arbitration to resolve the dispute.

Penalties

Possible penalties for violation of the Code of Ethics include:

- Letter of warning;
- Letter of reprimand;
- Education courses;
- Fines not to exceed $15,000;
- Probation for not less than 30 days or more than one year;
- Membership suspension for not less than 30 days or more than one year;
- Expulsion from membership for one to three years; and/or,

- Suspension or termination of MLS rights and privileges.

PATHWAYS TO PROFESSIONALISM

While the Code of Ethics establishes enforceable standards that Realtors® must follow, it does not set out standards of common courtesy or etiquette that Realtors® should use in their dealings with other Realtors® or the public. This is accomplished with NAR's set of professional courtesy standards called the Pathways to Professionalism.

There are three sections to the Pathways to Professionalism:

1. Respect for the Public
2. Respect for Property
3. Respect for Peers

These Professional courtesies are intended to be used by REALTORS® voluntarily. They cannot form the basis for a professional standards complaint.

Respect for the Public

1. Follow the "Golden Rule": Do unto others as you would have them do unto you.
2. Respond promptly to inquiries and requests for information.
3. Schedule appointments and showings as far in advance as possible.
4. Call if you are delayed or must cancel an appointment or showing.
5. If a prospective buyer decides not to view an occupied home, promptly explain the situation to the listing broker or the occupant.
6. Communicate with all parties in a timely fashion.
7. When entering a property, ensure that unexpected situations, such as pets, are handled appropriately.
8. Leave your business card if not prohibited by local rules.
9. Never criticize property in the presence of the occupant.
10. Inform occupants that you are leaving after showings.
11. When showing an occupied home, always ring the doorbell or knock—and announce yourself loudly before entering. Knock and announce yourself loudly before entering any closed room.
12. Present a professional appearance at all times; dress appropriately and drive a clean car.
13. If occupants are home during showings, ask their permission before using the telephone or bathroom.
14. Encourage the clients of other brokers to direct questions to their agent or representative.
15. Communicate clearly; don't use jargon or slang that may not be readily understood.
16. Be aware of and respect cultural differences.
17. Show courtesy and respect to everyone.
18. Be aware of—and meet—all deadlines.
19. Promise what you can deliver—and keep your promises.
20. Identify your REALTOR® and your professional status in contacts with the public.
21. Do not tell people what you think—tell them what you know.

Respect for Property

1. Be responsible for everyone you allow to enter listed property.
2. Never allow buyers to enter listed property unaccompanied.

3. When showing property, keep all members of the group together.
4. Never allow unaccompanied access to the property without permission.
5. Enter property only with permission, even if you have a lockbox key or combination.
6. When the occupant is absent, please leave the property as you found it (lights, heating, cooling, drapes, etc.) If you think something is amiss (e.g., vandalism), contact the listing broker immediately.
7. Be considerate of the seller's property. Do not allow anyone to eat, drink, smoke, dispose of trash, use bathing or sleeping facilities, or bring pets. Leave the house as you found it unless instructed otherwise.
8. Use sidewalks; if weather is bad, take off shoes and boots inside the property.
9. Respect sellers' instructions about photographing or videographing their properties' interiors or exteriors.

Respect for Peers

1. Identify your REALTOR® and professional status in all contacts with other REALTORS®.
2. Respond to other agents' calls, faxes, and e-mails promptly and courteously.
3. Be aware that large electronic files with attachments or lengthy faxes may be a burden on recipients.
4. Notify the listing broker if there appears to be inaccurate information on the listing.
5. Share important information about a property, including pets, security systems, and whether sellers will be present during the showing.
6. Show courtesy, trust, and respect to other real estate professionals.
7. Avoid the inappropriate use of endearments or other denigrating language.
8. Do not prospect at other REALTORS®' open houses or similar events.
9. Return keys promptly.
10. Carefully replace keys in the lockbox after showings.
11. To be successful in the business, mutual respect is essential.
12. Real estate is a reputation business. What you do today may affect your reputation—and business—for years to come.

The above is from the 2021 NAR Code of Ethics and Arbitration Manual, Pathways to Professionalism, page vii. https://www.nar.realtor/code-of-ethics-and-arbitration-manual/pathways-to-professionalism

Commitment to Excellence (C2EX)

Commitment to Excellence (C2EX) from the National Association of REALTORS® empowers REALTORS® to evaluate, enhance, and showcase their highest professional levels. It is not a course, class, or designation—it is an Endorsement that REALTORS® can promote when serving clients and other REALTORS®.

The NAR Board of Directors has requested that all Board of Directors, committee members, and leadership complete the C2EX program. To date, over 50,000 Realtors® have completed this program.

SNAPSHOT REVIEW: UNIT NINETEEN

NAR CODE OF ETHICS

NAR'S CODE OF ETHICS

- was established in 1913. Its primary goal is to protect the public from land scams and to promote homeownership.

Structure of the Code of Ethics

- The Code of Ethics has four parts: The Preamble, Duties to Clients and Customers, Duties to the Public, and Duties to Realtors.

SECTION I: PREAMBLE

- serves as a vision statement and lays out the duties and responsibilities for Realtors®.

SECTION II: DUTIES TO CLIENTS AND CUSTOMERS

- Standards of practices are more detailed requirements of each Article within the Code of Ethics.

ARTICLE 1

- promotes honesty to all.

ARTICLE 2

- Realtor's® actions must have transparency to them.

ARTICLE 3

- promotes cooperation among brokers unless it is not in their client's best interest.

ARTICLE 4

- Realtors® must disclose that they have a real estate license when buying, selling, or renting their own property.

ARTICLE 5

- Realtors® must disclose any conflict of interest before providing professional services.

ARTICLE 6

- Realtors® may not accept any compensation without the written consent of all parties.

ARTICLE 7

- Realtors may not accept compensation from more than one person without disclosing the fact to all parties.

ARTICLE 8

- addresses the handling of escrow funds.

ARTICLE 9

- states that all documents must be in clear and concise language.

SECTION III: DUTIES TO THE PUBLIC

ARTICLE 10

- Realtors® must give equal professional service to all clients and customers irrespective of race, color, religion, sex, handicap, familial status, national origin, sexual orientation, or sexual identity
- Realtors do not discriminate in their employment practices

ARTICLE 11

- Realtors® must be knowledgeable and competent in their fields of practice
- If not competent, must get assistance from a knowledgeable professional or disclose any lack of experience to their client

ARTICLE 12

- Realtors® must be honest and truthful in their communications
- must present accurate descriptions in advertising, marketing, other public representations

ARTICLE 13

- Realtors® must not engage in the unauthorized practice of law

ARTICLE 14

- Realtors® must willingly participate in an ethics investigation and enforcement actions.

SECTION IV - DUTIES TO REALTORS®

Article 15

- Realtors® must be truthful, make objective comments about other real estate professionals.

Article 16

- respect exclusive brokerage relationships of other Realtors® with their clients

Article 17

- arbitrate financial disagreements with other Realtors® and with their clients.

COMPLAINT PROCESS

- **complaint process** begins with filing of a complaint by anyone against a Realtor®.
- First, **Grievance Committee** reviews complaint, forwards to Professional Standards Committee if a violation of Code of Ethics occurred.
- **Professional Standards Committee** decides on punishment if a violation.

- recommendations forwarded to the Board of Directors to enforce

Pathway to Professionalism

- sets forth etiquette standards Realtors® should follow
- three categories of etiquette: Respect for the Public, Respect for Property, Respect for Peers

C2EX

- new program introduced by NAR, to date, 50,000+ Realtors® have completed program.

==

Check Your Understanding Quiz:

Unit Nineteen: NAR Code of Ethics

Carefully read each question and provide your best answer based on what you learned in this unit. Then check your answers against the Answer Key which immediately follows the quiz questions.

1. The central theme of Article 1 of the NAR Code of Ethics is to

   a. deal honestly with everyone no matter what type of relationship.
   b. disclose all defects of a home you are selling.
   c. use skill, care, and diligence if working with exclusive clients.
   d. do not violate fair housing laws.

2. A broker is selling his home as a For Sale by Owner. A potential buyer comes to look at the house, and the broker shows him around. The buyer puts in a 95% offer, and the seller accepts it. After closing, the buyer finds out the seller is a real estate broker and never disclosed it. Has this broker violated the Code of Ethics? Why or why not?

   a. No, since the buyer is only a customer
   b. No, since the offer was ultimately accepted
   c. Yes, since one must disclose his or her licensed status
   d. Yes, since the property was a For Sale by Owner

3. According to Article 13, when Broker Tom gave his seller client advice on how to remove liens from the property's title, Tom violated the Code of Ethics by practicing

   a. medicine
   b. law.
   c. accounting.
   d. appraising.

4. According to Article 17, because Broker Jerry and Broker Richard are in a transaction dispute, both brokers should be willing to _____ the dispute.

   a. arbitrate
   b. litigate
   c. ignore
   d. accept

5. Realtors® follow the Pathway to Professionalism to show respect for

   a. the public, their peers, and their customers.
   b. the public, the property, and their clients.
   c. the public, the property, and their peers.
   d. the property, their peers, and their customers.

6. C2EX is a new program that

   a. is required by every Realtor®.
   b. was developed by local boards.
   c. is the most recent NAR designation.
   d. allows agents to show a high level of professionalism.

7. NAR was formed with the goal of

   a. protecting the public and promoting homeownership.
   b. guiding real estate agents in acquiring property listings.
   c. developing educational programs for real estate licensees.
   d. creating state rules and regulations to govern real estate licensees.

8. In January 2021, the following was added to the Preamble of the Code of Ethics.

   a. Under all is the land.
   b. Realtors® must maintain and improve the standards of their calling.
   c. Licensees should not dishonor the real estate profession.
   d. Realtors® are responsible for acting with integrity and honesty.

9. Which of the following is a standard of practice under Article 1 of the Code of Ethics?

   a. A Realtor® must not participate in doctoring the numbers on any contract.
   b. No dual agency.
   c. Realtors® must not give false information about the availability of property to be shown.
   d. Realtors® must reveal their ownership or interest in the property in writing before entering into any contract.

10. Article 7 requires Realtors® to have a specific consent in writing. What is this specific consent?

   a. The consent for the Realtor® to enter into a contract involving the Realtor®'s own property
   b. The consent for the Realtor® to disclose variable rate commission
   c. The consent for the Realtor® to accept compensation from more than one person
   d. The consent for the Realtor® to mix personal money in the same account with money held in trust for others

11. Broker Alicia was named in a Code of Ethics violation. She is angry about the accusations and threatened the person who filed the charges against her. She then refused to turn over information to the Professional Standards Committee. Which of the following Articles has Alicia now violated?

    a. Article 14 regarding not interfering with an investigation or hearing
    b. Article 1 regarding honesty as a critical virtue of any licensee
    c. Article 2 regarding the need for transparency in all transactions
    d. Article 17 regarding the commitment to move unsettled disputes to binding arbitration

12. A Realtor®'s website shall disclose the brokerage's name and licensure state in a readily apparent manner. This is a standard of practice under which Article?

    a. Article 15 regarding not making misleading statements about a Realtor®'s own business or practices
    b. Article 2 regarding the need for transparency in all transactions
    c. Article 12 regarding honesty in advertising and marketing
    d. None of the above

13. If a residential Realtor® attempts to handle the short sale of a commercial building, which Article is the Realtor® violating?

    a. Article 1 regarding honesty as a critical virtue of any licensee
    b. Article 11 regarding Realtors® working within areas in which they have sufficient knowledge
    c. Article 16 regarding not stealing another broker's client
    d. Article 12 regarding honesty in advertising and marketing

14. What change was made to Article 10's Standards of Practice in November 2020?

    a. Sexual orientation was added as a protected class.
    b. Realtors® were warned to be careful when using demographic information in advertising.
    c. The standards were broadened to cover all of a Realtor®'s activities.
    d. A standard was added to protect a Realtor®'s First Amendment rights.

15. What is the Code of Ethics' requirement for Realtors® when working electronically with a client?

    a. Article 1 regarding honesty as a critical virtue of any licensee
    b. Article 11 regarding Realtors® working within areas in which they have sufficient knowledge
    c. Article 2 regarding the need for transparency in all transactions
    d. Article 9 requires brokers to ensure all transaction documents are in clear, concise language

16. A client asks his Realtor® to recommend a lending institute where he could get a mortgage loan. The Realtor® tells the client that he can recommend one in particular because he has a relationship with the lender who pays him a bonus for every recommendation. The client is thrilled and signs the consent form for the Realtor® to receive the bonus. Has this Realtor® violated the Code of Ethics?

    a. Yes, because one of the Articles prohibits kickbacks, rebates, etc.
    b. Yes, because he is receiving compensation from more than one party, i.e., the client and the lender
    c. No, because he has a business relationship with the lender
    d. No, because he obtained the client's written consent to accept the bonus

17. Which Articles prohibit discrimination based on a protected class?

    a. Articles 3 and 10
    b. Articles 5 and 8
    c. Articles 1 and 10
    d. None of them prohibit this.

18. Which of the following statements is true?

    a. The requirement to arbitrate includes disputes between Realtors® from different states.
    b. When a Realtor® leaves a brokerage, his listing goes with him.
    c. Realtors® should communicate to the customer or client and not the co-brokering Realtor®.
    d. Realtors® can use MLS information to solicit potential customers.

19. Which of the following statements is false?

    a. A Realtor® should not disclose any information they learned at an ethics hearing.
    b. The brokerage name must appear in all advertising.
    c. A Realtor® can be found guilty of a Code of Ethics violation whether or not the infraction is related to a transaction.
    d. Realtors® may not provide demographic information of a neighborhood.

20. Which of the following statements is false?

    a. Realtors® are required to disclose any conflict of interest before providing any professional services.
    b. Realtors® may not change the cooperative compensation.
    c. Realtors® should make listed property available to other brokers.
    d. Realtors® must disclose cooperation with other brokers.

21. When a complaint is filed with a local association of Realtors®, it is then forwarded to the

    a. Professional Standards Committee.
    b. Board of Directors.
    c. Grievance Committee.
    d. National Association of Realtors®.

22. When is a complaint hearing to be scheduled?

    a. When the Grievance Committee believes there is sufficient evidence of an ethics violation
    b. When the Professional Standards Committee recommends a hearing to the Board of Directors
    c. When the complaint is sent to the local Board's Ombudsman program
    d. When the parties did not resolve the dispute through mediation

23. Which of the following is not an allowable penalty for Code of Ethics violations?

    a. Letter of reprimand
    b. Fines not to exceed $15,000
    c. License suspension
    d. Termination of MLS rights and privileges

24. Under what circumstances is a Code of Ethics violation sent to the Ombudsman program?

    a. If the violation involved discrimination against a protected class
    b. If the violation involved a monetary issue
    c. If the violation was also a license law violation
    d. All violations are sent to the Ombudsman program.

25. The Pathways to Professionalism includes

    a. Respect for the Employer.
    b. Respect for Clients.
    c. Respect for the Law.
    d. Respect for Property.

26. Who handles a professional standards complaint for a violation of the Pathways to Professionalism?

    a. Professional Standards Committee
    b. Ombudsman program
    c. Grievance Committee
    d. The Pathways to Professionalism cannot form the basis for a professional standards complaint.

27. "Avoid the inappropriate use of endearments or other denigrating language" is included in the _____ section of the Pathways to Professionalism.

    a. Respect for the Public
    b. Respect for Property
    c. Respect for Peers
    d. None of the above

28. "Promise what you can deliver—and keep your promises" is included in the _____ section of the Pathways to Professionalism.

    a. Respect for the Public
    b. Respect for Property
    c. Respect for Peers
    d. All of the above

29. What penalty may be imposed on a Realtor® who violates the Pathways to Professionalism?

    a. Letter of warning
    b. Probation for not less than 30 days or more than one year
    c. Education courses
    d. None because following the Pathways to Professionalism is voluntary

30. Commitment to Excellence (C2EX) is

    a. a designation.
    b. an endorsement.
    c. a class.
    d. a course.

==

Answer Key:

Unit Nineteen: NAR Code of Ethics

1. a. deal honestly with everyone no matter what type of relationship.
2. c. Yes, since one must disclose his or her licensed status
3. b. law.
4. a. arbitrate
5. c. the public, the property, and their peers.
6. d. allows agents to show a high level of professionalism.
7. a. protecting the public and promoting homeownership.
8. c. Licensees should not dishonor the real estate profession.
9. b. No dual agency.
10. c. The consent for the Realtor® to accept compensation from more than one person
11. a. Article 14 regarding not interfering with an investigation or hearing
12. c. Article 12 regarding honesty in advertising and marketing
13. b. Article 11 regarding Realtors® working within areas in which they have sufficient knowledge
14. c. The standards were broadened to cover all of a Realtor®'s activities.
15. d. Article 9 requires brokers to ensure all transaction documents are in clear, concise language
16. d. No, because he obtained the client's written consent to accept the bonus
17. a. Articles 3 and 10
18. a. The requirement to arbitrate includes disputes between Realtors® from different states.
19. d. Realtors® may not provide demographic information of a neighborhood.
20. b. Realtors® may not change the cooperative compensation.
21. c. Grievance Committee.
22. a. When the Grievance Committee believes there is sufficient evidence of an ethics violation
23. c. License suspension
24. b. If the violation involved a monetary issue
25. d. Respect for Property.
26. d. The Pathways to Professionalism cannot form the basis for a professional standards complaint.
27. c. Respect for Peers
28. a. Respect for the Public
29. d. None because following the Pathways to Professionalism is voluntary
30. b. an endorsement.

UNIT 20:

RISK MANAGEMENT

Unit Twenty Learning Objectives: When the student has completed this unit, he or she will be able to:

- Describe the primary areas of risk to include agency relationships; property disclosures; listing, selling, and contracting processes; fair housing; antitrust; financing, etc.
- Identify the four risk management strategies and explain each.
- Explain the relationship between education, disclosure, documentation, and insurance and risk management.

RISK

Risk is the chance of losing something. Its two dimensions are the probability of occurrence and the extent of exposure to monetary or non-monetary consequences. Since most risks are related to judgments and decisions, the real estate licensee, who makes numerous complex decisions every day, faces a high degree of *risk potential*.

Risk management is a structured approach to dealing with the uncertainties and consequences of risk. In real estate practice, the aim is to reduce risk to an acceptable level through anticipation and planning.

PRIMARY AREAS OF RISK

Risks for licensees are present every day in business transactions. Many of these risks carry legal implications as well as possible financial and professional consequences.

Agency

The risks involved in agency relationships generally will occur in one of two areas:

- the requirement to inform and disclose
- the requirement to carry out an agency duty.

Disclosure requirements. In Georgia, agency relationships are in writing and must be disclosed to all parties to a transaction in a timely manner, but no later than when any party first makes an offer to purchase, sell, lease, or exchange real property. Licensees must provide written disclosure to both parties in the transaction, revealing the party or parties for whom the licensee's firm is acting as an agent or dual agent. If the firm is not acting as agent of either party, written disclosure must be given regarding which party will be paying the brokerage commission.

Duties. A licensee who acts for a principal in a real estate transaction is required by law to assume certain responsibilities toward the parties to the transaction.

Agency disclosures and duties are discussed in further detail in Unit 10 Brokerage Relationship in Real Estate Transactions Act (BRRETA).

Penalties. Possible penalties for breach of agency relationships include rescission of transaction, loss of compensation, fees and costs, punitive damages, ethics discipline, and license discipline.

Property disclosures

Property condition. While Georgia licensees are required to disclose adverse material facts they know about the property and can be penalized for not doing so, property condition disclosures are not required. The licensee may also be subject to legal action for deliberately distorting the facts (intentional misrepresentation) or cheating any party (fraud).

Lead-based paint and other disclosures. Federal law requires sellers of houses built before 1978 to make a lead-based paint disclosure before accepting an offer to purchase.

Property and environmental disclosures are discussed in detail in Unit 11 Property and Environmental Disclosures.

Listing and selling process

Nature and accuracy of the listing agreement. When listing a property, especially important facts for a broker or agent to verify are the property condition (keep in mind a property condition disclosure is not required in Georgia, but agents are required to disclose adverse material facts about the property), ownership status, and the client's authority to act. An agent who does not to act with a reasonable degree of due diligence in these matters may be exposed to liability if it turns out that the property is not as represented or the client cannot perform the contract as promised.

Comparative Market Analysis (CMA). In preparing a Comparative Market Analysis, licensees should guard against using the terms "appraisal" and "value," which are reserved for the use of certified appraisers. Misuse of these terms could lead to a charge of misrepresenting oneself as an appraiser. If the CMA leads the seller to list at a price that is too high, the seller may blame the agent when the transaction fails because of an appraisal that comes in below the selling price. To minimize this risk, it is best to be conservative in the CMA and retain documentation that the seller went above the recommended price in spite of the agent's advice.

Advertising. State and federal laws regulate advertising, including the federal Fair Housing laws as they pertain to discriminatory advertising and providing of services. Advertising must be consistent with company image and legal requirements. The license laws of most states list illegal advertising actions subject to discipline such as substantial and intentional misrepresentation and making false promises through affiliate brokers, other persons, or any advertising medium.

Authorizations and Permissions. Licensees should stay within the bounds of the authority granted by the agency agreement or must not do anything requiring permission without first getting that permission in writing. Examples include posting a sign on the property or using a multiple listing service.

Scope of expertise. Agents must be particularly careful about the temptation to misrepresent themselves as experts and offer inappropriate expert advice. Disclaimer and referral are always the best risk control procedures to forestall an accusation of misrepresentation from a consumer who claims to have been harmed by reliance on the licensee's non-existent expertise. Further, an agent who fails to live up to prevailing standards may be held liable for negligence, fraud, or violation of state real estate license laws and regulations.

Contracting process

According to the Statute of Frauds, all contacts for real estate must be in writing to be enforceable. Contracts that contain incorrect information or are inadequately prepared can pose a serious liability for a licensee. To avoid such a situation, it is imperative for the contract to reflect the terms that the parties have agreed upon in the most accurate and honest manner. Violations can jeopardize the enforceability of a listing or sales contract, in addition to resulting in criminal prosecution.

Common risks and errors in the contracting process include using an illegal form, failing to state inclusions and exclusions, failing to track the progress of contingency satisfaction, and mistakes in entering data in a form.

Unauthorized practice of law. The unintentional practice of law without a license is a great risk in the contracting process, as well as in the representation process. It is illegal for real estate professionals who are not attorneys to draw up contracts for transactions they are not involved in or to charge a separate fee for preparing a contract. Licensees may fill in blanks or make deletions on a preprinted contract form prepared by a lawyer. It is also illegal for real estate licensees who are not lawyers to give legal advice or interpret contract language.

Fair Housing

The risk of violating fair housing laws can be minimized through ongoing education that addresses both the content and the intent of the laws. It is especially necessary for paperwork and documentation to be accurate and concise in a situation where a fair housing issue could arise.

Fair housing laws and their requirements are discussed in detail in Unit 1 under Unfair Trade Practices and in Unit 2 under Fair Housing.

Advertising. Risk can be reduced by the use of street names or other non-biased geographical references when stating where the property is located, and by describing the property rather than the type of persons who might live in or around it.

Answering questions. When faced with questions that might lead to a *steering* charge or other violation of fair housing laws, it is best for the licensee to limit the response to features of the home and to the process of selling, buying, and listing properties. It is illegal for the licensee to voice an opinion based on race, religion, color, creed, national origin, sex, handicap, elderliness, or familial status. The agent should explain this fact to the buyer and be wary of any situation where the agent's behavior might be construed as discriminatory.

Offers. A seller cannot refuse to sell a property to an individual based on the individual's belonging to a protected class. The best risk reduction procedure is to treat all buyers and sellers equally, showing no preference for one over another.

Antitrust

Antitrust laws forbid brokers to band together to set a price on their services in listing and selling property. Even being overheard discussing commission rates or being present at such a conversation can lead to charges of *price fixing*.

The Sherman Antitrust Act, the Clayton Act, the Federal Trade Commission Act, and the related enforcement and penalties for violations are discussed in detail in Unit 2 under Antitrust Laws.

Rules and regulations

State real estate laws and commissioners' rules and regulations attempt to cover every possible risky situation. Non-compliance poses a direct threat to the legal and financial status of licensee and license in the following general ways:

- license expiration – due to failure to maintain E & O insurance when required, meet education requirements, and observe correct renewal procedures.
- license revocation or suspension – due to obtaining a license under false pretenses, committing a prohibited act, neglecting to comply with offer requirements, failing to include all required terms and conditions in a sales contract, and improperly handling escrow funds.
- licensee discipline – civil penalty imposed due to violations of a statute, rule, or order.
- suit for damages – by the Department of Justice, Federal Trade Commission, a state real estate commission, a human rights commission, another licensee or firm, or an individual consumer.

Misrepresentation

Unintentional misrepresentation. This type of misrepresentation occurs when a licensee _unknowingly_ conveys inaccurate information to a consumer concerning a property, financing or agency service. False or inaccurate information that the licensee, as a professional, should have known to be false or inaccurate may be included in the definition. Those found guilty generally have to pay fines and may be disciplined by state real estate regulators and professional organizations.

Intentional misrepresentation. Also known as fraud, this kind of misrepresentation occurs when a licensee _knowingly_ conveys false information about a property, financing or service. Fraud is a criminal act that may result in fines and incarceration, in addition to discipline from state regulators and professional organizations.

Recommending providers

There are several risks related to the recommendation of vendors and service providers to a consumer. First, the consumer may not be satisfied with the performance of the recommended party and blame the licensee. Second, in cases where a recommended provider performs illegal acts, there may be legal consequences for the licensee. Third, if a licensee has a business relationship with a recommended vendor or provider and neglects to disclose the fact, there are license violation consequences.

The major risk management technique is to shift the responsibility for choosing a vendor to the consumer.

Financing and closing

Licensees have an obligation to inform and educate their clients throughout the transaction process. Surprises and accusations of incompetence or misrepresentation are among possible results of failing to keep the party informed.

Discrimination. Of course, it is important to comply with relevant laws. Licensees must be mindful of the requirements of ECOA and refrain from participating in any manner of discriminatory lending. _See Unit 12 for a detailed discussion of the Equal Credit Opportunity Act._

Progress reporting. All inspection and testing progress reports should be accurate, timely, in writing, and free of speculation. If a consumer has a question about the meaning of something in an inspection report, the licensee should refer the consumer to the person who wrote the report rather than trying to explain it. This method transfers some of the risk inherent in interpreting the report.

Qualifying buyers. Many transactions fail because a buyer has been improperly qualified before the offer is presented. Using a lender to qualify the buyer saves time and protects the agent against leading a seller to believe a purchaser is fully qualified when this may not be the case. *See Unit 12 Financial Qualification for details on how borrowers are qualified for mortgage loans.*

Lending fees disclosure. The licensee should explain loan fees, charges, amounts, timing, and responsibilities. The fact that a high origination fee and points may make a loan with a low interest rate unattractive to a borrower is important information for the agent to provide, and providing it may protect the agent against a later complaint that the buyer suffered a loss because of the agent's failure to inform.

Appraisal problems. Delays and appraised value are the typical problem areas. Failure to inform parties about delays can compromise the transaction. An under-appraisal will require the buyer to make a larger down payment or the seller to lower the price. If the property appraises for more than the purchase price, the seller may blame the agent for suggesting the lower price. In such a case, the seller's agent's defense is that the seller agreed to the listing price and that the price was a factor in attracting the buyer to the property.

RESPA Violations. The licensee's risks regarding RESPA primarily relate to failing to ensure that the consumer is informed about his or her rights under the law and giving or receiving an illegal kickback. *RESPA and its requirements are discussed in detail in Unit 16 under Real Estate Settlement Procedures Act.*

Trust fund handling

State laws prescribe how licensees must handle any escrow or earnest money deposits they receive. Failure to comply with these laws, such as commingling or converting funds, puts the licensee at risk of imposed penalties. *Trust fund handling and trust account requirements are discussed in detail in Unit 8.*

RISK MANAGEMENT STRATEGIES

Four well-established strategies for managing risk include avoidance (elimination), reduction (mitigation, sharing), transference (outsourcing, insuring), and retention (acceptance and budgeting). Not all of these strategies are always possible or available, but a real estate firm or licensee who fails to make a conscious effort to employ one or more of them increases the likelihood of loss from the many potential risks that are always present in the real estate business.

Avoidance

Avoidance includes refraining from an activity that carries risk. Avoiding risks also means missing the opportunity to benefit from the avoided activity. Complete avoidance of risk in real estate practice is almost impossible. A broker, for instance, may believe that hiring only experienced affiliates eliminates the risk that affiliates will commit license law violations. However, even experienced practitioners may not know the law, and, sometimes, people break the law deliberately. The risk may be reduced, but it remains.

Reduction

Reduction involves taking steps to reduce the probability or the severity of a potential loss. However, this strategy may result in reducing risk in one area only to increase it in another. A familiar example is a sprinkler system that dispenses water to reduce the risk of fire but at the same time increases the risk of water damage.

In real estate practice, one risk reduction tactic is to share responsibility for making a decision. The agent provides the consumer with expertise, and perhaps some advice, but lets the consumer decide how much to offer. In this way, the agent gets some relief from the risks inherent in the buyer's decision to purchase.

Transference

Transference means passing the risk to another party, by contract or other means. In the real estate business, transference is typically and most successfully accomplished by means of an errors and omissions (E&O) insurance policy, either on the individuals in a firm or on the firm itself. State law may require such insurance.

Retention

Retention of risk means entering into an activity in spite of known risks and taking full responsibility for the consequences. This is, in effect, self-insurance, the only strategy left when risk cannot be reduced or transferred and one has decided not to avoid it because of the desirability of the potential benefits.

RISK MANAGEMENT PROCEDURES

Experience shows that the most practical strategies for risk management in real estate practice are reduction and transference, with procedures focusing on education, disclosure, documentation, and insurance.

Education

Education is the first line of defense against risk. When agents are familiar with the forms provided by the office, how and when to complete them and where to send them, the likelihood of errors is reduced. Likewise, agents need to be able to identify and understand common contract elements, complete contract forms developed by attorneys, and evaluate offers received from co-op agents on their listings without committing a license violation or breach of law.

In Georgia, brokers have a legal obligation to provide training to affiliated licensees. As a matter of risk management, the broker should also have ongoing training covering fair housing laws, contract law, environmental issues, changes in financial laws and trends, etc. Licensees should also seek out appropriate education and training outside the brokerage to ensure that they know how to comply with the law.

Disclosure

By ensuring that all parties have the information they are entitled to, proper disclosure reduces the risk that clients and customers will accuse a licensee of misleading or inducing them to make a decision with incomplete information. Further, laws in every state require disclosures of one kind or another.

Required disclosures usually include:

- agency relationships
- property condition
- duties and obligations
- personal interest in the transaction
- personal interest in referrals

Documentation and Record keeping

Documentation provides evidence of compliance with laws and regulations. It proves what clients and customers and licensees said and did in a transaction. Some documentation is required by law.

The components of a thoroughly documented paper trail include the following:

Policy and procedures manual. A written and uniformly enforced company policy lets everyone in the firm know what to expect before problems arise. A procedures manual should spell out how to handle every aspect of the company's business that agents and brokers need to know. Adherence to a procedures manual reduces the risk that an individual will inadvertently commit an unlawful act.

Standard forms. Standard forms save time and protect against the unauthorized practice of law. They are most often prepared by lawyers familiar with the market area; however, a licensee often needs to adapt a standardized form for a client by assisting with filling in blanks, modifying terms, and attaching addenda. To avoid risk, the licensee must always remain aware of the limitations the state has placed on such activities.

Communication records. Retaining evidence that information has been communicated is a necessary procedure. Maintaining a good record of communications is useful for resolving disagreements where parties dispute what has been said because it allows the agent to produce a dated document that resolves the issue definitively.

A transaction checklist is a good tool for managing risk associated with the failure to make required communications to all principals and for keeping track of required communications from co-op agents. Electronic communications should be archived on suitable electronic media. Copies of mailed or faxed communications should be maintained in the transaction folder.

Transaction records. State laws require licensees to document transactions. Firms are required to keep written records of all real estate transactions for three years after closing or termination.

Accounting. In addition to other accounting records, there is the requirement to maintain written accounting of escrow funds. For each transaction, property, and principal, escrow records will include depositor, date of deposit, date of withdrawal, payee, and other information deemed pertinent by the real estate commission.

Other documents. Additional documents may be required by law or regulation or should be kept simply as protection in case of disputes and lawsuits. These would include copies of advertising materials, materials used in training agents, records of compliance with continuing education requirements, safety manuals, and anything else that shows how the firm conducts its business and safeguards its staff as well as the rights of consumers.

Insurance

General Liability. General liability insurance provides coverage for risks incurred by a property owner when the public or a licensee enters the owned property (**public liability**). The insurer pays the covered claim and legal fees, costs, and expenses, including medical expenses, resulting from owner negligence or other causes. This type of insurance does not cover **professional liability,** for which an Errors & Omissions policy is necessary.

Errors and Omissions. The primary method for transferring the professional liability risks of brokers, managers, and licensees is Errors & Omissions (E&O) insurance. A standard E&O policy provides coverage for "damages resulting from any negligent act, error or omission arising out of Professional Services." Professional liability is of two general types:

1. Unprofessional conduct – a claim that one has failed to carry out fiduciary duties and provide an acceptable standard of care

2. Breach of contract – a claim that one has failed to perform services under the terms of a contract in a timely manner

E&O insurance, in short, covers "mistakes" but not crimes.

Fire and hazard. The risks of property damage caused by fire, wind, hail, smoke, civil disturbance, and other such causes are covered by fire and hazard insurance.

Flood. The risks of property damage caused by floods, heavy rains, snow, drainage failures, and failed public infrastructures such as dams and levies are covered by a specialized flood policy. Regular hazard policies do not include flood coverage.

Other insurance. Other common types of insurance coverage for income and commercial properties include:

- **casualty**—coverage for specific risks, such as theft, vandalism, burglary, illness and accident, machinery damage
- **workers' compensation**—hospital and medical coverage for employees injured in the course of employment, mandated by state laws
- **contents and personal property**—coverage for building contents and personal property when they are not actually on the building premises
- **consequential loss, use, and occupancy**—coverage for the business losses resulting from a disaster, such as loss of rent and other revenue, when the property cannot be used for business
- **surety bond**—coverage against losses resulting from criminal or negligent acts of an employee

SNAPSHOT REVIEW: UNIT TWENTY

RISK MANAGEMENT

PRIMARY AREAS OF RISK

Agency

- main failures: to inform and disclose, to fulfill duties
- disclosures: written, agency relationship and duties
- duties: to all parties to transaction
- penalties for breach of agency

Property disclosures

- adverse material facts and lead-based paint required, property condition disclosure not required; failure to disclose may be construed as misrepresentation or fraud

Listing and selling process

- areas of risk include listing agreement accuracy, Comparative Market Analysis results, advertising, authorizations and permissions, exceeding expertise

Contracting process

- contracts for real estate must be in writing; inaccuracy endangers contract; other risks: illegal form, omitted elements, lapsed contingencies, wrong data
- unauthorized practice of law: non-lawyers may fill in blanks and delete words on standard contract forms; no legal advice to public allowed

Fair Housing

- risk minimized through education and accurate documentation, careful advertising, no steering when answering questions, offers not to be refused based on protected class

Antitrust

- Sherman Antitrust Act outlaws restraint of trade; Clayton Act outlaws practices that harm competition; Federal Trade Commission Act outlaws unfair methods of competition
- violations punishable by government criminal and civil actions as well as by private lawsuits; fines, damages, and imprisonment possible

Rules and regulations

- violators of state rules and regulations risk license expiration, revocation, suspension, and other discipline
- prime causes of discipline include commission of prohibited acts, practicing with an expired license, disclosure failures, earnest money mishandling

Misrepresentation

- unintentional: inaccurate information conveyed unknowingly; subject to fines and license discipline; occurs most often in measurements, property descriptions

- intentional: fraud, knowingly conveying false information; criminal act subject to fines, license discipline, and incarceration

Recommending providers

- risks include consumer dissatisfaction, possible vicarious liability for illegal acts committed by a recommended provider, undisclosed business relationship
- best practice: shift responsibility for choosing vender to the consumer

Financing and closing

- risk areas include fair housing and ECOA violations; failed progress reporting; buyer not qualified for loan; no lending fee disclosure; appraisal problems; RESPA violations

Trust fund handling

- risk areas include mishandling of earnest money deposits; commingling and conversion of trust funds

RISK MANAGEMENT STRATEGIES

Avoidance

- refrain from risky activity

Reduction

- reduce probability; share responsibility

Transference

- pass risk by contract; insurance

Retention

- accept risk; self-insurance

RISK MANAGEMENT PROCEDURES

Education

- train in laws, forms and procedures, job performance

Disclosure

- provide information to reduce misunderstanding & lawsuits; agency, property condition, duties, personal interest

Documentation and record keeping

- maintain evidence of compliance; manuals, forms, records, contracts, accounting, other documents

Insurance

- general liability, E&O, fire and hazard, flood, casualty, workers, personal property, consequential loss, surety bond

==

Check Your Understanding Quiz:

Unit Twenty: Risk Management

Carefully read each question and provide your best answer based on what you learned in this unit. Then check your answers against the Answer Key which immediately follows the quiz questions.

1. The probability of occurrence and the extent of exposure to monetary or non-monetary consequences are the two dimensions of

   a. law violations.
   b. management issues.
   c. risk.
   d. error.

2. To avoid risk in Georgia, an agency relationship must be disclosed to all parties to a transaction no later than

   a. when an offer is first made on real property.
   b. when the property is shown to a prospective buyer.
   c. both parties signing the sales contract.
   d. The disclosure is not required in Georgia.

3. To avoid risk of law violation in Georgia, a property condition disclosure must be provided to a potential purchaser

   a. when showing the property.
   b. prior to the seller accepting an offer.
   c. at least 5 business days prior to transaction closing.
   d. The disclosure is not required in Georgia.

4. When preparing a comparative market analysis, licensees who use the term "appraisal" could be charged with

   a. operating without a license.
   b. misrepresentation.
   c. false advertising.
   d. fraud.

5. Licensees who represent themselves as experts when they are not and then fail to live up to the standards of the particular field of expertise may be held liable for

   a. negligence.
   b. fraud.
   c. violation of state real estate license laws and regulations.
   d. All of the above

6. If a licensee charges a separate fee for preparing a sales contract, that licensee is guilty of

   a. misrepresentation.
   b. unauthorized practice of law.
   c. illegal acceptance of a kickback.
   d. false advertising.

7. The risk of violating fair housing laws can be minimized through

   a. education.
   b. avoiding relationships with specific protected classes.
   c. steering.
   d. voicing an opinion based on any protected class.

8. Several brokers meeting to discuss proposed commission rates can lead to charges of

   a. fair housing violations.
   b. fraud.
   c. price fixing.
   d. misrepresentation.

9. Which of the following violations could possibly result in the licensee being incarcerated?

   a. Steering
   b. Intentional misrepresentation
   c. Unintentional misrepresentation
   d. Price fixing

10. When a consumer does not understand something within an inspection report, to avoid the risk of an incorrect explanation, the licensee should refer the consumer to

    a. an attorney.
    b. the licensee's employing broker.
    c. the inspector who wrote the report.
    d. the seller who is familiar with the property.

11. Which of the strategies for managing risk is most successfully accomplished with the purchase of an E&O insurance policy?

    a. Avoidance
    b. Reduction
    c. Transference
    d. Retention

12. Entering into an activity in spite of known risks and taking full responsibility for the consequences is a risk management strategy known as

    a. avoidance.
    b. reduction.
    c. transference.
    d. retention.

13. In risk management, _____ is considered the first line of defense against risk.

    a. disclosure
    b. education
    c. documentation
    d. insurance

14. Which type of insurance provides coverage for risks, such as injuries, incurred by a property owner when a licensee enters the property?

    a. Errors and Omissions
    b. Workers' Compensation
    c. General Liability
    d. Consequential Loss

15. Which type of insurance policy covers a claim that a licensee has failed to carry out fiduciary duties and provide an acceptable standard of care?

    a. Consequential Loss
    b. Workers' Compensation
    c. General Liability
    d. Errors and Omissions

==

Answer Key:

Unit Twenty: Risk Management

1. **c. risk.**
2. **a. when an offer is first made on real property.**
3. **d. The disclosure is not required in Georgia.**
4. **b. misrepresentation.**
5. **d. All of the above**
6. **b. unauthorized practice of law.**
7. **a. education.**
8. **c. price fixing.**
9. **b. Intentional misrepresentation**
10. **c. the inspector who wrote the report.**
11. **c. Transference**
12. **d. retention.**
13. **b. education**
14. **c. General Liability**
15. **d. Errors and Omissions**

UNIT 21:

SAFETY PRECAUTIONS

Unit Twenty-One Learning Objectives: When the student has completed this unit, he or she will be able to:

- Identify steps agents can take to protect their safety and the safety of their clients.
- Describe how firms can protect their agents' safety, including the use of technology.

SAFETY PRECAUTIONS

A major concern for realtors is personal safety. Because no one can guarantee your personal safety, the best way to keep yourself safe is to employ safety measures as a matter of common sense and habit. You cannot be too cautious about your personal safety or that of your client.

What you can do to protect yourself

As a real estate agent, you will often work outside of the office and away from your colleagues. You will find yourself in situations where you are in the company of one or more strangers at a property or inside an unoccupied structure. Consequently, for your own safety, get into the habit of taking the following steps:

- **Always meet a new client at your office.** On the first meeting, do not meet at a property. Before meeting outside the office or alone, get as much personal information as possible. A copy of the driver's license is a good start not only for safety but also for the client database.

- **Show properties before dark.** Evening showings can be dangerous. Inform home buyers that you only do viewings during the day. If you must show a property after dark, turn on all lights and don't lower any shades or draw curtains or blinds throughout the house.

- **Don't get lost.** Always know the exact address of where you are going. If you are relying on your GPS in an unfamiliar area, make mental notes of landmarks, points of interest, and intersections. This makes a quick exit easier.

- **Practice the buddy system.** Bring a colleague or buddy with you when you meet clients at a property. Having a second person often adds to the safety and comfort of the situation. The buddy can drive separately or wait in the car after you let him or her know you feel comfortable enough to continue the showing alone. Don't allow a client to ride in your car unless you know them well.

- **Make your location known.** Always tell your office mates or broker where you are going, who you will be with, when you will return, and when you will next be in touch. Leave the name and phone number of the client you are meeting. Make sure the person you are meeting knows that you've given your office this information. Also, schedule a time for your office to call you to check in. Beforehand, establish a method of being able to relate an emergency situation to the office or a contact person. Have a secret word or phrase to notify the office you are in trouble, one that can be worked into any conversation for cases where you feel that you are in danger.

For example: "Hi, this is Jennifer. I'm with Mr. Henderson at the Elm Street listing. Could you email me the RED FILE?"

- **Park on the street.** If you park in the driveway, another car can block you in. You want to have a clean escape route if necessary. Park in a well-lit, visible location. Keep the keys to your vehicle and your cell phone with you at all times. Keep your handbag and other valuables locked in the trunk of your vehicle.

- **Take two seconds to pause and look around as you enter your destination.** Does anything seem out of place? Is anyone present who shouldn't be there or who isn't expected? Are there potential hiding places? Have a plan for what to do if something or someone doesn't seem right.

- **Never turn your back to a client.** Always let the client enter a doorway and go upstairs first. Stay in the doorway of each room. Never let your client get between you and the exit. Make sure you have previewed the property and know all of the accessible exits and how to contact the closest neighbors. Leave the doors unlocked for easy exit and leave one door open at all times, if possible. Do not enter attics or crawl spaces. Allow the clients to do so if they wish, but you should remain outside.

- **Open house safety.** Don't hold an open house alone. Inform a neighbor that you will be hosting an open house, and ask if he or she would keep an eye and ear open for anything out of the ordinary. Be alert to visitors' comings and goings, especially groups near the end of showing hours. There have been reports of some group members distracting the agent while others go through the house and steal anything they can quickly take. Also, don't assume that everyone has left the premises at the end of an open house. Check all of the rooms and the backyard prior to locking the doors. If you find yourself to be the last one in an open house and your car is not in the immediate vicinity of the venue, then make a phone call as you walk. Assailants will be less willing to attack if you are in mid conversation with another person.

- **Prepare to defend yourself.** Never assume that you can talk your way out of a situation. Learn some self-defense skills. Also, while carrying pepper spray may seem extreme, it can save your life if you have it on hand. Know how to use it and any self-defense moves, and do not hesitate to use either if you are threatened or attacked.

- **Dress appropriately.** Wear practical clothing that makes it easy to escape a dangerous situation. This might mean swapping heels for sensible flats and wearing something with pockets to hold your keys and cell phone. Also, never wear expensive jewelry.

- **Limit the amount of personal information you share.** This means avoiding mention of where you live, whether you live alone, your after-work or vacation plans, and similar details.

- **Set up your cell phone.** Check in advance to be sure your phone is serviceable in the area in which you are showing the property and that the phone is fully charged. Always remain aware of your surroundings when utilizing electronic devices such as cellphones and iPods. To best prepare for an emergency, pre-program important numbers into your cell phone. These may include your office, your roadside assistance service or garage, and 911.

- **Be careful with cash.** If you must transport cash deposits, use the buddy system or arrange for a security service or police escort.

- **Don't invite criminals.** Do not advertise a property as vacant. Report suspicious activity, i.e., a person's conduct or action that does not fit the norm of the neighborhood. If you think or feel that something is wrong or suspicious, it probably is. Most agents who have been victims of crime said they felt something was off but didn't do anything. If something feels out of place, don't hesitate to stop a showing or open house and leave immediately.

What the office can do to protect its agents

- **Keep a file on each agent's vehicle.** Record each vehicle's make, year, model, color, and license number.
- **Keep daily schedules.** Keep a schedule of agents' outside appointments with times, locations, and client names.
- **Require guest registries.** Require that agents set up a guest registry for persons attending an open house or viewing a model home.
- **Do not include personal information on business cards.** No home addresses or telephone numbers on the agents' business cards.
- **Maintain a record of agents' health conditions.** Be prepared to alert emergency responders to any existing health conditions that may result in a sudden and dangerous situation.
- **Require a buddy system.** Not only should agents not show properties alone, but they should not be alone in the office after hours.
- **Protect from scams and theft of personal information.** Keep up to date on email scams and warn agents. Shred documents containing personal and financial information. Train agents on recognizing telephone scams, adware, and malware.

What an agent can do to protect the client

- Tell your clients not to show their home by themselves, not to talk to other agents or buyers, and to refer all inquiries to you. Tell sellers if someone they don't know walks up to the home asking for a showing, don't let them in.
- Remind your clients that strangers will be walking through their home during showings or open houses.
- Do a walk-through with the client to make sure you have identified everything that needs to be removed or secured, such as medications, valuables, and personal information.

Make use of technology

Technology is available that can track the agent's location, sound an alarm, send a distress signal to a contact list and more. There are several apps and devices on the market provide safety for real estate agents. Some are tiny, wearable devices connected to professional monitoring services and to smartphones. When a crisis or threat occurs, the agent would press the device, and the monitoring team will send emergency resources to the agent's location without requiring the agent to say a single word.

National Association of Realtors® has information, tips, courses, training videos, and other resources on their website at https://www.nar.realtor/safety. The site also includes information on safety products, programs, and smartphone applications.

SNAPSHOT REVIEW: UNIT TWENTY-ONE

SAFETY PRECAUTIONS

SAFETY PRECAUTIONS

Protect yourself

- Do not meet strangers alone after dark and away from the office
- Be aware of your location, exit routes, and anything that seems out of place
- Use extra safety during open houses
- Prepare for defending yourself by knowing self-defense, dressing appropriately, not sharing personal information, not carrying cash, and setting up your cell phone

Office to protect agents

- Maintain agent vehicle records, daily schedules, health conditions
- Require buddy system and guest registries for open houses and model homes
- Train on email and phone scams and ID theft

Protect the client

- Tell client not to show home alone or without agent
- Perform walk-through to identify items to be removed or secured

Use technology

- Use tracking devices, cell phone apps, monitoring services
- Check NAR's website for further information

==

Check Your Understanding Quiz:

Unit Twenty-One: Safety Precautions

Carefully read each question and provide your best answer based on what you learned in this unit. Then check your answers against the Answer Key which immediately follows the quiz questions.

1. Which of the following statements is false?

   a. Female agents should keep their purses with them at all times when away from the office.
   b. Agents should have visitors enter doorways ahead of the agent.
   c. Agents should not let the person they are meeting know the office has been given the person's name and location of the meeting place.
   d. Agents should rely only on their GPS in unfamiliar areas.

2. The purpose of having a secret word or phrase when contacting the office is to

   a. let the broker know if the potential buyer has submitted an offer.
   b. let the office know the potential buyer did not arrive for the property showing.
   c. let the office know the agent is in trouble.
   d. let the office know the open house is over and the agent is leaving.

3. Why should the broker keep a record of agents' health conditions?

   a. To judge the agent's performance
   b. To determine the agent's workload
   c. To alert emergency responders
   d. To select appropriate health benefits

4. Which of the following items should clients secure in preparation for an open house?

   a. Artwork
   b. Toys
   c. Large televisions
   d. Prescription medications

5. Which of the following would be a safety concern during an open house?

   a. A group of visitors near the end of the day
   b. A neighbor's interest in the event
   c. Finding the house completely empty prior to the agent leaving
   d. An agent talking on her cell phone when walking to her car

===

Answer Key:

Unit Twenty-One: Safety Precautions

1. b.   Agents should have visitors enter doorways ahead of the agent.
2. c.   let the office know the agent is in trouble.
3. c.   To alert emergency responders
4. d.   Prescription medications
5. a.   A group of visitors near the end of the day

PRACTICE EXAMINATION

1. Which of the following is an unfair trade practice?

   a. A licensee failing to respond to a GREC request
   b. A licensee failing to include an expiration date in a listing agreement
   c. A licensee paying a fee to the GREC with an insufficient funds check
   d. A licensed salesperson performing broker duties

2. What is the maximum Recovery Fund payment amount per transaction?

   a. $5,000
   b. $75,000
   c. $10,000
   d. $25,000

3. Failure to display a standard HUD fair housing poster in a brokerage office may be construed as

   a. a misdemeanor.
   b. a criminal violation of GA law.
   c. discrimination.
   d. the broker exercising the right to free speech.

4. What is the main purpose of the ADA?

   a. To define what constitutes a disability
   b. To assure people with disabilities have the same rights and opportunities as everyone else
   c. To assure that those with disabilities are easily recognized while in public
   d. To provide special privileges to those with disabilities

5. An example of _____ is when Broker Bob agrees to limit his practice to sale and rental of condominiums if Broker Bill agrees to limit his practice to sale and rental of single-family homes.

   a. market allocation
   b. tie-in agreements
   c. price fixing
   d. creating monopolies

6. The Georgia Residential Mortgage Fraud Act does not apply to

   a. single-family homes in GA.
   b. residential duplexes located in GA.
   c. apartment properties which contain 5 or more units.
   d. single-family homes that include a mother-in-law suite.

7. Under what circumstances may a mortgage loan borrower be denied a refund of the application fee?

   a. When the borrower changes his mind and cancels the loan application
   b. When the lender denies the loan based on a misrepresentation on the application
   c. When the property sale is canceled
   d. Under no circumstances

8. The qualifying broker for a corporation must be

    a. a partner.
    b. a member.
    c. the broker owner.
    d. an officer.

9. Which of the following must be designated to sign documents and disburse trust funds when the qualifying broker of a corporation dies?

    a. An immediate family member of the deceased broker
    b. An officer of the corporation
    c. The salesperson with the most seniority within the corporation
    d. Such designation is not required

10. Whether a sales agent is an employee or an independent contractor, the broker

    a. must withhold income taxes from compensation.
    b. is responsible for the sales agent's actions.
    c. must provide benefits.
    d. can impose methodology for work to be performed.

11. Steve just sold a home for $350,000 with no cooperating broker. His affiliated broker's sales commission policy is 6% of the sale price. Steve's share of that commission is to be 90% due to his outstanding sales performance. How much commission will Steve receive for this sale?

    a. $9,400
    b. $17,010
    c. $18,900
    d. $21,000

12. Which of the following acts is an unlicensed support person prohibited from performing?

    a. Assembling documents for closings
    b. Computing commission checks
    c. Placing signs on properties
    d. Making cold calls

13. Internet advertising of real estate must include _____ on every viewable webpage of the site.

    a. the advertising licensee's phone number
    b. the name of the licensee's affiliated broker
    c. the name and phone number of the licensee's firm
    d. the advertising licensee's name

14. Which of the following is discriminatory advertising?

    a. Beautiful 3-bedroom home for sale near public park
    b. Stately home for sale located in lovely Jewish community
    c. Lakefront property available for residential construction
    d. Apartment for rent in complex with pool and community recreation center

15. What is the purpose of a company having written policies, rules, and procedures?

    a. To spell out how to handle critical aspects of the company's business
    b. To reduce the risk that an individual will inadvertently commit an unlawful act
    c. To keep the business running smoothly and professionally
    d. All of the above

16. Which of the following statements is false?

    a. A company's written policies, rules, and procedures should include that licensed activities be only performed by licensed personnel.
    b. Each managing broker most likely has his or her own philosophy on how the firm's business should be conducted.
    c. Advertisement requirements for real estate transactions should be included in the company's policies and rules.
    d. Written procedures should spell out how to handle every aspect of the company's business that agents, brokers, and unlicensed staff need to know.

17. If a licensee owns less than 100% interest in a property for which he receives trust funds, the licensee must

    a. open a trust account in his name and the name of the other party who owns the remaining interest in the property.
    b. turn the funds over to the Commission to be held in trust.
    c. deposit the funds into the firm's trust account.
    d. turn the funds over to the licensee's affiliated broker prior to closing.

18. A broker may maintain more than one trust account if

    a. the broker receives funds from more than one client at the same time.
    b. the broker provides required account information to the Commission.
    c. the broker has affiliated licensees who receive trust funds.
    d. The broker may only maintain one trust account.

19. When obtaining offers, the seller's agent

    a. should suggest to a customer what price the seller will accept.
    b. should freely develop offer terms on the seller client's behalf.
    c. should weed out unacceptable offers.
    d. should abide by fiduciary obligations to the client.

20. The step(s) in obtaining listings include

    a. safety precautions.
    b. prospecting.
    c. facilitating closings.
    d. providing financing assistance.

21. Who compensates a cooperating broker?

    a. The listing broker
    b. The seller
    c. The buyer
    d. The MLS organization

22. Which of the following duties does a broker owe a client after the brokerage relationship has terminated?

    a. Promoting the client's best interest
    b. Accounting for all client funds handled
    c. Complying with BRRETA's duties
    d. Performing ministerial activities

23. What cause of action may a party take against a broker for revealing information that is required by BRRETA?

    a. Filing suit against the broker for fraud
    b. Filing suit against the broker for breaking confidentiality
    c. Seeking monetary compensation for breach of contract
    d. No cause of action may be taken for this compliance.

24. Other than lead-based paint, what is another environmental hazard that requires disclosure when selling residential properties?

    a. Occupants infected with contagious diseases
    b. Poor air quality
    c. Mold
    d. Asbestos

25. What is Georgia's property condition disclosure requirement?

    a. Approved and regulated disclosure form must be provided to buyer.
    b. Material facts related to the physical condition of the property must be disclosed.
    c. Only issues discovered during an inspection must be disclosed.
    d. Georgia has no property condition disclosure requirement.

26. Which of the following is NOT a factor when determining income stability?

    a. How long the applicant has been employed at the current job
    b. How many properties the applicant owns
    c. How education level may affect continuation of the current income level
    d. How likely secondary income is to continue on a regular basis

27. A lender's "firm commitment" is

    a. a straight forward offer to make a specific loan at a specific interest rate for a specific term.
    b. an offer to lend a specific amount for a specific term at a specific interest rate that is subject to an expiration date.
    c. an offer to make a loan if certain provisions are met.
    d. an offer to make a loan that will pay off and replace another lender's loan.

28. Most conventional lenders require that this ratio be *no greater than 25-28% of gross income*.

   a. Income ratio
   b. Debt ratio
   c. Monthly housing expense
   d. Monthly debt obligations

29. Which valuation approach includes estimating and deducting accrued depreciation?

   a. Income approach
   b. Cost approach
   c. Sales comparison approach
   d. Market data approach

30. In the sales comparison approach, what is the principle of substitution?

   a. One comparable can easily be substituted for another.
   b. Features in one comparable can be substituted for different features in another comparable.
   c. A buyer will pay no more for the subject property than would be sufficient to buy a comparable property.
   d. Specific characteristics can be substituted for others to add value to a property.

31. Which of the following statements is true?

   a. Both oral and written sale contracts are enforceable.
   b. Conditions under which a buyer can cancel a sale contract without default are contingencies.
   c. When the buyer signs the contract, he or she gains equitable title to the property.
   d. Signing a contract that has blank spaces is allowed as long as the spaces are filled in prior to closing.

32. A spouse with an ownership interest in a property fails to sign the sale contract. This can result in

   a. homestead rights being released to the buyer at closing.
   b. the contract being invalidated.
   c. an encumbered title.
   d. the transaction not closing.

33. The first step of a conventional transfer of real estate ownership happens

   a. when buyers and sellers exchange offers to negotiate the transfer terms.
   b. when the buyer obtains a firm loan commitment.
   c. when an offer is accepted and signed.
   d. when the offeree rejects the offeror's offer.

34. The exact point at which the offer becomes a contract is

   a. when one party presents an offer to the other party.
   b. when the listing agent's employing broker signs the offer.
   c. when the offeree gives the offeror notice of offer acceptance.
   d. when the negotiation process begins.

35. John is selling his rental property, and the closing date is June 3. If that closing day belongs to the buyer and the property rents for $1,200 a month already paid for June, what proration would show on the Closing Disclosure Statement?

   a. Credit buyer $1,120; Debit seller $1,120
   b. Credit seller $1,120; Debit buyer $1,120
   c. Credit buyer $1,080; Debit seller $1,080
   d. Credit seller $1,080; Debit buyer $1,080

36. The annual property taxes on John's rental property are estimated at $2,737.50 for the current year. John is selling the property and has not yet paid the taxes. The closing date is June 3, and the day belongs to the buyer. Consequently, what proration for property taxes would show on the Closing Disclosure Statement?

   a. Credit seller $1,147.50; Debit the buyer $1,147.50
   b. Credit buyer $1,147.50; Debit the seller $1,147.50
   c. Credit seller $1,590; Debit the buyer $1,590
   d. Credit buyer $1,590; Debit the seller $1,590

37. How much will documentary stamps cost for a property selling for $625,900 with a tax rate of $1.00 per $100?

   a. $62.59
   b. $625.90
   c. $6,259
   d. $62,590

38. The HO-2 insurance policy is known as the

   a. renters' policy.
   b. most comprehensive policy.
   c. peril policy.
   d. condo policy.

39. The National Flood Insurance Act requires flood insurance coverage for properties located in a designated flood-hazard area if

   a. the property is seller financed.
   b. the property is financed through a federally related loan.
   c. the property was not inspected by a professional property inspector.
   d. the purchaser paid cash for the property.

40. The process of enforcing a lien by forcing sale of the lienee's property is called

   a. execution.
   b. attachment.
   c. foreclosure.
   d. subordination.

41. A _____ occurs when a property owner owes more than the resale value and loan pay-off.

   a. strict foreclosure
   b. short sale
   c. non-judicial foreclosure
   d. lis pendens

42. In a strict foreclosure, what happens first?

   a. The lender files suit in court.
   b. The legal title gets transferred to the lender.
   c. The lender gives the borrower official notice.
   d. The owner is given a period of time to repay the amounts owed.

43. What is the purpose of the Commitment to Excellence (C2EX)?

   a. To educate Realtors® on their duties to clients
   b. To illustrate how Realtors® are to respect their peers
   c. To provide Realtors® a designation for completion of Pathways to Professionalism education
   d. To empower Realtors® to promote their highest professional levels to clients and peers

44. Which Article's Standard of Practice did Paula violate when she failed to disclose her license status when she listed her own property for sale?

   a. Article 12 regarding the requirement to be honest in all advertising and marketing
   b. Article 10 regarding the prohibition of discrimination against anyone in a protected class
   c. Article 35 regarding the requirement to disclose any conflict of interest when providing a professional service
   d. Article 3 regarding cooperation among brokers

45. Which of the following is not a protected class under Article 10 of the Code of Ethics?

   a. Sex
   b. Familial status
   c. Age
   d. Gender identity

46. Which of the following is a Code of Ethics violation?

   a. Broker Sarah charged a buyer a commission in a short sale transaction.
   b. Broker Charlie failed to disclose his ownership interest in a property he sold.
   c. Broker Sean refused to show an available property to a buyer based on the buyer's finances.
   d. Against the buyer's wishes, Broker Tom deliberately used a standardized sales contract to close the transaction.

47. Which of the following is a common risk relating to the agency relationship?

   a. Failing to inform and disclose the relationship properly
   b. Failing to take a personal interest in a transaction
   c. Acting as an exclusive agent without an oral agency agreement
   d. Forgetting to record the listing agreement

48. Even though Georgia does not require a property condition disclosure, the licensee may still be subject to legal action for

    a. failing to detect customer misrepresentations.
    b. failing to disclose known, material adverse facts.
    c. relying on publicly available market information.
    d. advising the purchaser to exercise due diligence.

49. How does having a lender qualify a buyer protect a licensee?

    a. It guarantees that a buyer will have a loan.
    b. It reduces the chance of presenting an offer from an unqualified buyer.
    c. It relieves the licensee of his or her due diligence responsibilities.
    d. It allows the licensee to avoid asking embarrassing questions.

50. Which of the following steps is not advised for an agent's safety?

    a. Checking in advance if the agent's cell phone service is working in the property's area.
    b. Carrying pepper spray.
    c. Carrying her handbag at all times during an open house.
    d. Parking on the street during an open house.

PRACTICE EXAMINATION ANSWER KEY

1. b. **A licensee failing to include an expiration date in a listing agreement**

2. d. **$25,000**

3. c. **discrimination.**

4. b. **To assure people with disabilities have the same rights and opportunities as everyone else**

5. a. **market allocation**

6. c. **apartment properties which contain 5 or more units.**

7. b. **When the lender denies the loan based on a misrepresentation on the application**

8. d. **an officer.**

9. b. **An officer of the corporation**

10. b. **is responsible for the sales agent's actions.**

11. c. **$18,900**

12. d. **Making cold calls**

13. c. **the name and phone number of the licensee's firm**

14. b. **Stately home for sale located in lovely Jewish community**

15. d. **All of the above**

16. a. **A company's written policies, rules, and procedures should include that licensed activities be only performed by licensed personnel.**

17. c. **deposit the funds into the firm's trust account.**

18. b. **the broker provides required account information to the Commission.**

19. d. **should abide by fiduciary obligations to the client.**

20. b. **prospecting.**

21. a. **The listing broker**

22. b. **Accounting for all client funds handled**

23. d. **No cause of action may be taken for this act.**

24. c. **Mold**

25. b. **Material facts related to the physical condition of the property must be disclosed.**

26. b. **How many properties the applicant owns**

27. a. a straightforward offer to make a specific loan at a specific interest rate for a specific term.

28. c. Monthly housing expense

29. b. Cost approach

30. c. A buyer will pay no more for the subject property than would be sufficient to buy a comparable property.

31. b. Conditions under which a buyer can cancel a sale contract without default are contingencies.

32. c. an encumbered title.

33. a. when buyers and sellers exchange offers to negotiate the transfer terms.

34. c. when the offeree gives the offeror notice of offer acceptance.

35. a. Credit buyer $1,120; Debit seller $1,120

36. b. Credit buyer $1,147.50; Debit the seller $1,147.50

37. c. $6,259

38. c. peril policy.

39. b. the property is financed through a federally related loan.

40. c. foreclosure.

41. b. short sale

42. c. The lender gives the borrower official notice.

43. d. To empower Realtors® to promote their highest professional levels to clients and peers

44. a. Article 12 regarding the requirement to be honest in all advertising and marketing

45. c. Age

46. b. Broker Charlie failed to disclose his ownership interest in a property he sold.

47. a. Failing to inform and disclose the relationship properly

48. b. failing to disclose known, material adverse facts.

49. b. It reduces the chance of presenting an offer from an unqualified buyer.

50. c. Carrying her handbag at all times during an open house.

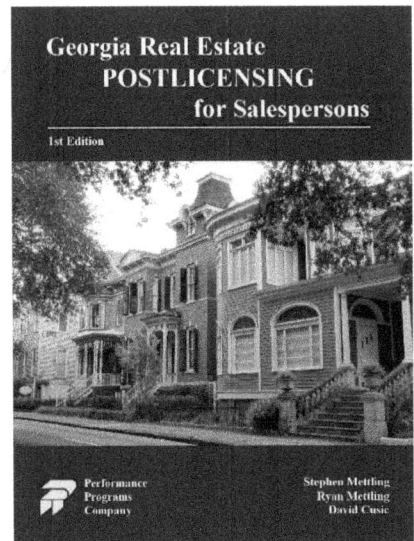

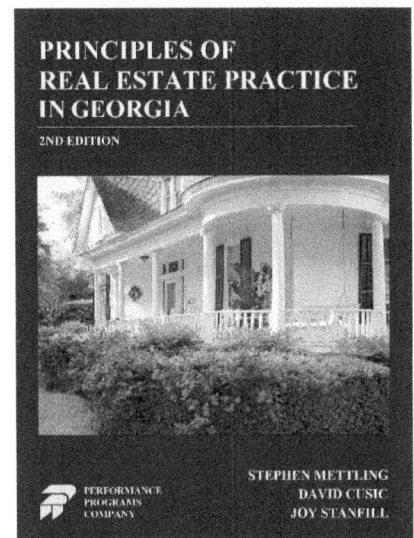

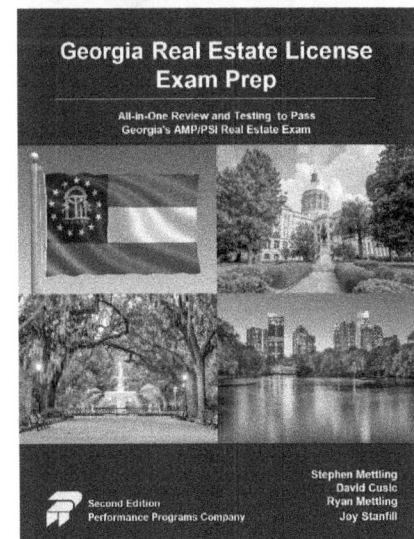

www.ingramcontent.com/pod-product-compliance
Lightning Source LLC
Chambersburg PA
CBHW080532220326
41599CB00032B/6290